1980

THE WORD OF THE LORD GROWS

THE WORD OF THE LORD GROWS

An Introduction to the Origin, Purpose,
and Meaning of the NEW TESTAMENT

BY MARTIN H. FRANZMANN

Publishing House
St. Louis

Concordia Publishing House, St. Louis, Mo. 63118

ISBN 0-570-03222-9

Library of Congress Catalog Card No. 61-13453
© 1961 Concordia Publishing House
Manufactured in the United States of America

PREFACE

I have attempted to write the sort of introduction to the New Testament for which I myself was searching in my student days and never really found. I was looking for a book which would enable me to wear a path through my New Testament both historically and theologically, a book which would enable me to move about in the New Testament with confidence and would give me solid ground under my feet for future more detailed exploration. I have attempted, therefore, to make the historical materials serviceable theologically by taking the Holy Spirit seriously as the paramount power in history. I have sought to write a book which encourages a maximum of observation of the text itself. I have reduced the theoretical and hypothetical to a minimum and have contented myself with the barest indication of views which diverge from my own.

This attempt — to produce a book which would leave the student, for the first, alone with his New Testament — brings with it certain inevitable drawbacks, of which I am acutely conscious. For one thing, I have been forced to be somewhat more authoritarian in the expression of my views than I actually care to be. For another, since it seemed best for this purpose to do without footnotes, I run the risk of appearing careless of the debt which I owe to the many scholars who have worked and are at work in this field. I therefore here gratefully acknowledge that "I am a part of all that I have met," as every student in this field must.

I should like to acknowledge a special debt to that giant among New Testament scholars, Adolf Schlatter.

I wish to express my gratitude to Concordia Publishing House and the Literature Board of The Lutheran Church — Missouri Synod, who provided me with a generous portion of leisure for work on this book. It is my prayer that a gracious Lord may bless the work which they have furthered.

Thankful acknowledgment is also herewith expressed for permission to quote from the Revised Standard Version of the Bible, copyrighted 1946 and 1952 by the Division of Christian Education of the National Council of Churches and published by Thomas Nelson & Sons.

MARTIN H. FRANZMANN

CONTENTS

The Table of Dates

30	Pentecost; Birthday of the New Testament Church
32	Death of Stephen and Conversion of St. Paul
43	Founding of Gentile Church at Antioch; Paul Summoned to Antioch by Barnabas
44	Death of James the Son of Zebedee
c. 45	EPISTLE OF ST. JAMES
46—48	St. Paul's First Missionary Journey
48	EPISTLE TO THE GALATIANS
49	Apostolic Council
49—51	St. Paul's Second Missionary Journey
50 (early)	1 THESSALONIANS; 50 (summer) 2 THESSALONIANS
52—56	St. Paul's Third Missionary Journey
55 (spring)	1 CORINTHIANS; 55 (summer or fall) 2 CORINTHIANS
56 (early)	ROMANS
56—58	St. Paul's Caesarean Imprisonment
58—59	St. Paul's Voyage to Rome
59—61	St. Paul's Roman Imprisonment
59—61	COLOSSIANS, PHILEMON, EPHESIANS, PHILIPPIANS (The Captivity Letters)
50—60	GOSPEL ACCORDING TO ST. MATTHEW
c. 60	GOSPEL ACCORDING TO ST. MARK
62—63	1 TIMOTHY
63	TITUS
64	Fire in Rome. Neronian Persecution

CHAPTER I: The Historical Character of the New Testament Word

READINGS: ACTS 1–12

"The word of the Lord grew" — three times in the Book of Acts Luke uses this sentence to sum up a period of the history of the first church (Acts 6:7; 12:24; 19:20). These words are a telling expression of the Biblical conception of the divine word. Our Lord Himself compared the word with a seed that is sown and sprouts and grows: "The seed is the word of God" (Luke 8:11). The word of the Lord is a power and is active; it "prevails mightily," as Luke puts it in one of the passages just referred to (Acts 19:20). Paul speaks of the Gospel as "bearing fruit and growing" (Col. 1:6), and Peter speaks of the "living and abiding word of God" as an "imperishable seed" (1 Peter 1:23).

This "living and active" word (Heb. 4:12) is therefore a force in history; it "speeds on" in the world and "triumphs" there (2 Thess. 3:1), in time and place and among men; it is enmeshed in events, tied up with the world, and it involves people. The word of God is God in action; for God is not a lecturer but the God who is "working still," as Jesus said of His Father, and of Himself the Son (John 5:17). God is the Lord of all history, reveals Himself by His mighty acts in history, and the word which He gives His prophets to utter interprets those acts and makes them an enduring force in the world. His word and His work are so closely connected that both the Old Testament and the New Testament speak of God's great acts simply as the activity of His *word*. Psalm 107, which praises the LORD as the Deliverer from all evils, describes His act of delivering those who "because of their iniquities suffered affliction . . . and drew near to the gates of death" with the words, "He *sent forth His word,* and healed them, and delivered them from destruction" (Ps. 107: 17-20). And Peter in his sermon in the house of Cornelius can sum up the whole story of the sending of the Son of God into the world thus: "You know the *word* which He [God] sent to Israel, preaching good news of peace by Jesus Christ." (Acts 10:36)

If, then, we are to hear the divine word of our New Testament on its own terms (and that is the whole task and function of interpretation), we must study it historically. We must learn to see it as the growing and working divine word, as God Himself active in history. We must come to know it and comprehend it as a word that has its point of origin (as a divine word) in human history, as a word that gets its form and its contours from history, as a word that is essentially history (a recital of "the mighty works of God," Acts 2:11), and as a word that has history-making power, as a dynamic and creative personal power of God at work among men.

Students of comparative religion tell us that the Book of Acts is unique in the history of religions. Nowhere else in the religious life of man do we find this sober and religious sense of history, this absolute conviction that God is the God of history, who clothes Himself in a garment of mighty deeds in order to reveal Himself to men. Here only do we find the conviction of faith that His word is a force, is in fact *the* force in history. The Book of Acts is therefore uniquely valuable for our study of the whole New Testament. It is valuable because it provides us with the historical information which is indispensable for reconstructing the historical background of many New Testament books, especially the letters of Paul. But not only for that reason; we appreciate and value the Book of Acts as students of history, of course; but we are never merely historians when we seek to interpret the New Testament — we are always first and foremost theologians and believers, for whom the historical is a means to a higher end, the end namely that we hear the New Testament speak to us as the living voice of God *now.* And it is to the theologians and believer that the Book of Acts is really uniquely valuable. Since it is the history of the first church, conceived of and told not as the history of another religious society but as the history of the growth, the progress, and the triumph of the divine word, the Book of Acts can determine not only the method of our study but also the basically religious attitude of our study.

Thus the first twelve chapters of the Book of Acts will provide us with the materials which enable us to reconstruct the historical setting and the original function of the Epistle of James and will give us an insight into the genesis and the background of the mission to the Gentiles which gave rise to the letters of Paul. However, we shall do well to use these twelve chapters first as a means of getting a basic, theological insight into the character of the New Testament word of God. This does not mean that we ignore the historical; it does mean that we see in history the revelation of God — our God. "When my love walks, she treads upon the ground," a poet once said in appreciation of a lady who was less "heavenly" than the ladyloves of more exuberant poets. We might say the same of our God: "When our God walks, He treads upon the ground." He does not remain a remote and shadowy sort of philosopher's God; He condescends to enter history and does His gracious work there, for us men and for our salvation. If we study historically the life of the first church and the nature of the apostolic proclamation which called that first church into being, we shall be enabled to hear God speaking to us now.

THE LIFE OF THE FIRST CHURCH

The New People of God Under the Lordship of Jesus Christ

What sort of life was this life of the first church, that life which was the historical framework of our New Testament, the seedbed in which it sprouted and grew? Its first and most obvious characteristic is that it is a life wholly dominated by the Lord Jesus Christ. Luke makes it very plain that the Book of Acts (which is the second book of a two-volume work, of which his Gospel is the first) is the direct continuation of the Gospel of Jesus Christ: "In the first book . . . I have dealt with all that Jesus *began* to do and teach" (Acts 1:1). The human figure of Peter may loom large on the stage of history in the first part (chaps. 1—12) and that of Paul in the second (chaps. 13—28);

but they are both dwarfed by, and completely subordinated to, Him who is the real and sole Actor in this Book of Acts — this Jesus who continues to do and to teach. It is His word that grows and speeds and triumphs here, not Peter's or Paul's, a fact which Peter and Paul are the first to assert.

His word grows; His will is done. For He is the exalted Lord of invincible majesty, the Lord who has been "taken up" into heaven, to the world of God (Acts 1:2, 9, 11), "exalted at the right hand of God" (Acts 2:33) as "Leader and Savior" (Acts 5:31), the "Lord of all" (Acts 10:36). The dying Stephen prays to this Lord, just as Jesus Himself had on the cross prayed to His Father. (Acts 7:59, 60; cf. Luke 23:34, 46)

He is the exalted Lord by virtue of His resurrection from the dead: "This Jesus God raised up. . . . Being therefore exalted at the right hand of God. . . . God has made Him both Lord and Christ" (Acts 2:32, 33, 36). It is the God who has raised Him from the dead who has exalted Jesus as Leader and Savior at His right hand (Acts 5:30, 31). "God raised Him on the third day and made Him manifest" (Acts 10:40). The exalted Lord is the Lord risen from the dead; that ties Him firmly and forever to the Lord who was made man for us men and for our salvation, to the Lord Jesus who went in and out among His disciples, whom John the Baptist heralded and proclaimed (Acts 1:21, 22), the *man* Jesus of Nazareth whom God attested to Israel with mighty works done in the midst of the men of Israel (Acts 2:22), the Jesus of Nazareth whom God anointed with the Holy Spirit and with power, who went about doing good and healing all that were oppressed by the devil (Acts 10:38).

He is Lord because He went that way of gracious ministry to the utmost. He is the chief stone of the new temple of God because He was the stone rejected by the builders (Acts 4:10, 11), because He was betrayed by His own disciple, arrested by His own people (Acts 1:16), and killed and crucified (Acts 2:23; 3:13-15; 4:10; 7:52).

The new people of God know and proclaim their Lord as the Servant of God. The term "Servant" is used more frequently of Him in these early chapters of Acts than anywhere else in the New Testament (Acts 3:13, 26; 4:27, 30; cf. 8:32, 33). No other single term could, perhaps, so fully denote His peculiar and all-encompassing Lordship as this one. For with this term Jesus was proclaimed as the fulfillment of those prophecies of Isaiah which fixed the hope of God's people on the Servant of the LORD, that servant whom the LORD endowed with His Spirit for a mission of merciful ministry to all nations in order that He might be "a covenant to the people" Israel (that is, that He might bring about fully and forever the intent of God's covenant-mercy and covenant-fidelity for God's chosen people), and in order that He might be "a light to the nations" — that in Him the dawn of God's great day of salvation might break on all men everywhere (Is. 42: 1-9). The Servant is described by the prophet as going down into the depths of humiliation and rejection in His ministry (Is. 49:4, 7; 50:6), a ministry whose goal is the restoration of Israel and the salvation of all nations, that the LORD'S "salvation may reach to the end of the earth" (Is. 49:6). The servant is pictured by the prophet as going through ministry and humiliation to a triumphant exaltation:

> Behold, My servant shall prosper,
> He shall be exalted and lifted up,
> and shall be very high . . .
> kings shall shut their mouths because of Him.
>
> (Is. 52:13, 15)

But the triumph is not His until He has gone the downward way of ministry to the full, not only "despised and rejected by men" (Is. 53:3), but bruised and put to grief by the LORD Himself (Is. 53:10), who numbers Him with the transgressors (Is. 53:12) and lays upon Him and punishes in Him the iniquity of all (Is. 53: 5, 6). Only when the Servant has gone down into a vicarious, penal, atoning death for a sinful people, only when He has borne the sins of many, led like a lamb to the slaughter for their guilt, only then does He rise to new life and triumph (Is. 53:10-12). With the term "Servant" the apostles and the new people of God after them could sum up the whole glory of their Lord. The glory of the ministering Messiah, the crucified Messiah, the risen Messiah, the exalted Messiah was all comprehended in that term; and the dark mystery of His cross was illumined by it.

The prophet had said of the Servant:

When He makes Himself an offering for sin,
He shall see His offspring, He shall prolong His days;
the will of the LORD shall prosper in His hand;
He shall see the fruit of the travail of His soul and be
satisfied.   (Is. 53:10, 11)

The Servant-Messiah of the new people of God is anything but
a mere memory for them; He is for them no departed hero, no
commemorated martyr. He is their present, living, and actively
working Lord. Peter tells the people, "God, having raised up His
servant, sent Him to you first, *to bless you*" (Acts 3:26). We
can see this actively blessing character of the church's Lord clearly
in the way in which Luke speaks of His "name" in Acts; for the
"name" of God in Biblical language means God turned toward
man, God entering into communion with man, God making and
shaping man's history. So also the "name" of the Lord Jesus
Christ signifies the Lord in action. If a miracle is done "in the
name" of the Lord Jesus, if Peter says to the lame man at the
Beautiful Gate of the temple, "In the name of Jesus Christ of
Nazareth, walk" (Acts 3:6), that means: the Lord who in the
days of His flesh went about doing good is still graciously and
omnipotently at work in the world; the Author of Life is restoring
God's ruined creation to full and whole life (Acts 3:15, 16; 4:10;
cf. 9:34). Men must call on the name of Him whom God has
made both Lord and Christ if they would be saved (Acts 2:
21, 36); they are summoned to repent and to be baptized in the
name of Jesus for the forgiveness of sins (Acts 2:38); for "every
one who believes in Him receives forgiveness of sins through
His name" (Acts 10:43). In Jesus Christ, through His active
grace in Baptism and the Word, men are saved from judgment
(Acts 2:40), brought to God, reconciled, forgiven, made members
of the new people of God. Salvation is in His name and in His
alone (Acts 4:12), for He is God's own royal and lavish grace
in person. He is the present kingdom of God; when Luke says
of Philip that he "preached good news about the kingdom of
God and the name of Jesus Christ" in Samaria (Acts 8:12), he
is not implying that Philip's preaching had two themes (Philip
had but one theme — "he proclaimed to them the Christ," Acts

8:5) but is describing the one theme of his preaching in two ways. "The name of Jesus Christ" is another way of saying "the kingdom of God." Where the Lord Jesus is at work, there God Himself is at work establishing His royal reign of grace among men.

The exalted Lord works in history, through men. Men are His "instruments" (Acts 9:15) whom He chooses in sovereign grace — the persecutor Saul must bow before that royal grace and carry this Lord's name "before the Gentiles and kings and the sons of Israel" and must suffer for the sake of that name (Acts 9:15, 16). He makes men His apostles, messengers who are determined wholly by the will of the sender and are completely dependent upon Him, wholly obedient to Him. As such they speak His word and represent Him and confront men with Him. The apostles' deeds of power are therefore the Lord's deeds; "many wonders and signs were done *through the apostles*" (Acts 2:43; cf. 5:12). Concerning the lame man whom he had healed, Peter tells the rulers, elders, and scribes, "By the name of Jesus Christ of Nazareth, whom you crucified, whom God raised from the dead, *by Him* this man is standing before you well" (Acts 4:10). Perhaps the most striking expression of the fact that the apostle is the "chosen instrument" of the Lord Jesus Christ (no less than that, but also only that) is in the words which Peter spoke at the bedside of the paralytic man at Lydda: "Aeneas, *Jesus Christ heals you*" (Acts 9:34). As instruments of the Lord the apostles are completely selfless: "Why do you stare at us, as though by our own power or piety we had made him walk?" Peter says to astounded people in Solomon's portico (Acts 3:12). And when Cornelius fell down at Peter's feet, Peter responded with, "Stand up; I too am a man" (Acts 10:25, 26). It is because the apostles are the self-effacing, chosen instruments of the Lord, because they are no more and no less than the human vehicles of the Lord's presence, that their word shapes and directs the whole life of the new community: "They devoted themselves to the apostles' teaching." (Acts 2:42)

The apostles are not religious geniuses, whose insights enrich and enlarge the accumulated religious stores of mankind. They are recipients of revelation, witnesses to a Person and an act in history — and this Person and this act completely overshadow and dominate them. They are important, not for themselves, but for what they bear witness to. They receive divine power for one purpose only, for witnessing (Acts 1:8). In fact, the Lord must completely invert their own human thinking before He can use them as chosen instruments. They are curious as to times and seasons, and they think of a reign in Israel: "Lord, will You at this time restore the kingdom to Israel?" (Acts 1:6) He turns their thoughts from curiosity as to times and seasons to a sober submission to the sovereign will of the Father, from the idea of reign to the duty of ministry, from the narrow horizon of Israel to the wide world. They are to be His witnesses, not only in the land and among the people they know and love, but also to the Samaritans whom they hated, and to the ends of the earth, the wide world of the Gentiles, about whom they were by nature indifferent (Acts 1:8). The Lord sets them to witnessing to Jew and to Gentile, for He is Lord of all (Acts 10:36) and determines all history. The eighth verse of the first chapter of Acts not only indicates the plan of the Book of Acts; it marks out the course of all history for the church, until the time when the Son of man returns to end and judge and crown all history.

Thus the life of the new people of God is a life under the Lordship of Jesus Christ; the men upon whom God's new day has dawned behold "the light of the knowledge of the glory of God *in the face of Christ,*" as Paul puts it (2 Cor. 4:6). But they behold the glory of God; the Lordship of Jesus does not obscure God but reveals Him. The name of Jesus is the revelation of the kingdom of God (Acts 8:12; cf. 28:31); to be under the Lordship of Jesus is to live a life in communion with God.

The same history which reveals Jesus as Lord and Christ reveals God the King as the gracious and omnipotent Lord of history. God foretold the coming of His Christ, His anointed King, "by the mouth of all the prophets" (Acts 3:18; cf. 4:25, 26). God attested the man Jesus of Nazareth with mighty works and wonders and signs (Acts 2:22); God anointed Jesus with the Holy Spirit and with power; God "was with Him" (Acts 10:38). When Jesus went down in death at the hands of His enemies, God was still in control; they crucified and killed Him "according to the definite plan and foreknowledge of God" (Acts 2:23). When they wrought their rebellious will upon God's Servant, they were still doing what God's hand and God's plan had predestined (Acts 4: 27, 28). God, we hear it again and again, raised Jesus from the dead (Acts 2:24; 3:15; 10:40). God exalted Him on high and glorified His Servant (Acts 2:33; 3:13; 5:31). God has ordained Him to be Judge of the living and the dead (Acts 10:42). The exalted Christ has received from the Father the promised Holy Spirit which He pours out upon His own — and that Spirit moves men to tell of "the mighty works of *God*" (Acts 2:11). The persecuted and praying church bows before God as the absolute and sovereign Lord of history, whose enemies cannot but do His will. (Acts 4:24-28)

The church which submits itself wholly to God as the Lord of history (Acts 4:28, 29) also adores Him as Creator; the church's prayer begins, "Sovereign Lord, who didst make the heaven and the earth and the sea and everything in them" (Acts 4:24). When God sent His Son into the created world, into history, into humanity, He was speaking an unmistakable yea to His very good creation; and not only the prayer of the church, but the whole life of the church is witness to the joyous conviction that "everything created by God is good" (1 Tim. 4:4). The witness of the church does not pass over or seek to minimize the full humanity of Jesus, His very human history, His sufferings, His death. Moreover, the new community did not withdraw to a wilderness asylum, but stayed and worked and witnessed where the Creator of the world and the Lord of history had placed them. And there was nothing sequestered or monastic about their fellowship. Their fellowship was a table fellowship; "they partook of food with glad and generous hearts, praising God" (Acts 2: 46, 47). It was a fellowship of families — they broke bread from house to house (Acts 2:46), a fellowship from which woman was not excluded (Acts 1:14; 6:1; 8:3), a fellowship in which woman played a rich and honorable part, as the example of Tabitha shows (Acts 9:36-41). A common care for the physical needs of the community was an important part of the church's life from the beginning (Acts 2:44, 45; 4:32-35). The apostles did not permit it to encroach upon or overshadow their prime task of prayer and the ministry of the word, but they did recognize its impor-

tance and made provision for it as a work which only the Holy
Spirit could enable a man rightly to do. (Acts 6:1-6)

These men knew God the Creator as the Father of the Lord
Jesus Christ and therefore as their Father too; they knew Him as
men living under the heaven of the forgiveness of sins. This
transformed their lives and gave them a remarkable freedom from
care and anxiety. It gave them "glad and generous hearts" (Acts
2:46). It enabled them to welcome suffering in their lives as
another good gift from the Creator's hand (Acts 5:41). It filled
their lives with the music of prayer which accompanied all that
they did and all that befell them (Acts 2:42; 4:24-30; 6:4; 12:
5, 12). It set them free for love toward one another, so that "the
company of those who believed were of one heart and soul, and
no one said that any of the things which he possessed was his own"
(Acts 4:32). It was no wonder that people felt a certain awe
for them (Acts 2:43; 4:21; 5:13, 26); they lived lives which were
an enacted doxology to God the Father of our Lord Jesus Christ.

The church has rightly called our New Testament, the book
which incorporates the word that grew on this soil, "The New
Testament of our Lord and Savior Jesus Christ"; for it is the
book which on every page calls Jesus Lord and gives to men the
light of the knowledge of the glory of God in the face of Christ.
But it is for that very reason the book of the Holy Trinity, for in
it Jesus is called Lord to the glory of God the Father. And the
New Testament is a book of the Holy Spirit too, an inspired book.
This brings us to the second major aspect of the life of the
first church.

The New People of God Under the Power of the Spirit

The Book of Acts has aptly been called the Gospel of the
Holy Spirit. The book opens with the promise of the Spirit
(1:5, 8), and the New Testament church is born when the Spirit
is given in the fullness and universality which neither the Old
Testament people of God nor the disciples of Jesus had as yet
experienced (Acts 2:1-42). The disciples knew the Holy Spirit
from the Old Testament as the creative personal presence of God
which makes and shapes and interprets history, the power which
moved over the face of the waters at creation (Gen. 1:2); the
power that came upon the Judges of Israel (Judg. 6:34; 14:6)

and upon Israel's kings (1 Sam. 16:13, 14) and enabled them to
do great things for the LORD and the LORD's people. They
knew the Spirit as the power that enabled the prophets to say,
"Thus says the LORD" — to interpret history as the arm of the
LORD laid bare and to foretell what the LORD would yet do
for the salvation of His people and all nations (Acts 1:16; 4:25).
They knew that when the Children of Israel resisted the leaders
and prophets sent to them by God they were resisting the Holy
Spirit (7:51). They knew that the Spirit of the LORD was to
rest upon the Messiah-Prince of the line of David and enable
Him to establish God's rule of right over His people and to restore
God's ruined creation to the peace of paradise (Is. 11:1-10), that
the Spirit of the LORD would come upon the Servant-Messiah
and make Him the Covenant of the people and the Light to lighten
the Gentiles (Is. 42:1; 61:1). They knew that Jesus of Nazareth
had been anointed by God with the Holy Spirit and had thus
performed the mighty works which attested Him as Messiah and
Savior (Acts 10:38). They knew that it was "through the Holy
Spirit" that their risen Lord had given commandment to His
chosen apostles (Acts 1:2). They had received the promise of
the Spirit for themselves from Him, both in the days of His flesh
(Luke 12:12) and in the forty days after the resurrection (Acts
1:5, 8). But it was not until the day of Pentecost had come that
they experienced what their Lord had promised, what the prophet
Joel had foretold for the last days (Acts 2:16, 17), the "pouring
out" in unprecedented fullness of the Spirit of God upon "all flesh."

The twelve apostles received the Spirit (Acts 2:4; 4:8; 5:32;
10:19; 11:12), and Paul, the apostle "untimely born" (1 Cor.
15:8), received the Spirit too, in peculiar fullness and strength.
But what they received was not given to them to have and to
hold as their private possession and prerogative; they were not
only recipients of the Spirit; they also became vehicles of the
Spirit (e. g., Acts 2:38; 8:18). The Spirit is poured out not only
on apostles, but also on prophets like Agabus (Acts 11:28), on
the Seven and on evangelists (Acts 6:3, 5, 10; 7:55; 8:29, 39);
on great and kindly leaders like Barnabas (Acts 11:24), on all
believers (Acts 2:38; 4:31), on Jews, on Samaritans (Acts 8:
15-18), and even (to the amazement of some Jewish Christians)
on Gentiles (Acts 10:44, 45, 47; 11:15).

The Spirit filled the whole church; and the Spirit animated and governed the whole life of the new people of God. It is not only in ecstatic utterance and in enraptured vision that the Spirit's working is manifested, though these are found in the life of the first church too: the men who spoke in other tongues at Pentecost were so far carried beyond the way of normal and ordinary speech that mockers could call them drunken (Acts 2:13); when the Spirit "fell" on the men of Samaria, the results were so striking that Simon the sorcerer wanted to purchase the power of the Spirit from the apostles — it seemed to him a very potent kind of magic (Acts 8:17-19); when the Spirit fell on Cornelius and his friends at Caesarea, they "spoke in tongues," in ecstatic doxology (Acts 10:44-46; 11:15). Stephen, "full of the Holy Spirit," saw "the heavens opened and the Son of man standing at the right hand of God." (Acts 7:55, 56)

But Luke's record attributes to the working of the Holy Spirit utterances and actions which our secularized thinking would consider ordinary and normal. Not only the enraptured Peter of Pentecost is filled with the Holy Spirit; the Peter who must speak in sober defense before the Sanhedrin is no less Spirit-filled (Acts 4:8). As his Lord had promised, the Spirit teaches him in that hour what he ought to say (Luke 12:12). The Spirit is for the apostles functional power, a power which equips them for their task of witnessing to the act of God in Christ, to the fact in history that spells the salvation of mankind (Acts 1:8; 5:32; 9:17, 20). The Spirit is working guidance for the apostle (Acts 10:19) and for the evangelist (Acts 8:29, 39). When the Spirit inspires the prophet Agabus, he produces no startling and exciting apocalyptic novelties to satisfy the religious curiosity of man; he foretells a famine, in order that the church may carefully plan and duly carry out her work of charity (Acts 11:28-30). The Spirit enables men to "serve tables" in the church, to provide for the widow and the fatherless in wise and sober charity; the Seven chosen for this task must be, Peter tells the church, "men . . . full of the Spirit and of wisdom" (Acts 6:1-6). The martyr's vision of the opened heavens is not the only fruit of the Spirit in the life of Stephen, one of these seven men; the Spirit enabled him to do his work as servant of the church for the poor and to acquit himself well in his disputes with the men of the synagog. (Acts 6:10)

The church prayed in her hour of need (Acts 4:23 ff.), prayed for courage to endure persecution, not for escape from persecution. God manifested His presence among them: "the place in which they were gathered together was shaken, and they were all filled with the Holy Spirit" (Acts 4:31). What is the fruit of the Spirit? What is the result of this inspiration? The result is characteristic of the whole piety of the first church under the power of the Spirit; the aim and goal of its religious life is not self-enrichment or self-fulfillment; there is no trace of egotistical piety here. The result is the will to unity and the will to witness: "They . . . spoke the word of God with *boldness*" (Acts 4:31). The word which we are forced to translate with "boldness" is the outstanding characteristic of the Spirit-filled church in action. It signifies that free, glad, courageous confidence, that robust health of faith which comes from the assurance of free access to God the Father given in Christ by the Spirit. It is the energetic religious health which makes Peter and John say, "We cannot but speak of what we have seen and heard" (Acts 4:20); it is that high confidence of faith which makes Saul, when he has received the Holy Spirit (Acts 9:17) proclaim Jesus as Son of God in the synagogue "immediately" (Acts 9:20), "preaching boldly" both in Damascus and in Jerusalem (Acts 9:27-29).

This boldness is boldness under the Lordship of Jesus. It is the church which walks "in the fear of the Lord," which enjoys the "comfort of the Holy Spirit" (Acts 9:31). It is a boldness under the reign of God, who gives His Spirit "to those who *obey* Him" (Acts 5:32). This disciplined and obedient character of the church's boldness is especially apparent in the church's use of the Old Testament. As Jesus in the days of His flesh was led by the Spirit, not beyond Scripture, but into it, so that He repelled Satan with "It is written" (Luke 4:1-13), so the apostles were led into Scripture by the guidance of the Spirit. They used the Old Testament gladly and freely, in the confidence that in it God was by His Spirit speaking to them there and then in their own day; they appropriated it fully as *their* book, the book of the New Testament people of God. Peter's sermon at Pentecost is typical. "The man is crammed with Scripture" is Luther's comment on it. And when Philip, prompted by the Spirit, joined the Eunuch who was reading from the prophet Isaiah, he opened his mouth, and *"beginning with this Scripture* he told him the good news of Jesus" (Acts 8:35). The Spirit-filled church under the living word of the apostles was far from feeling any aversion to the written word of God's elder revelation; she perceived in the written Old Testament the voice and the operation of the Holy Spirit and gratefully used the inspired book.

The robust religious health of mind and will which the Spirit gave the first church is apparent also in the language of the church. In a sense, the Holy Spirit did create a new language in the last days, as every student of the New Testament learns, a language richly individual, with forces and connotations all its own. But there is nothing strained, far-fetched, or esoteric about it; there is no mumbo-jumbo. It is a perfectly natural and open language, rooted in the life and history of the Jew and Greek to whom the church bore witness.

That is the second major aspect of the history which produced our New Testament. It is a history in which the Spirit of God moves creatively upon the waters. To speak of the word which grew on this soil and sped and triumphed in this history as an *inspired* word, wholly inspired, is not to impose an alien theory upon the word; it is simply a recognition of its character as a part of the history of the New Testament people of God. It is inspired because God the Lord of history made it so; it is verbally inspired because God deals with men on person-to-person terms, in terms of converse with men; it is the product of the Spirit of the living God and vehicle of that Spirit still, inspired and inspiring.

The New People of God in the World's Last Days

The third major aspect of the history which is the seedbed of our New Testament is the fact that the church is conscious of being the eschatological people of God, that is, the people of God in the world's last days. The Spirit is the gift of God given "in the last days" (Acts 2:17). And the gift is given in order that men may bear witness to the fact which decisively ushers in the last days, the resurrection of Jesus from the dead (Acts 2:

32-36). That fact means that Jesus is enthroned as Christ and
Lord (Acts 2:36), soon to return (Acts 3:20). The "day of the
Lord" of which Joel had spoken is full in view (Acts 2:20), and
it is for the new people of God "the day of our Lord Jesus Christ."
The kingdom of God is "at hand" more imminently and more
urgently than when John the Baptist cried out in the wilderness
(Matt. 3:2) or even when Jesus proclaimed it in Galilee (Matt.
4:17). The risen Lord is proclaiming it; the word of His messengers is establishing it (Acts 1:3, 6, 8). When the "good news
about the kingdom of God and the name of Jesus Christ" is being
proclaimed (Acts 8:12), the Kingdom is there, the Christ is
taking up His power and is beginning to reign; it is the beginning of the end. The last days have dawned.

All previous revelation of God has led up to and prepared
for this: "All the prophets who have spoken . . . also proclaimed
these days" (Acts 3:24); the prophets, whom a rebellious Israel
persecuted, "announced beforehand the coming of the Righteous
One" (Acts 7:52). All subsequent history is determined by this
single, unparalleled, eschatological fact, the fact of the resurrection of Jesus. For this is not merely the fact that Jesus of Nazareth
is alive, that "He presented Himself alive after His Passion"
to His apostles (Acts 1:3). His resurrection is the great turning
point, from death to life, for all men and all creation. He is the
Author of life (Acts 3:15). The apostles proclaim *the resurrection
from the dead* "in Jesus" (Acts 4:2) — they proclaim that the
man Jesus has crossed the frontier of death into everlasting life
for all men. All history is moving with divine inevitability, with
the "must" of the will of God (Acts 3:21), toward the goal of all
God's ways, toward the return of the Christ, the time of "refreshing . . . from the presence of the Lord," and the restoration of all
creation, the establishing of all things that God spoke by the mouth
of His holy prophets from of old (Acts 3:19-21).

With the resurrection of Jesus the new life, the real and eternal
life of the world to come, has become a present reality, breaking
miraculously into the present world of men living under the sign
of death. To proclaim and to impart this new life, that is the
mission of the apostles. To the apostles, the witnesses of the
resurrection of Jesus (Acts 1:3; 1:22; 10:41), the angel of the

Lord says, "Go and stand in the temple and speak to the people all the words of this life" (Acts 5:20). The signs and wonders done through them are the enacted proclamation of "this life." They are "the powers of the age to come" active even now, tokens and predictions of the new world of God, in which disease and death shall be no more. The "name of Jesus" is strong to save and can restore the lame man to perfect health because God has raised Him from the dead and made Him to be the Author of life. (Acts 3:15, 16)

This consciousness of being the people of God in the world's last days, of being witnesses to the accomplished fact of the Resurrection, the fact which is the dawn of the last day and the assurance of its perfect coming, fills the church with a joy that nothing can quench, not even death. The dying Stephen is the characteristic representative of the New Testament church. The church sees the heavens opened, the world of God welcoming man, and sees the Son of man standing at the right hand of God, about to return, that Son of man who came to seek and to save (Luke 19:10); and the church knows that He will save to the uttermost, that His coming will be the end of the world's agony and the time of eternal refreshing for His people (Acts 3:19, 20). The church is "born anew to a living hope through the resurrection of Jesus Christ from the dead." (1 Peter 1:3)

The church knows too that "the Son of man is to come" in judgment and "will repay every man for what he has done" (Matt. 16:27); and the church lives and works and hopes with a sober sense of responsibility. The church knows that the present is pregnant with the future and has in it the issues of salvation and judgment. The Lord God has in Jesus raised up the Prophet whom Moses had foretold; men must give heed to His word or be destroyed (Acts 3:22, 23). The apostles' cry is: Repent! Be saved from the judgment now, be saved in Him whose name alone can save (Acts 2:21, 38, 40; 4:12), before He comes to judge the living and the dead (Acts 10:42).

The New Testament which grew up amid this history, history interpreted by the Spirit of God and understood by faith as events in time moving surely toward God's goal of ultimate salvation and final judgment, is a book of buoyant eschatological hope and a book of sober and realistic eschatological responsibility. It is a book of the last days through and through and speaks with the urgency and finality of the last days:

> Today, when you hear His voice,
> do not harden your hearts.

THE APOSTOLIC PROCLAMATION IN THE FIRST CHURCH

The Book of Acts pictures the new people of God as living by the apostles' word. The church living thus lives in faith and love under the Lordship of Jesus, animated by the Spirit which He has poured out upon all believers, in joyous, active, and responsible expectancy of the return of the Lord in glory. The impress of this first history of God's people is on the whole new New Testament, and the first apostolic preaching (often referred to by its Greek name, *kerygma,* "herald's news, proclaimed Gospel") has given all the New Testament writings their characteristic color and contour.

The first 12 chapters of Acts give us the best and fullest examples of that apostolic *kerygma* in their record of the preaching of Peter (Acts 2:14-40; 3:12-26; 4:8-12; 10:34-43) and Stephen (Acts 7:2-53); we may round out the record with the sermon of Paul in the synagog at Pisidian Antioch recorded in Acts 13:16-41. The message of these sermons is essentially a reproduction of the basic proclamation of Jesus Himself, now told in the light of His resurrection and exaltation. Jesus had opened His Messianic ministry in Galilee with the words,

> The time is fulfilled,
> and the kingdom of God is at hand;
> repent, and believe in the Gospel.
> (Mark 1:14)

"The time is fulfilled." Jesus marked His appearance as the fulfillment of the prophet's prediction and of Israel's hope. And the most obvious fact about the apostolic *kerygma* is the assertion that what happened in Jesus of Nazareth happened "according to the Scriptures," the assertion that He is in the whole compass of His history the fulfillment of Old Testament prophecy. Whether it be Peter preaching it to Jews (Acts 2:16, 25; 3:18, 22, 24;

4:11) or to Gentiles (Acts 10:43), or whether it be Paul (Acts 13:23, 27, 32), or whether it be the Spirit-filled Stephen (Acts 7:52), the apostolic *kerygma* is unanimous in proclaiming: All the voices of the Old Testament, all the hopes of Israel are fulfilled in Him whom we proclaim as Lord and Christ. As Paul put it: "All the promises of God find their yes in Him." (2 Cor. 1:20)

"The kingdom of God is at hand." When Jesus spoke these words, He meant nothing less than this: "The kingdom of God is present in My person." The whole record of Him in the Gospels says just this, that God is establishing His reign in these last days by making Jesus Lord in the power of the Holy Spirit. Jesus can say to those who blasphemously reject Him: "But if it is by the *Spirit* of God that *I* cast out demons, then the kingdom of *God* has come upon you" (Matt. 12:28). If, then, the apostolic proclamation asserts that Jesus is Lord and Christ, it is proclaiming the kingdom of God, just as Jesus' word had proclaimed it. If Peter says, "God has made Him both Lord and Christ, this Jesus whom you crucified" (Acts 2:36), or if Philip preaches "good news about the kingdom of God and the name of Jesus Christ" (Acts 8:12), that is consentient witness to one great fact, one great act of God. For Jesus is Lord to the glory of God the Father, the Father who did great works through Jesus, gave Him up into death as the Servant who makes "many to be accounted righteous" (Is. 53:11), exalted Him at His right hand, and gave Him the Spirit to pour out upon His own. To proclaim the kingdom of God and the Lordship of Jesus is therefore necessarily to proclaim the Holy Spirit too, for the Spirit is indissolubly connected with both. The presence of the Spirit in the earthly life of Jesus is the evidence of His Lordship even then (Acts 10:38); the gift of the Spirit is the witness to His exaltation (Acts 2:33-36) and the means whereby the exalted Lord exercises His gracious Lordship for the salvation of men (Acts 2:28; 5:32).

The kingdom of God, the Lordship of Jesus the Christ, the outpouring of the Holy Spirit, all mark the days in which this news is uttered as the last great days, the age of fulfillment, the beginning of the end, the time when the new life of the world to come has broken into the old world of death in the person of Him who is the Author of life. And this life becomes man's possession by the Spirit, the Lord and Giver of life. All history now moves from this event with a new and unheard-of urgency toward the end of the end, toward the judgment on all who refuse this new life, toward the consummation of all things, the new heaven and the new earth in which the righteousness of God is forever and fully at home.

"Repent, and believe in the Gospel." Jesus by His words and deeds demanded a decision of men: "He who is not with Me is against Me" (Matt. 12:30). The apostolic proclamation of Jesus' words and deeds is news, is history. It is real, vital news; the story of the life, death, and exaltation of Jesus of Nazareth is not a tale that can be told or left untold at will. It does not diminish in immediacy and importance as the passage of days removes it from the present. It is an ever-present reality in the inspired Word that conveys it; it confronts, stirs, shakes, and moves men now. It calls for repentance, and it moves men to repentance and faith. In Jesus the Lord God has laid bare His arm for the last time in history, and man is confronted with the choice, now, of having that almighty arm for him or against him. There is no neutral corner where a man may stand, no place where a man may stay and await developments, as Gamaliel hoped to do. (Acts 5: 38, 39)

The word of the Lord grew. The whole New Testament is the rich and various unfolding of this proclamation. The Gospels expand it; the epistles restate, point up, and apply it; the Book of Revelation unfolds its utmost eschatological reach. And nowhere, in any aspect of it, does this word lose its character as history. It *has* a history, being the crown and fulfillment of God's previous actions and promises; it *is history* — the recital of the mighty works of God which culminate in that epochal history when God dealt decisively with the sin of man in His Servant Jesus of Nazareth; and it *makes* history — it is the word of the Lord, and the Spirit of the Lord moves creatively in it. It calls upon men to turn, and turns them, and thus catches men up into God's last great movement in history toward God's last goal.

CHAPTER II: The Implanted Word in Judaic Christianity: The Letter of James

Luke pictures the life of the early Judaic church (Acts 1—12) as a life of faith and hope under the apostolic word, a life under the dominion of the Lord Jesus to the glory of God, empowered by the Spirit and straining in joyous and earnestly responsible expectancy toward the return of the Lord in glory. That life moved on a high level; it was marked by a bold courageousness of confession that nothing could silence. Persecution might disperse the church, but its members went about as a witnessing church nevertheless, and the disciples' joy in suffering was in itself the most eloquent witness to the new life which had arisen in them. That life was marked by a unanimity and a will to mutual service that was in striking contrast to the bitter and often brutal factionalism of the Old Israel. (Acts 2:44, 45; 4:32—5:4)

Externally, the first church remained essentially Judaic in character. The disciples observed the Law as all good Jews did, even in such points as the distinction between clean and unclean foods (Acts 10:14); they observed the traditional hours of prayer, both in Jerusalem and when they were away from the holy city (Acts 3:1; 10:9, 30); they taught in the temple precincts (Acts 5:20, 25, 42); and they sought contact with the synagog (Acts 6:9, 10). They were faithful and devoted to their immediate mission to Israel (Acts 1:8) and lived in the midst of Israel in the spirit of Jesus' words to His disciples concerning the temple tax: Jesus had taught His disciples that they were children of God and therefore free from any obligation to support financially the house of the Divine

King, their Father, since kings impose taxes on strangers and not on their children; but Jesus had also laid upon them the velvet yoke of His love; to avoid offending the Jews, they were to pay the temple tax and to remain, with inner freedom, bound to the forms of the piety of God's ancient people (Matt. 17:24-27). Only so could they fulfill their mission to Israel; had they broken with the temple, they would have branded themselves as renegades and atheists, to whom no pious Jew would give ear.

They were thus placed squarely into the midst of Judaism, enmeshed in the life of Judaism; and they there called Israel to a radical reversal of repentance, to faith in the Lord Jesus Christ, and to baptism in His name. This made their situation difficult in the extreme. It put them under the persistent pressure of opposition, of official and unofficial persecution, and brought them poverty (cf. Gal. 2:10). The qualities which they displayed in their communal life and the wondrous deeds wrought by the hands of their leaders certainly won them the respect of the masses of the people, who even viewed them, in the beginning at least, with a certain awe. But official Judaism was against them from the beginning. This opposition was intensified by the success of the new movement and particularly by the fact that "a great many of the priests" went over to it and "were obedient to the faith" (Acts 6:7). And apparently the will of Israel's leadership imposed itself more and more upon the people generally; about A. D. 44 Herod saw that the execution of the apostle James had (as he had hoped and intended) "pleased the Jews" (Acts 12:2, 3), and he imprisoned Peter, "intending after the Passover to bring him out to *the people*" (Acts 12:4).

In these circumstances it was not easy to maintain the high level of missionary fervor and communal love which were the basic characteristics of the new community. Luke is in the Book of Acts telling the story of how the word of the Lord grew, how the Good News triumphed and sped on from Jerusalem to the end of the earth. We cannot therefore expect from him a full history, much less a sociology, of the first church. Nor should we assume that his picture of the life of the church is an idealized one; he is interested in indicating only the salient features of the new life which the word produced in men who responded to it

with repentance and faith. And even his succinct and schematic
presentation of the life of the first church makes it clear enough
that this level of life under the Lord was by no means a self-
evident and automatic possession of the church, but involved
a constant and strenuous struggle. The story of Ananias and
Sapphira (Acts 5:1-11) shows that men within the new people
of God could and did resist the Spirit and that the church had
need of stern discipline in order to remain the pure new people
of God. The words of Barnabas to the Gentile converts at Antioch
reflect the hard-won experience of Judaic Christianity: "When
he came and saw the grace of God, he was glad; and he exhorted
them all to remain faithful to the Lord *with steadfast purpose"*
(Acts 11:23). And Luke's continual emphasis on the place of
prayer in the life of the apostles and the apostolic church shows
that the church stood in perpetual need of renewal and sought
renewal of strength and purpose from the Lord of the church.

But it is in another document of the early church, in the
Letter of James, that we see most clearly how constant and severe
the struggle must have been, how little the high qualities of this
new life were the once-for-all and static possession of the church,
how they had to be constantly rewon and reasserted in repentance
under the implanted word of the Lord. The letter also shows how
vigorously the leaders of the church aided the church in that
struggle, with what agonized and conscientious consecration they
strove to keep the word once implanted in the church implanted
and active in the hearts of the men of the church. We see what
a concentrated energy of inspired pastoral wisdom, "wisdom from
above," went into the human word which ensured the growth of
the word of the Lord and gave it firm and deep rootage in the
lives and words and deeds of men. And the Letter of James shows
us more clearly than the Book of Acts another and very important
feature in the life of the first church; it shows us how thoroughly
apostolic the "apostles' teaching" (Acts 2:42) was — the mark
of the apostle is that he is the voice and the representative of the
Lord who sent him (Matt. 10:40; Luke 10:16; John 13:20; 2 Cor.
13:3), and we can see in the Letter of James how the very words
of Christ were the basic substance of the apostolic teaching, the
air which the first church breathed and lived by.

The Persons Addressed in the Letter

The Letter of James is addressed to Jewish Christians. The words of the salutation, "To the twelve tribes in the dispersion" (James 1:1), in themselves do not necessarily mark the readers as Jewish, since the New Testament constantly appropriates the titles and attributes of Israel for the New Testament people of God (cf. Gal. 6:16; Phil. 3:3; 1 Peter 1:1, 17; 2:9, 10; Rev. 7:4 ff.; 14:1); but these words are part of the generally Judaic coloring of the letter. The situation presupposed among the Christians addressed in the letter — that of a poor, tired, oppressed, and persecuted church — corresponds to what we know of the Jerusalem church of Acts 1—12; and what held for Jerusalem very probably held for other Jewish churches in Palestine and in the dispersion also. The sins which the letter particularly deals with are the sins of Judaism in their Christianized form; the problem of sexual license, for instance, which looms so large in gentile Christianity and is constantly dealt with in letters addressed to gentile churches, is not touched on here, while the prime sin of Israel under the leadership of scribe and Pharisee, that of cleavage between profession and practice (Matt. 23:3), which evoked Jesus' most stringent polemics, is scored heavily by James. The place of worship is called by the same name as the Jewish synagog (James 2:2), a practice which was long observed in Judaic Christianity, but was never frequent elsewhere in Christendom. The author takes all his examples from the Old Testament (Abraham, Rahab, Job, the prophets, Elijah), and this tells us something about the readers as well as the author.

Date of the Letter

The letter is apparently addressed to Judaic Christians of the early days, during the period covered by Acts 1—12. The church is still firmly enmeshed in Judaism, a part of historic Israel, so much so that one modern scholar has argued that the letter is addressed to *all* Israel, stressing all that Christians and Jews have in common, and is intended to be a missionary appeal, by way of admonition and a call to repentance, to all Jews. Although this theory amounts to an overstatement of the case and can hardly be accepted in the form in which it is advanced, it does

call attention to the essentially Judaic character of the persons
addressed, and it recognizes the fact that there are portions in
the letter which address the readers particularly as members of
historic Israel (4:1 ff.) and passages which are apostrophes directed to the Judaic world around the church rather than admonitions spoken directly to the church (4:13-17; 5:1-6). Judaism
has not yet definitively expelled the new community. Furthermore,
there is no indication in the letter of the tensions and difficulties
which arose when gentiles came into the church in large numbers,
those tensions which gave rise to the Apostolic Council (Acts 15)
and occasioned Paul's Letter to the Galatians. A date prior to
Paul's first missionary journey is therefore most probable, about
A. D. 45; and the phrase "twelve tribes of the dispersion" is
intended to designate the new people of God at a time when it
consisted primarily and predominately of converted Jews.

Author of the Letter

The only indications of authorship in the letter itself are the
name James in the salutation and the general tone and character
of its content. If we ask which of the various men named James
in the New Testament could expect to be recognized and identified when he calls himself simply "James, a servant of God and of
the Lord Jesus Christ" (1:1) and could speak with such massive
authority to Judaic Christianity as he does in this writing, the
most probable answer is, James, the brother of the Lord. (The
much debated question whether the brethren of the Lord were
His cousins, half brothers, or full brothers need not detain us here;
the last alternative, that they were the children of Joseph and Mary,
would seem to be the most probable; that they were his half
brothers is possible; the theory that makes them his cousins is beset by almost insuperable difficulties.)

This James had, like his brothers, refused to accept his brother
as the Christ during His lifetime (John 7:5). It was not, apparently, until the risen Lord appeared to him that his doubts were
overcome and he became the servant of Him whom he henceforth
called "the Lord Jesus Christ" (cf. 1 Cor. 15:7; Acts 1:14).
Active in the life of the church from the beginning, he seems to
have confined his work to Jerusalem. Possibly he undertook missionary journeys within Palestine, like his brothers (1 Cor. 9:5).

At any rate, it was in Jerusalem that he became and remained prominent. As early as A. D. 44 he was the acknowledged leader of the Jerusalem church, as Peter's words in Acts 12:17 show. About to leave Jerusalem after his deliverance from jail, Peter bids the people assembled in Mary's house tell of his release and departure "to James and to the brethren." At the Apostolic Council the voice of James is the final and decisive voice in the discussion (Acts 15:13-29). When Paul at the end of his third missionary journey reports to the Jerusalem church and brings the gifts of the gentile church to the saints at Jerusalem, he reports to James (Acts 21:18). The picture we have of James in Acts is confirmed by what we find in the letters of Paul; Paul can refer to him simply as "James" and reckon on being understood (1 Cor. 15:7); he practically ranks him with the apostles in Gal. 1:19; and even mentions him before Peter and John as one of the "pillars" of the church (Gal. 2:9). James is, for Paul, so integral a part of the life of the Jerusalem church that he can describe Jerusalem Christians who came to Antioch by saying, "Certain men came *from James*" (Gal. 2:12). Jude can in his letter identify himself to his readers by calling himself "brother of James." (Jude 1)

A later Jewish-Christian tradition preserved for us by Eusebius (*HE* II, 23, 4) pictures James as a paragon of Judaic piety in the sense that he was deeply interested in, and devoted to, the ritual side of that piety; but none of the New Testament notices of him confirms this. He is, according to the New Testament, a Christian Jew, devoted to his mission to Israel and therefore faithful to the temple and to the Law so long as the temple stands and there is an Israel that will hear him. Reliable tradition has it that he was faithful to his people to the end and died a martyr's death A. D. 66. So strongly had his piety and his love for his people impressed men that even pious Jews called him the Just and saw in the Jewish wars and the fall of Jerusalem God's righteous visitation upon Israel for putting this righteous man to death.

Occasion of the Letter

The Epistle of James shows that the author is acquainted with the situation of his readers, but none of the references is so specific that it enables us to point to any particular event or set of

circumstances as the immediate occasion for writing. Still, it
is probably not accidental that the epistle opens with a summons
to find cause for joy in "various trials" (1:2) and closes with an
admonition to restore the brother who "wanders from the truth"
(5:19). The "twelve tribes" are under the twin pressures of
poverty and persecution; they are tempted to grow depressed,
bitter, and impatient — depressed at the fate of the doomed people
of which they remained a part, a fate which loomed ever more
clearly and more terribly against the stormy skies of Palestine;
bitter at the fact that they were offering the grace of God in vain
to this doomed people; and impatient for the "times of refreshing" and the establishing of all things (Acts 3:19-21) which the
resurrection of Jesus Christ from the dead had promised and
assured.

They were tempted, in this apathetic slackening of their ener-
gies, this declension in their Christian stamina, to relapse and
accommodate their life to the life of the world which pressed on
them from every side and sought to put its mark and impress
upon them. For them, accommodation to the "world" meant, of
course, accommodation to the Judaism from which they had es-
caped, Judaism with its distorted piety, its encrusted and inactive
faith, its superficial and fruitless hearing of the word, its arrogant
and quarrelsome "wisdom," its ready response to the seduction
of wealth, its mad thirst for liberty. The danger of apostasy was
for members of this church anything but remote and theoretical;
it was immediate and real. (5:19, 20)

In such a situation, in a church beset from without and within,
faced with the necessity of constant correction and discipline, it
is small wonder that the love of many grew cold, that the church
was troubled by inner dissensions, that men were ready to speak
against and to judge one another, that the spontaneous mutual
ministrations of the first glad days were in danger of lapsing and
being forgotten.

Content of the Letter of James

To these Judaic churches in this characteristically Judaic situation the leader of Judaic Christianity addressed a thoroughly
Judaic letter, or rather, a homily in letter form; for the letter is
a letter chiefly in form — and even the letter form is not com-

plete; the personal conclusion, characteristic of Paul's letters, is absent here. A phrase like *"Listen,* my beloved brethren" (2:5) shows that we have to do with a writing which is simply the extension of the spoken "implanted word"; and the whole style of the letter bears this out. The leader and teacher whose word is the vehicle of the will of God to the Jerusalem church is speaking to the Judaic churches in Judea, Samaria, Galilee, Syria, Cilicia — perhaps the letter went even farther afield than that.

The features that characterized the life of the first Judaic church are the basic presuppositions of the letter of James, and the basic notes of the proclamation which produced and sustained that life recur in the word of James. Jesus is proclaimed as Lord and Christ, with divine authority; James' first word is a confession to God and to Jesus, and his relation is the same to both; he is "a servant of God and of the Lord Jesus Christ" (1:1). Jesus is "the Lord of Glory" (2:1), just as God is "King of Glory" and "God of Glory" in the Old Testament (Ps. 24:7; 29:3), and He is the object of faith (2:1); and He is Lord to the glory of God the Father, to the glory of the God whose nature is that He is the Giver of good gifts (1:5, 17), the God who has given to men the supreme gift of new life in the "word of truth," the Gospel (1:18). The presence and work of the Spirit is touched on too. God has made the Spirit to dwell in the men who constitute the new twelve tribes in the dispersion whom James is addressing (4:5). The wisdom that is God's gift to the believing man (1:5, 6) is in complete contrast to the "earthly, *unspiritual,* devilish" wisdom of natural man; it is wisdom which comes down "from above" (3:17) — we are reminded of the combination used by Luke in Acts: "Spirit and wisdom" (Acts 6: 3, 10). The consciousness of living in the world's last days finds the most explicit and vigorous expression. Christ is the Author of life, of the new and eternal life, in James as in the first apostolic proclamation. The word of truth which proclaims Him and presents Him produces a new birth in men; and James views this new life as the "first fruits," the beginning and the pledge of the renewal of all life (1:18). The new people of God await the "coming of the Lord" as the farmer waits for the harvest which will crown his year and his labors (5:7). The poor and oppressed people of

God are "heirs of the kingdom" (2:5) and look forward to the crown of life which God will give to those who love Him (1:12).

But the characteristic thing about this letter is the fact that these great, fundamental statements are so rigorously and completely subordinated to the one imperative that is based upon them, to the command, "Repent!" Many students of the Letter of James have found it passing strange that the letter is, on the one hand, so distinctly Christian and, on the other hand, so reticent about the basic Christian facts: the cross and resurrection are not even mentioned in any outspoken fashion. All manner of theories have been advanced to account for this strange double aspect of the letter. Some scholars, for instance, have suggested that the letter is really a Jewish writing lightly worked over to make it Christian, or that it incorporates an earlier Jewish work with Christian additions and modifications. Such theories are, of course, almost purely conjecture and do not carry us any farther toward understanding the epistle in a really historical sense. One scholar, one of the greatest students of James, has suggested an answer to the problem which has a solid basis in the facts of James' history and is therefore at least a fruitful suggestion: James, he notes, was a brother of Jesus and had witnessed Jesus' work, but had not come to faith in Him until he was confronted by Him as the risen Christ, the "Lord of Glory." Furthermore, James, after his conversion, worked in Jerusalem and sought to win Israel for the Christ and therefore kept the church of Jerusalem within the framework of Judaism; he stayed in Jerusalem and confronted Jerusalem with the Christ until his countrymen killed him. This history turned James away from all speculative wisdom and from everything that smacked of generality and theory. He has seen in Jesus' death and resurrection that he, James, with his ideas about God and Christ had been in the wrong and that Jesus, who gave God a whole love in word and deed, in life and in death, was in the right. He had seen how the "wise and prudent" of his people had rejected Jesus because their theoretical knowledge about God had blinded them to God's presence and God's action in Jesus before their very eyes and in their very midst. And James saw that it was because Israel's teachers and leaders thought they knew what the Messiah should be that they persisted in rejecting the Messiah proclaimed by the apostles and so led their people to refuse Him. James had learned, both in his own life and in the life of his people, how thoroughly a presumptive knowledge of God can lead a man astray and turn man from God as He actually reveals Himself. What James held fast, therefore, as the best and dearest possession that Jesus had left him was Jesus' call to repentance, that call which condemned Israel's pride and Israel's religious hypocrisy and proffered Israel God's grace. Only by repentance (which in Jesus' proclamation always includes faith) can man come to God; and the church can remain the twelve tribes of God's people only by repentance; it can hope to win Israel only as a perpetually repentant church, as the church which itself heeds Jesus' call of "Repent, for the kingdom of Heaven is at hand," heeds it and lives it in the whole compass of its life — for only so will Judaism be brought to see that God is in the midst of her.

Whether this or some other fact which we can no longer determine be the reason for it, it is obvious that James' whole letter is one great call to repentance, repentance as the Old Testament prophets, John the Baptist, and Jesus Himself had proclaimed it: the turning of the whole man wholly to his God, in a complete and radical break with his evil self and his evil past, a turning in submissive trust and obedience, a turning which is always ultimately God's own act in man (cf. Acts 5:31; 11:18). James stands in the New Testament as a prophet, and his cry is the prophet's cry: "Turn ye!" (Cf., e. g., Jer. 25:5.)

The "miscellaneous" character of James' admonitions has often been exaggerated, sometimes in the interest of theories concerning the origin of the book. This miscellaneous character is more apparent than real, being due to the Semitic habit of thought which sets down related thoughts side by side without explicitly co-ordinating them or subordinating one to the other as we are accustomed to do. James' call to repentance breaks down, upon closer investigation, into six rather massive units, each of which again usually has two aspects.

Turn Ye!

I. 1:2-27. Turn to your God, the good Giver of perfect gifts

    A. 1:2-18. Turn to the God who perfects you by trial

    Turn from your folly, 5, from your wavering double-

mindedness, 6-8, your doubt of God's goodness, your Judaic
fatalism which attributes man's sin to God, 13-15.

Turn to your God and find in Him the power to speak
a glad assent to the trials which He sends you, 2; find in Him
the tried and tested faith which gives steadfastness, 3, and
perfection, 4; find in Him, by the prayer of faith, the wisdom
which will enable you to bear your trials, 5, a wisdom which
enables the poor man to see in his poverty his exaltation, 9,
and gives to the rich man the power to see his greatness
elsewhere than in himself and his riches, 10, 11. Turn to God
and find in Him the unchanging and unchangeable Giver of
all good gifts, the Giver of the supreme gift, the gift of new
birth by His word, a rebirth which is the beginning and pledge
of creation's rebirth, 18. Thus empowered, endure your trials
manfully and joyfully and receive from Him the crown of
life, 12.

Since the gift of new life comes by the word of truth,

B. 1:19-27. Turn to the God who has implanted His word
of truth among you

Turn from the pride which breaks out in self-assertive
speech before it has heard the Good Giver out, turn from the
anger which resents His judgment on man's sin, 19, from the
filthiness and wickedness which insulates a man against the
wholesome fires of God's judgment and against the life-giving
warmth of His grace, 21. Turn from speaking to hearing,
from self-assertive anger to the meekness which hears God
out on His terms, 19-21, turn to God and receive from His
word the righteousness which God alone can work, 20, receive
it in a repentance which strips off the filth and wickedness of
self and in its naked helplessness receives from God salvation
of the soul, 21.

When you have so heard the word in repentance and faith,

Turn from the self-deception which thinks that God's word
is a word to be contemplated, that a man may hear God's
word without being moved by it, 22, 26; turn from such mere
and forgetful hearing of His word, 22, 24, 25, to a persevering
and vital hearing of it, turn to a doing of the word which

God's great gift has made for you a perfect law of liberty,
a law which sets you free for God and for your fellow men, 25,
that law which leads man to a pure and undefiled worship
of God, which hallows his speaking, makes his deeds deeds
of mercy, and sets him apart from the defilement and the
doom of this dark world, 26, 27.

II. 2:1-26. Turn from a self-contradicting faith and from a faith
    that exhausts itself in words to the true and active faith which
    the Lordship of Jesus demands

    A. 2:1-13. Turn: Break with the partiality toward the rich
       which is a self-contradiction for believers in the Lord of
       Glory

       Turn from a partiality which fawns on the rich and dis-
honors the poor, 1-3, for that is for you a cleavage of yourself
and a transgression of your Lord's command of "Judge
not," 4; it involves an impious judgment upon the poor and
a false and unrealistic judgment upon the rich, 5-7.

       Turn from the pious self-justification which pleads the law
of love to excuse partiality toward the rich, 8; free yourselves
of the last traces of the Judaic theory of compensation, which
seeks to offset the transgression of one commandment with
the fulfillment of another, 9-11; turn from the mercilessness
which you can conceal from yourselves but will not be able
to conceal from God in the Judgment, 12, 13.

       Turn to the Lord Jesus Christ, who will bestow the glory
of the kingdom of God upon the poor and has made the poor
rich even now as heirs of the Kingdom, 1, 5, who lifts those
who believe in Him above the petty difference between rich
and poor. Rise in faith to the vision which sees men, both
poor and rich, with the eyes of God, the poor as heirs of God,
the rich as the oppressors of the people of God and the
blasphemers of the holy name pronounced upon the believer
at his baptism, 5-7. Return to a real and repentant confron-
tation with the will of God — see in the law of love the
royal law which gives meaning to all the commandments and
includes them all; and remember that you will be judged under
the law of liberty, that law which sets you free for God and
for your fellow man; remember that only a faith whose work

is mercy can hope for mercy in the merciful judgment of
God, 8-13.

B. 2:14-26. Turn from a mere profession of faith to a living
and active faith

Turn from a merely verbal faith, for a faith that exhausts
itself in words is as useless as a charity that exhausts itself
in gracious phrases, 14-16; turn from a faith that is in reality
no faith at all, but dead, 17, and unable to save, 14.

Turn: Cease trying to excuse yourselves with a pious
sophistry which makes an impossible cleavage between faith
and works by distributing them as several gifts, faith to one
man, works to another, 18; this reduces faith to a merely
intellectual grasp of truths about God — demons have that
kind of faith, and they know that it cannot save them; they
shudder at the judgment that is to come upon them, 19.

Turn from this delusion about your barren faith, a faith
as impotent and as inactive as a corpse, 20, 26. Turn to that
faith which is a living faith and must needs evince itself in
works, 18, a faith which justifies because it is a faith that
commits a man wholly to his God and is therefore a working
faith, such a faith as Abraham's was: He was ready to give
to God the best gift God had given him, his son; Abraham's
faith was active in his works and found its fullest expression
in works, 21, 22. In the fact that believing Abraham showed
in deed that he held God dearer than God's dearest gift there
was seen the full meaning of the words, "Abraham believed
God, and it was reckoned to him as righteousness," 23, 24.
Abraham, the believing friend of God, was friend in word
and deed, and so one can even say that man is justified by
works and not by faith alone, for faith is never alone, as
even the example of Rahab shows: Hers was a simple and
unfinished faith, and yet this believing woman, with her stained
and ruined past, acted out her faith in works, and she too
was thus justified by works, as one whose faith made her the
doer of the will of God, 25.

Turn to the faith which is the creation of the God who is
God of the living and not of the dead, a faith that is a body
animated by a living soul, not a corpse, 26.

III. 3:1-18. Turn, you who would be teachers in the church, from your hopelessly sinful selves and from your human wisdom to the God who gives true wisdom from on high

A. 3:1-12. Turn from your sinful selves, from man to God

Turn from the blithe self-assurance which presses boldly into the teaching office, unmindful of the fearful responsibility imposed on human frailty by that office, 1, 2; consider what a struggle is involved in the control of the tongue, 2, what fearful power for evil this small member wields, how fierce and untamable this ruthless evil, this very embodiment of the godless world, is, 3-6. Turn from the delusion that any man can tame this evil — man is lord of creation but is not master of his tongue, 7, 8. Turn from that unnatural cleavage of the soul which makes the tongue the means by which men both bless God and curse man, the creature made in the image of God, 9-12. Since *no man* can tame the tongue, turn to Him who alone can overcome the evil in man. (This is implicit in "no man can tame the tongue"; the positive side of the call to repentance is really expressed in B.)

B. 3:13-18. Turn from your earthbound, unspiritual, demonic wisdom to God, who gives true wisdom from on high

Turn from a wisdom which in its selfish bitterness creates divisions and produces every vile practice and thus gives the lie to the truth which God has given you in His word of truth, 13-16. Turn from a wisdom that is earthly, unspiritual, and devilish, 15. Turn to God, who gives true wisdom and understanding, who alone can save man from his fruitless and arrogant wisdom and give him true wisdom, characterized by meekness and productive of good, 13, a wisdom whose purity attests its divine origin, an active and graciously productive wisdom that goes its way in the certitude and candor of faith, 17. Turn in the strength of this wisdom to a life devoted to the making of peace, as teachers who by their words and deeds plant seeds which grow and ripen into righteousness, 18.

IV. 4:1-12. Turn from assimilation to the world, with its passionate strife and its passionate enmity against God, to God the Giver of the Spirit and all grace

A. 4:1-10. Turn from assimilation to the world to God, the
  Giver of the Spirit

Turn from the world's passionate wars and fierce fightings,
1, 2. Turn from the world's worldly, self-centered, and therefore fruitless prayers, 3. Turn from your friendship with the
world which is infidelity to God and enmity against Him,
and turn from the devil, the author of all enmity against God,
4, 7. Turn from your impurity and double-mindedness, from
your secular laughter and your worldly joys, 8, 9.

Turn to the God who has made His Spirit to dwell in
you and yearns jealously for that Spirit — you dare not receive the grace of God in vain, 5. Turn to God who opposes
the proud but gives grace to the humble, who will welcome
all who penitently draw near to Him, 6, 8. Turn to the God
who exalts those who speak a resolute no to the devil and
thus submit to God and humble themselves before Him, 7, 10.

B. 4:11, 12. Turn from the world's evil-speaking to the God
  who is able to judge and to save

Turn from that refined form of murder, cf. 2, the malicious
word against your brother, 11. Turn from your quarrel with
God, which is what your words against your brother come to;
for when you condemn your brother you condemn God's Law,
which demands of you a whole and unbroken love for your
brother, 11. Turn in fear to Him who has power to destroy,
the one Lawgiver and Judge whose office you dare not
usurp, 12. Turn in faith and hope to Him who is able to
save as well as to destroy, 12.

V. 4:13—5:6. Turn from the world in its haughty and godless
self-assurance

This section does not address the church directly but
rather apostrophizes the world in the midst of which the
church lives, just as the Old Testament prophets apostrophize
the "nations" round about Israel. Note that (a) the address
"brethren," found in every other section of the epistle, does
not occur here; (b) the brusque and peremptory expression
"come now," 4:13 and 5:1, occurs only in this section. The
warning to the world is, of course, significant to the church
in the world; the church lives in the midst of the world, is

threatened by the world, and can be infected by the world. Also, the church is thus kept aware of the fact that God's call to repentance is a universal call, as universal as the grace of God, with whom nothing is impossible, not even the conversion of the ungodly rich. But because it is the world that is primarily addressed here, the positive aspects of the command to "turn" are here only implicit.

A. 4:13-17. Turn from the world's self-assurance in planning

Turn from the secular self-assurance of the trader, who lays his plans under the huge delusion that man is lord of his tomorrows, forgetting the frailty and transience of all human life and forgetting Him who is Lord of the morrow, 13-17. Turn to the Lord who rules all life and all its tomorrows and learn to say "If the Lord wills" in all your planning, 15, for to know the Lord and not to live constantly under His Lordship is sin, 17.

B. 5:1-6. Turn from the world's ruthless and impious accumulation of wealth

Turn from the world's callous and brutal pursuit of riches, its heaping up of possessions beyond any conceivable need, its fat and wanton luxury; for the rich live luxuriously under the very shadow of judgment, unmindful of the fact that the last days are already upon them, that the slaughter-day of judgment, Jer. 12:3, is imminent, that day on which their treacherously gotten and unused wealth will rise up to witness against them. They employ the Law to kill the righteous man, as they used it to condemn and kill the Righteous One, and they find in the patient submission of the righteous the assurance that all is well, 1-6.

VI. 5:7-20. Turn to the returning Lord: Rest in the Lord, wait patiently for Him, and let your whole life be attuned to His coming

A. 5:7-12. Rest in the Lord, wait patiently for Him

Turn from the impatience of the wavering heart, 7, 8. Renounce all grumbling against the brother; all our attempts to have the last word now show that we have forgotten Him who will come to have the last word soon, 9. Renounce all

swearing; when we invoke the presence of the Lord on some
of our words, we show that we have forgotten the coming
Lord who is the remembering witness of our every word, 12.

Turn to the patience of the farmer who waits but knows
why he must wait and what he waits for — the precious
harvest which crowns his year with festal joy, 7-9. Turn to
the comforting knowledge of the Lord's ways given you in
the Scriptures, to the example of the prophets who spoke the
word of the Lord as you are speaking it now, who suffered
for that speaking as you are suffering now, who suffered
with a patient endurance which you must emulate; for you
know from the example of Job what the purpose of the Lord
in all man's suffering is; you know Him as the compassionate
and merciful Lord, 10, 11, and you know that steadfastness
under His Lordship brings a great reward, 11. Turn to that
speaking which always has the end in view, so that your every
word to your brother is a word of love and your simple yes
and no is an oath, spoken in the presence of Him who comes
to judge and to reward, 9, 12.

B. 5:13-20. Let your whole life be attuned to His coming

Turn: Let every aspect of your life, your suffering and
your joy, be hallowed by the word of God and by prayer, 13.

Turn: Let the life of the church be one of ministering
love to the sick, a love which deals with suffering man in the
believing confidence that forgiveness and healing are *there* by
God's giving, there for the reaching hand of the prayer of
faith; faith can pray as Elijah prayed, 14-18.

Turn: Let the love of the seeking Shepherd live in you,
that love which pursues the brother who has wandered from
the truth, and brings him back, back from death to life, from
sin to the forgiveness of sins, 19, 20.

Characteristics of the Letter

Two things stand out at once as characteristic of this letter;
it is practical in content and poetic in form. Both these qualities
put the work of James into the literary classification of the Christian "psalm." Paul speaks briefly of this form of edifying speech
in 1 Cor. 14:26 and more fully in Eph. 5:19 and Col. 3:16. In

the first passage the "psalm" (or "hymn," as the RSV translators have rendered it) is coupled with "a lesson" over against three other forms of utterance which are clearly very closely related to one another: "a revelation, a tongue, or an interpretation." The purpose of all these is "edification" (1 Cor. 14:26). Since Paul goes on to regulate the utterance of revelation, tongue, and interpretation in the interest of an orderly and edifying worship by the church (1 Cor. 14:27-31), we may assume that both the psalm and the lesson (to which he devotes no further attention) are less enthusiastic and therefore more readily intelligible forms of utterance that present no particular problem in the control of worship. This is confirmed by the other two passages, in which the psalm appears as a form of inspired teaching and admonition "in all wisdom" (Col. 3:16), in which Christians admonish one another. The psalm, it would seem, was a poetic form of the "word of Christ" (Col. 3:16) which addressed itself particularly to the practical problems of Christian living, as the immediate context of the passages in both Ephesians and Colossians shows (Col. 3:12 ff.; 3:18 ff.; Eph. 5:15-18, 21 ff.). The Letter of James, with its 54 imperatives in 108 verses, is very decidedly "teaching and admonition" in poetic form. As such it naturally bears a strong resemblance to what is called the "Wisdom literature" of the Jews, such works as the Book of Proverbs and Ecclesiastes in the Old Testament and apocryphal works like the Wisdom of Solomon and Ecclesiasticus. Indeed, the letter is strongly Old Testamental in tone and content, much more so than the number of actual quotations from the Old Testament (there are only five of them) would seem to indicate. A glance at the margins of a cross-reference Bible will show how rich the letter is in allusive reminiscences of the Old Testament.

But the work is anything but a mere continuation of the Old Testament-Judaic Wisdom tradition. What gives the Letter of James its distinctive flavor and its distinctive content is not the influence of the Old Testament or anything in the tradition of Judaism. It is, rather, the all-pervasive influence of the words of Jesus, whom James calls Lord. Though James never quotes Jesus directly, he is constantly recalling and echoing words of Jesus in a way which shows that they were for him and his hearers

the basic and self-evident influence in their lives, the authority
beyond which there is no appeal. Cross-references and statistics
(a recent study lists 26 allusions to the words of Jesus in the
letter) cannot really convey the true and full impression; the best
way to measure the impact of Jesus upon James is to come fresh
from a reading of the Gospel According to Matthew to the Letter
of James. Then one can see how the Lord who is so rarely
mentioned by James nevertheless casts His bright light across
every page and can see that James' work is essentially the recalling of the words of the Lord Jesus Christ, with comment and
explication which applies that word to His church here and now.

Even in literary form James bears a strong resemblance to
Jesus. His imagery, like that of Jesus, is drawn largely from the
outdoors — the stars of the heavens, the sea and the winds, the
fields and the sun, fig tree and vine, the early and latter rain and
the harvest, fountains, the morning mist, the horse, the birds and
beasts and fish and creeping things, the forest and the forest fire.
Some of James' images may be due to the direct influence of
Jesus; other similarities are due, no doubt, to their common experience as men of Galilee. Furthermore, Jesus' words are poetic;
the Beatitudes are direct descendants of the Psalter, and scholars
have found that the Lord's Prayer, for instance, when translated
back into Jesus' mother tongue comes out as Semitic poetry.
James' words too have a pronounced poetic rhythm throughout.
Even a translation will give one the feel of it, especially if one
reads aloud and notes the natural division suggested by the sense.

One of the best modern commentators on James has well
characterized his style as energetic, lively, and vivid. James dis-
likes the abstract and likes to make his meaning clear by concrete
and plastic images, which he often expands into little narratives,
such as that of the farmer waiting for the harvest (5:7); or he
makes his point by means of crisp and telling dramatic sketches,
such as the scene of fuss and flutter when the rich man makes
his appearance in the Christian assembly (2:2, 3). James button-
holes his reader by means of questions, direct address, and imperatives; no one goes woolgathering while this prophetic preacher
is speaking. None of these devices is a merely literary device,
however; all are in the service of an inspired and passionate
pastoral concern.

Structurally the letter is a series of "psalms" rather than the ordered and continuous development of a single theme such as we find in Paul's Letter to the Ephesians or Letter to the Romans. Still, the letter is not merely a loosely strung series of little admonitory paragraphs, as is often said. James walks round his theme, as it were, a theme which one might sum up as "The People of God in the Last Days As It Ought by God's Grace to Be," and deals successively with various aspects of it; he is not at pains to make obvious the connection between the various aspects. But that there is an inner connection between the larger units (as well as between the smaller sections) can hardly be denied; there is a natural, if not inevitable, progression from Part One of the outline given above, which calls for a believing acceptance of suffering and a believing submission to the word of God and, moreover, closes with the appeal that Christians be both hearers and doers of the word, to Part Two, which deals with faith as a working, active faith. From faith, which must document itself in deeds if it is faith at all, to Part Three, which portrays the active and peaceable wisdom from above which overcomes the invincible malice of the tongue and makes men teachers worthy of the name, is again an easy and not unnatural transition. The rebellious viciousness of the tongue and the self-centered worldly wisdom, which are the foil to the true wisdom in Part Three, suggest the theme of Parts Four and Five, the antithesis between the church and the world. The prediction of the last judgment in the denunciation of the rich in Part Five suggests the theme of Part Six: the life of the people of God attuned to the coming of the Lord.

Authenticity of the Letter

A good many modern scholars have doubted whether the Letter of James could be the work of James the brother of the Lord and have advanced various theories of authorship to explain the fact that the letter is, on the one hand, so markedly Judaic and, on the other, so specifically Christian and yet silent on the great redemptive facts of the life, death, and resurrection of Jesus. The theories can be roughly divided into two classes: According to one, James' letter is viewed as an earlier Jewish writing, worked over and Christianized by a later writer, not James the brother of the Lord. According to the other, the letter is considered to be a Christian work of the late first century or the first half of the second century, written either by an otherwise unknown James or by someone who wanted to have his work accepted as the work of James the brother of the Lord. These theories are, of course, highly conjectural and need not detain us long. The arguments used to disprove the authorship of James the brother of the Lord are of greater concern. They are chiefly the following:

   a. The absence of an early and definite tradition assigning the letter to James the brother of the Lord.
   b. The absence of any emphasis on ritualism in the letter — the fact that there is no mention of circumcision, the Sabbath, clean and unclean food, etc.
   c. The absence of concrete references of Jesus' history and Messiahship.
   d. The high quality of the Greek employed in the letter.

As for (a): It may be admitted at once that the ancient tradition which assigns the letter to James is not very early (*ca.* A. D. 200) or very strong, whatever the reason may be. But if the evidence in tradition is relatively slight, it must also be noted that there is no evidence whatever for anyone else as author, so that the tradition must be allowed to stand until *conclusive* reasons for denying the letter to James can be advanced.

With regard to (b): The absence of any reference to ritualism is not by any means conclusive evidence against the authenticity of the letter. There is nothing in the *New Testament* evidence to indicate that James was a rabid ritualist who could not speak to the church without touching on circumcision and the like. Indeed, the fact that he gave Paul the right hand of fellowship (Gal. 2:9), and his words in Acts 15:13-21 would seem to indicate that James, while he earnestly sought to keep Judaic Christianity Judaic in order not to forfeit its missionary opportunity in Israel, had no particular interest in Judaic ritual as such. The picture of James as a passionate devotee of ritual stems from second-century heretical Jewish-Christian sources, sources which moreover tend to discredit themselves by their fanciful and legendary character.

With regard to (c): The absence of concrete and clear references to Jesus' history is more serious. James does, of course, state the Messiahship and Lordship of Jesus in emphatic and weighty terms (James 1:1; 2:1), and the fact that his work is permeated by the words of Jesus must be allowed due weight. But when we ask why James should have said this much and no more, we can only guess in answer. Theoretically, it is highly unlikely that the apostle Paul, who said, "for me to live is Christ," should have written a whole chapter on love without once referring explicitly to Christ as the very embodiment and the sole source of that love. And yet Paul has done just that, 1 Cor. 13.

With regard to the fourth argument, (d), the allegation that the Greek employed in the letter (correct, cultured, eloquent, and in some respects literary rather than popular) is impossible for a Galilean Jew, it must be remembered that such verdicts can never be certain. They might be more certain if we knew for certain just what Greek James heard in Galilee and in Jerusalem, what Greek books he read or heard quoted, what kind of mind and memory James had — was it perhaps one like Shapespeare's, which sponged up and retained everything once heard, seen, or felt, and retained it with remarkable fullness and fidelity? We can point to the following facts: Greek was widely used in Galilee, with its many Hellenistic cities; Jesus no doubt knew Greek. According to Acts, Greek was so commonly known in Jerusalem that Paul might have addressed the mob in the temple court in that tongue; they were both surprised and pleased when Paul spoke Aramaic (Acts 22:2). The Jerusalem church had a component of Greek-speaking Jews in it from the very beginning, (Acts 6:1). If James wished to address Christian Jews outside Jerusalem and outside Palestine, he could address them only in Greek if he wished to be understood by all. For James the brother of the Lord, leader of the Jerusalem church and head of Judaic Christendom, Greek was a natural and necessary second language. It is precarious to make assertions as to how well or how ill he may have spoken it.

On the other hand, the authenticity of the letter is strongly supported by (a) the simplicity of the self-designation, James 1:1; a later writer seeking to impersonate James would almost certainly have emphasized the fact that he was the brother of the Lord; (b) the free way in which the words of Jesus are used in the

letter; a later writer would more probably have drawn upon the
Gospels and have quoted more directly; (c) the points of agreement in language and thought between the letter and the speech
of James (and the letter which he suggested) at the Apostolic
Council, Acts 15:13-21; 23-29; this argument is not, of course,
in itself conclusive, but it is remarkable that within the limited
scope of the few sentences in Acts the points of contact with the
letter of James should be so many (e. g., the use of "name,"
James 2:7; 5:10, 14 with Acts 15:14, 17, 26; the use of "brother,"
James 2:5 with Acts 15:13; the use of "keep," James 1:27 with
Acts 15:29); (d) the peculiarly Palestinian coloring of a number
of expressions in the letter: "the early and the late rain," peculiar
to Palestinian agriculture, James 5:7, and "three years and six
months" as the duration of the drought invoked by the prayer of
Elijah (James 5:17); the account in 1 Kings 17:1 and 18:1 does
not make it so long. Jesus, too, uses the same expression with
reference to this drought in Luke 4:25. It seems to be not
a popular exaggeration of the Old Testament narrative, but a popular Palestinian expression for "a couple of" (as the half of seven,
the number of completeness).

Canonicity of the Letter

The Letter of James is an antilegomenon. (For an explanation
of the terms "canonicity" and "antilegomenon" see Chapter XII.)

James and Paul

At the time of the Reformation the place of James in the
church's canon (that is, the collection of sacred books which are
authoritative for the faith of the church) was again questioned,
not only by Luther, but also by Roman Catholic scholars such
as Erasmus and Cajetan. Luther's objection to James is well
known; it is based chiefly on the section James 2:14-26, which to
Luther seemed to be in irreconcilable conflict with Paul and the
Gospel of salvation by grace through faith without the works of
the Law. But James' words on faith and works are not aimed at
Paul; neither do they really contradict Paul's teaching. They are
not aimed at Paul; the idea that faith is merely the certainty that
God is one, 2:19, has nothing to do with Paul; neither was Paul
the first to see in Abraham the exemplar of saving faith — the

rabbis had done that before him, as had Jesus Himself (Matt. 8:11; John 8:56). The polemics of James *may* be directed at a watered-down and distorted version of Paul's Gospel, such as might have been reported in Jerusalem from Antioch when Paul was preaching there (Acts 11:25, 26). But it is more likely that James is combating not a doctrine, but a practical threat to faith that came to his readers from their Judaic past and their Judaic surroundings. Jesus had said of the teachers of Judaism that they professed without practicing (Matt. 23:3) — what would be more natural than a recurrence of this Judaic fault in a Christianized form in Judaic Christianity? It should be noted, moreover, that the bold but monumentally simple argument of James would be pitifully weak, if not malicious, as a refutation of Paul's teaching. And the James whom we know from his letter is neither weak intellectually nor malicious morally. James is not attacking Paul.

Neither does James, at bottom, contradict Paul. Both Paul and James are moved to speak by love. Paul emphasizes the fact that our salvation is wholly God's grace and entirely His doing and that faith is therefore first and foremost pure receiving. Paul will leave no desperate sinner outside God's call of grace. James emphasizes the fact that faith is union and communion with God and commits us wholly, with all our thoughts and all our doing, to God; James will allow no brother to destroy his faith and himself by making of faith an intellectual acceptance of doctrinal propositions and emptying it of love and works. Paul speaks to the sinner's desperation; James speaks to Christian complacency. When James is speaking to the repentant sinner, he makes no mention of works but bids such a one in his desperation draw near to God, in the assurance that God will draw near to him like the father of the returning prodigal son (James 4:8). James describes man's redemption as a new birth from God, solely by the will and word of God (James 1:18); and he describes God's love for man as God's sole and sovereign choice, as God's election (James 2:5). Paul, on the other hand, can combine his own characteristic emphasis with that of James in a single sentence: "By grace you have been saved through faith; and this is not your own doing, it is the gift of God — not because of works, lest any man should boast. For we are His workmanship, *created in Christ Jesus for good works,* which God prepared beforehand, that we should walk in them." (Eph. 2:8-10)

The same Luther who objected so strenuously to James' conception of justification by faith has given us a description of faith which would delight the heart of James: "Faith is a divine work in us, which transforms us and gives us a new birth from God, John 1:13, and kills the old Adam. . . . Oh, it is a living, busy, active, and mighty thing, this faith; it cannot but be ever doing good. Faith does not ask if there are good works to be done, but has done them before one can ask and is ever a-doing. But whoever does not do such works is a man without faith; he goes groping about in search of faith and good works and knows neither what faith nor what good works are." And the first of Luther's theses, which makes repentance the beating heart of the Christian existence, might serve as a title to the Letter of James. The presence of this letter in the canon is a perpetual reminder to the church not to misconstrue Paul by making him the advocate of a lazy and workless faith, a reminder to hear and be guided by the real Paul, the Paul who entreats us "not to accept the grace of God in vain." (2 Cor. 6:1)

CHAPTER III: Gentile and Jewish Christian — Tension and Conflict: The Apostolic Council and Paul's Letter to the Galatians

READINGS: ACTS 13:1–15:35; GALATIANS

The word of the Lord grows; where it grows, the Lord Jesus Christ is present and at work; and He is always "a sign that is spoken against" (Luke 2:34). Where the word of the Lord grows, the kingdom of God is present; Jesus once described the presence and working of the Kingdom by comparing it with the working of leaven in dough; where the Kingdom is, there is ferment, disturbance, change, and upheaval. And so it is not surprising and in no way a contradiction of the fact that it is a divine word if the growth of the word brings with it tension and rouses conflict, not only between the church and the world, but also within the church itself. The first church experienced such tension and conflict when the word of the Lord began to grow on Gentile soil and the question of the relationship between the converted Gentile and the Christian Jew became an acute question, involving as it did the question of the relationship between the new, universal Gospel and the ancient Law given by God to Israel.

The apostles and the apostolic church knew from the beginning that the Christ is Lord of all and that the word of the Lord must grow on every soil under heaven. Jesus had made His apostles His witnesses, not only in Jerusalem and all Judea, but also in Samaria and to the end of the earth (Acts 1:8). The miracle of Pentecost spelled out in roaring wind, in apportioned flame, and in the gift of a speech that men of every nation could understand as their own the fact that the Spirit was to be poured out on "all flesh," that the Gospel was to go to all men in every tongue, that the promise for the last days, now being fulfilled in the outpouring of the Spirit, was not only to the Jews but also "to all that are far off, every one whom the Lord our God calls to Him." (Acts 2:39)

This knowledge did not remain mere theory; nor was it the active possession of only a few. When Samaria received the word of God preached there by Philip, the Jerusalem apostles acknowledged and welcomed the fellowship of the Samaritans and cemented the fellowship between the church of Samaria and the church of Jerusalem by sending Peter and John thither to confer upon them the gifts of the Spirit in full measure; and the apostles further extended that fellowship by "preaching the Gospel to many villages of the Samaritans" (Acts 8:4-25). Philip was prompted by the angel of the Lord to tell the good news of Jesus to the Ethiopian eunuch and to baptize him, thus bringing into the new people of God one who had been doubly excluded from the ancient people of God, excluded both by the fact that he was a Gentile and by the fact that he was a eunuch (Deut. 23:1). Thus the promise made for just such men through the prophet was fulfilled (Is. 56:3-8). Such incidents were surely not isolated — Luke records typical incidents in his compressed account of how the word of the Lord grew — nor were they unknown or forgotten in Jerusalem.

Another such incident, the conversion of the gentile Cornelius and his family and friends (Acts 10:1-48), is characteristic of the attitude of the Palestinian church. The account of Luke marks this incident as a turning point, an epochal event. He tells it very fully, with emphasis on the divine guidance given by visions vouchsafed to both Peter and Cornelius; he records the sermon delivered by Peter in the house of Cornelius; and he points to the striking manifestations of the Spirit in these Gentile converts, manifestations at which the Jewish Christians were "amazed." Luke also records the fact that Peter's Jewish reluctance to enter a Gentile house had to be overcome (Acts 10:9-16, 27) and that there were those in Jerusalem who were dubious and critical about the step Peter had taken (Acts 11:1-18). For Peter this incident was of decisive and lasting importance, as his reference to it at the Apostolic Council shows (Acts 15:7-9). That the doubts of the men of Jerusalem were not wholly overcome by Peter's answer to their objections (Acts 11:4-18) is evident from the subsequent course of events. Thus there were present in Judaic Christianity two conflicting impulses, both the will for the inclusion of the Gentiles and a Judaic reluctance to accept the uncircumcised Gentiles as brethren without reservation or limitation.

The beginnings and the seeds of conflict were there. The tension was made acute and brought into the open chiefly by three events: the conversion of Saul, the founding of a predominantly Gentile church at Antioch on the Orontes, and the missionary journey of Paul and Barnabas to Cyprus and the cities of Southern Galatia in Asia Minor. The conversion of the rabidly conservative Pharisee and persecutor Saul is marked, both in the three accounts of it in Acts (Acts 9:1-19; 22:3-21; 26:9-18) and in Paul's own reference to it in his epistles (Gal. 1:15, 16; 1 Cor. 15:8-10; Eph. 3:3, 8; 1 Tim. 1:12-16), as an absolutely creative act of the sovereign grace of God, an act which made Saul God's "chosen instrument" (Acts 9:15). The history of Saul, or Paul, his Roman name, by which he was known in his work among the Gentiles and is remembered in the church, shows us how the Lord of history had prepared His chosen instrument. Paul was a *Roman* citizen (Acts 16:37; 22:25); a citizen of Tarsus in Cilicia, no mean *Greek* city (Acts 21:39); and a *Hebrew* of the Hebrews (Phil. 3:5). Here was a man whose history had fitted him for the task to which the grace of God had called him. He was enabled by it to become all things to all men; he could, in a world dominated politically by Rome, bring the Gospel to men decisively influenced by Greek culture and speaking the Greek language. And he would be the last man to break ruthlessly with Judaic Christianity, even when the question of the relationship between Gentile and Jew in the church made fellowship between Jew and Gentile agonizingly difficult, for he remained in the highest sense a Hebrew of the Hebrews to the last (cf. Rom. 9:1-5). In Paul God gave the church the man whose word and work would inevitably heighten the tensions latent there, and also the man who would work wholeheartedly for a salutary resolution of those tensions.

Paul did not found the Gentile church at Antioch; some unnamed Jews, men of Cyprus and Cyrene, did that (Acts 11:20), or rather, the "hand of the Lord" did it through them (Acts 11:21). Paul is not quite the lone genius in pioneering Gentile missions and in establishing Gentile churches free from the Law that some romanticizing accounts make him out to be. Neither was he the first to work for contact and communion between the new Gentile community and the older Judaic churches. The Jerusalem church itself did that, by sending Barnabas, that "good man, full of the Holy Spirit and of faith" (Acts 11:24) to Antioch. And it was Barnabas who brought Paul to Antioch (Acts 11:25, 26). But the influence of Paul's preaching at Antioch must have been deep and decisive. How great Paul's influence was and how graciously ecumenical it must have been, we can measure by the fact that it was Paul whom the brethren chose to go with Barnabas to bring relief to the brethren in Judea during the famine (Acts 11:27-30), and by the fact that the Spirit chose him for the first organized mission to the Gentiles (Acts 13:1-3). It was no doubt largely due to Paul's influence that the church of Antioch remained a church free of the Law, a church that both cultivated a full and active fellowship with the Judaic church and became the base for mission work to the Gentiles.

On the missionary journey that took Paul and Barnabas to Cyprus and Asia Minor (Acts 13—14) Paul emerges as the leader; Luke now calls him by his Roman name, Paul (13:9), and now usually speaks of the two men in the order "Paul and Barnabas," whereas previously he has put the name of Barnabas first. From the time of their meeting with the Roman proconsul Sergius Paulus on Cyprus (Acts 13:6-12), Paul is the central figure in Gentile missions and dominates the rest of Luke's account of how the word of the Lord grew. The conduct of the mission which Paul undertook jointly with Barnabas is characteristic of the ecumenical outlook of Paul. He sought contact with the synagog everywhere and found a ready acceptance of his good news especially among the "devout converts to Judaism" (Acts 13:43), and those Gentiles whom Luke designates as "men who fear God," Gentiles who, without actually being fully converted to Judaism, still were on the fringes of the synagog, attracted by its pure preachment of the sole God and the high character of its moral teaching. Paul sought contact with the synagog and became a Jew to the Jew in his preaching by emphasizing how all God's previous dealings with Israel, from the time of the patriarchs to John the Baptist, have been leading up to and preparing for the message of Jesus as the Messiah, whom Paul now proclaimed to them (Acts 13:26-41). But at the same time he made it startlingly plain that his Gospel was, as the fulfillment of the promises of God, no mere supplement to the Law, but the end of the Law and the antithesis to it, that the word of God was now going beyond the confines of Israel into all the world, that through the Savior whom God had brought of David's line, *"everyone that believes* is freed [literally, "justified"] from everything from which you could not be freed by the law of Moses" (Acts 13:39). He threw the doors of the new temple of God wide open to all, to Jew, to proselyte, to Gentile, and gave all men direct access to God, in Christ and simply by faith. He was saying out loud and in so many words what had long been implicit in the miracle of Pentecost, in the evangelization of the Samaritans, and in the conversion of the Ethiopian eunuch, Cornelius, and the Gentiles of Antioch.

As a result, there came into the church large numbers of Gentiles, without circumcision, without submitting to the customs of Moses, not by way of Judaism, not as Jewish proselytes, but directly. And these people were, to some extent at least, conscious of the fact that they did not need to come into the church by way of Judaism, that they were full members of the new people of God, just as they were and as God had called them. This was bound to raise questions in the minds of Jewish Christians who had not yet or would not ever grasp the total newness of the New Testament, who could not or would not face all that was implicit in the words of John the Baptist when he said, "God is able *from these stones* to raise up children to Abraham" (Matt. 3:9), or all that Jesus had meant when He said, in view of one Gentile's faith, *"Many* will come from east and west and sit at table with Abraham, Isaac, and Jacob in the kingdom of heaven"

(Matt. 8:11). Not that anyone denied the Gentile the right to
membership in the church; the question was rather: *How* was
the Gentile to attain such membership? Were all God's ancient
ordinances, all the marks and tokens of His covenant with Israel,
simply to be set aside, disannulled, and discarded by the new
and culminating revelation of God in Christ? Was the ancient
people of God, the people who claimed Abraham the believer
as their father, simply to disappear, lost in the inbreaking wash
of Gentile converts? Thus was created the tension within the
church which led to the convocation of the Apostolic Council
and the writing of Paul's Letter to the Galatians.

THE APOSTOLIC COUNCIL

The immediate occasion of the Apostolic Council was the
arrival at Antioch of Jewish Christian men who insisted that
Gentile converts must come into the church by way of Judaism;
such men are commonly labeled "Judaizers." These Judaizers
came to Antioch with the demand that the Gentile Christians
be circumcised "according to the custom of Moses" (Acts 15:1;
cf. 15:5), and they demanded circumcision as necessary to salvation: "Unless you are circumcised . . . you cannot be saved"
(Acts 15:1). This party, or group, had its forerunners in men
of the type who had called Peter to account for entering the
house of the Gentile Cornelius (Acts 11:1-18). If Gal. 2:1-5
refers, as seems most probable, to Paul's visit to Jerusalem
A. D. 46 at the time of the famine (his second visit, Acts 11:30;
12:25), men of this sort had already collided with Paul when
they demanded that his Greek companion Titus be circumcised.
And Paul had stoutly resisted their demands. Some of them,
at least, were converted Pharisees (Acts 15:5). They were, then,
a group or party within the church and did not, so far as we
can see, expressly deny any part of the Gospel as preached by
Paul and the rest. In fact, they seem to have claimed the support
of the Jerusalem church and the Jerusalem apostles for their
demands (Acts 15:24); Luke is perhaps tacitly disallowing their
claim when he says that they came "down from *Judea*" (Acts
15:1) and not "from *Jerusalem*."

They were so insistent in their demands, argued so stubbornly and so skillfully with Paul and Barnabas, and so unsettled the minds of the Gentile Christians at Antioch (Acts 15:24), as well as elsewhere in Syria and Cilicia (Acts 15:23), that it was decided to carry the matter to the apostles and elders in Jerusalem (Acts 15:2). At the meeting in Jerusalem, which apparently included not only the apostles and elders, but also representatives of the "whole church" (Acts 15:22), the voices of Peter and James the brother of the Lord were raised decisively in favor of Gentile freedom from the Law (Acts 15:7-11, 13-21). This was quite in keeping with the position which they had previously taken over against Paul's Gospel and his apostolate to the Gentiles A. D. 46 (Gal. 2:1-10), and the Judaic church followed their leadership in refusing to impose on the Gentiles "a yoke . . . which neither our fathers nor we have been able to bear" (Acts 15:10). But it must be remembered that for Judaic Christianity the question of the freedom of the Gentiles had two facets. The one half of the question, Must a Gentile become a proselyte to Judaism in order to be saved? was answered at once and decisively by the Council. But the other half of the question needed to be answered also, and that was, What is the relationship between the circumcised, ritually clean Jewish Christian and the uncircumcised, ritually unclean Gentile Christian to be? How are they to live together, how are they to carry out that act which loomed so large as an expression of Christian fellowship, namely table fellowship — how are they to eat together? (It should be remembered that the common meal and the celebration of the Lord's Supper were closely connected in the early church.) For the radical Judaizers the answer was, of course, simple: Let the Gentiles be circumcised and become good Jews. For Jewish men of good will who sought to fulfill the mission to Israel which God had given them (Gal. 2:8, 9), a mission which made it impossible for them to assume the freedom which they had granted to the Gentiles, the answer was anything but simple. And in the light of this fact the words in the letter sent to the churches must be understood, the words namely, "It has seemed good . . . to us to lay upon you no greater burden than these necessary things: that you abstain from what has been sacrificed to idols and from blood and from what is strangled and from unchastity"

(Acts 15:28, 29). The "necessary things" requested of the Gentiles are not marked as necessary to salvation and are therefore not a reimposing of the Law upon them; this is a *request* addressed to the Gentiles, a request which asked them to abstain from foods and practices abominable to Jewish feelings, foods and practices which their pagan past and their pagan surroundings made natural and easy for them. It is understandable that abstention from "unchastity" should be included also in the request, when we remember how closely connected unchastity was with pagan worship, pagan festivals, and pagan life generally. The so-called Apostolic Decree is therefore anything but a triumph of Judaic legalism. If a burden of love was laid upon the Gentile brethren by it, the Judaic brethren also assumed no light burden in not expecting and asking more. The reception of the letter at Antioch (Acts 15:31), and later on in the province of Galatia (Acts 16:4, 5), shows that the Gentile churches did not view it as a defeat for Gentile freedom: "They rejoiced at the exhortation" (Acts 15:31) and "were strengthened in the faith, and they increased in numbers daily" (Acts 16:5).

The men of the church learned, as the word of the Lord grew among them, not to use their freedom as an opportunity for the flesh, but through love to "be servants of one another" (Gal. 5:13). Thus Christianity was safeguarded against a reimposition of the Law; the very real danger that Christianity might degenerate into a Judaic sect (and so perish with Judaism) was averted. And the unity of the church was preserved; the new Gentile church was kept in contact with the Judaic church, to which it owed the Gospel (cf. Rom. 15:27) and was thus kept firmly rooted in the Old Testament Scriptures — a great blessing, for the history of the church has shown how readily alien and corrosive influences beset the Gospel, once contact with the Old Testament is lost. To surrender the Old Testament is the first step toward misunderstanding, perverting, and so losing the Gospel of the New Testament.

THE LETTER OF PAUL TO THE GALATIANS

The struggle was in principle decided by the Council at Jerusalem. But that did not mean that the Judaizers were forever silenced or that their influence was completely neutralized. Their claims were decisively rejected by the church at Jerusalem; but they had, apparently, meanwhile gone on to spread their plausible mischief beyond Jerusalem and Antioch, in the churches which Paul and Barnabas had established in Southern Galatia on their first missionary journey, at Pisidian Antioch, Iconium, Lystra, and Derbe (Acts 13:14). They did so with considerable success, for what they proclaimed was a very plausible sort of substitute for the Gospel which Paul's converts had heard from him. To judge from Paul's polemics against them, they did not in so many words deny any positive teaching that Paul had brought to the Galatians; they acknowledged and proclaimed Jesus as the Messiah, the Son of God, the risen and exalted Lord, the Giver of the Spirit, in whose name is salvation; they did not deny that He would soon return in glory to consummate God's work in grace and judgment. The evidence does not even indicate that they completely ignored or obliterated the cross in its redemptive significance; Paul's repeated and passionate emphasis on the central and all-embracing significance of the cross in his letter does indicate that for them the Messiah of the cross was overshadowed by the Messiah in glory, that the cross of Christ tended to become an episode which His exaltation counterbalanced and reduced to relative insignificance.

They did not, on their own profession, come to destroy Paul's work, but to complete it (Gal. 3:3). The coming of the Messiah, in their proclamation, crowned Israel's history and consummated Israel; it did not therefore by any means signify the end of the Law and such sacred ordinances as circumcision and the Sabbath, which God himself had ordained as the mark and condition of the covenant between Himself and His people forever. The coming of the Christ did not free men from the Law; the Christ confirmed the teaching of the Law and deepened the obedience which it demanded. Salvation by the mediation of the Christ therefore most assuredly included the performance of the works of the Law. A Christian estate based on faith alone, without circumcision and without the Law, was a very rudimentary and unfinished estate; perfection lay in circumcision and in keeping the Law to which it committed a man. Thus a man became a true son of Abraham and the inheritor of the blessing promised to Abraham, a member of God's true and ancient people. To dispense with the Law would mean moral chaos, or at best a very dubious and dangerous sort of liberty.

Paul, these men insinuated, had not told them all that was necessary for their full salvation. He was, after all, not an apostle of the first rank, not on a par with the original Jerusalem apostles, through whom he had received his apostolate. His failure to insist on the keeping of the Law was a piece of regrettable weakness on his part, due no doubt to his missionary zeal, but regrettable nevertheless; he had sought to gain converts by softening the rigor of the genuine Gospel of God — he had, in other words, sought to "please men." They, the Judaizers, were now come to complete what Paul had left unfinished, to lead them to that Christian perfection which Paul's Gospel could never give them.

Their attack was thus a three-pronged one. It was (a) an attack upon the apostolate of Paul, (b) an attack upon the Gospel of Paul as omitting essential demands of God, and (c) an attack which pointed up the moral dangers which would result from a proclamation of salvation by mere faith in an absolutely free and forgiving grace of God.

The attack was subtle; it was also, apparently, an organized attack, under a single leadership; Paul refers to one personality as particularly responsible for the harm that had been done in the Galatian churches (Gal. 5:10). And the attack was ominously successful, understandably enough. For the converted Jew this new form of the Gospel promised a more relaxed relationship with his unconverted fellow Jews; the Gentile converts would be impressed by the authority of the Jerusalem apostles which the new preachers invoked for their cause. And the zeal of these uncompromising extremists no doubt impressed both Gentile and Jew.

Paul probably heard of the activity of these men and of their incipient success while he was still at Antioch on the Orontes. Since he was about to go up to Jerusalem to thresh out the question raised by the Judaizers with the apostles and elders there, he could not go to Galatia in person, as he might have wished (Gal. 4:20), to meet the attack and to combat the danger. He met it by writing the Letter to the Galatians, which is therefore to be dated A. D. 48 or 49.

That letter is a threefold fighting defense of Paul, his apostolate, and his Gospel, corresponding to the threefold attack upon him by the Judaizers.

Content of the Letter to the Galatians

I. The Defense of Paul's Apostolate, 1:1—2:21

After the salutation, which touches on all three of the main themes of the letter (the divine origin of Paul's apostolate, the centrality of the cross, and the new life which removes men "from the present evil age," where the compulsion and the condemnation of the Law has its necessary place, 1:1-5), Paul, without pausing for the thanksgiving and prayer which are his usual opening word, breaks into a severe reproach of the Galatians and an unqualified condemnation of the men who have misled them with "another gospel." With that he has disposed of the charge that he is a weak and affable "pleaser of men" and marks himself as the servant of Christ, 1:6-10. Thus the defense of his apostolate has already begun; he now asserts of his apostolate, which makes him the bearer of divine good news, that his apostolic authority

1. is independent of men, received directly from Christ and the God who set him apart for this work from before his birth, and is therefore purely the grace of God, 1:11-24;

2. has been recognized by the Jerusalem apostles as the grace of God conferred upon him, 2:1-10;

3. extended even to the rebuking of Peter when Peter's conduct at Antioch called into question the truth of the Gospel that salvation is by grace alone through faith alone, 2:11-21.

(Paul's words to Peter constitute the transition to the theme of the second part of his letter, the either-or of Law or Promise, Law or Gospel.)

II. Defense of the Gospel of Free Grace, Without the Works of the Law, 3:1—4:31

A. Three Witnesses to the True Nature of Gospel and Law, 3:1-14

1. Paul appeals to the witness of the experience of the Galatians: they owe their conversion to the proclamation of the
   crucified Christ (the Cross is God's rejection of all the
   works of man); it was by "hearing with faith," in utter
   passivity and not by works, that they received the Spirit
   and witnessed the mighty works done among them, 3:1-5.

2. He then meets the Judaizers on their own ground by appealing to the witness of the Old Testament concerning
   Abraham; Abraham is the father of the people of God
   as a justified believer, and those who believe are his true
   sons, 3:6-9.

3. He further appeals to the witness of the Old Testament
   Law itself concerning the Law: the Law spells a curse on
   man, a curse from which Christ alone could and did redeem man, by becoming a "curse" in man's stead, 3:10-14.

B. The Relationship Between the Promise of God and the
   Law, 3:15-29

1. God's promise, His basic and primal word to man, is like
   a man's will. Now a will once ratified (by the testator's
   death) cannot be annulled or supplemented; so also God's
   Law cannot be thought of as in any way annulling or modi-
   fying His promise, 3:15-18.

2. The function of the Law is not to annul the promise of
   God; rather, it has a negative and temporary function in
   relation to the promise, 3:19, 22, limited to the nation
   Israel (this seems to be the meaning of the difficult
   verse 20); the Law cannot and does not therefore contradict or limit the promise of God but subserves the
   gracious purpose of the promise; it performs a "custo-
   dian's" service over God's people until the time of the
   fulfillment of the promise, 3:19-24.

3. With the fulfillment of the promise in Christ, all the dis-
   tinctions set up by the Law, all the orders of this world,
   lose their significance for man in the presence of God;
   all who are baptized (not only the Jew) are Christ's and
   are heirs according to the promise, 3:25-29.

C. Three Aspects of Sonship Which Confirm the Truth of the
   Gospel of Free Grace, 4:1-31

(This section has at first glance a rather miscellaneous
character; but the three subsections are tied together by
the idea of the blessings of sonship, sonship being emphasized in each section, cf. 4:7, 19, 31.)

1. The position of Israel under the Law was that of son and
   heir, but a *minor* heir, without liberty, no better than
   a slave. For the Jew to return to the Law and its bondage
   would be a turning from manhood to childhood, from
   a freedom which the Father Himself has bestowed to a self-
   chosen slavery. For the Gentile to turn from the Gospel
   to the Law would be practically a return to idolatry —
   he would be worshiping the outworn and discarded gar-
   ments of God, not the living God Himself as revealed in
   His Son, 4:1-11.

2. The Galatians have known what joy it is to be children of
   God in Christ. Paul gave them a new birth with his Gospel
   of free grace, v. 19. Will they turn from him, whom they
   loved so fervently, count him their enemy, and listen to
   the flattering persuasion of men who woo them now in
   order to lord it over them later? 4:12-20

3. Those who seek to subject the Galatians to the Law
   promise them that they will make them "sons of Abraham." Paul's reply is: "Which son of Abraham will
   you be?" If you set store by physical descent from Abraham and all that is connected with that physical descent
   from Abraham, your sonship is that of Ishmael, the son
   "born according to the flesh," son of the slave woman,
   who is typical of the covenant of Mt. Sinai (which, with
   its imposition of the Law, could as little be the final redemptive word of God as the birth of Ishmael could be
   the fulfillment of the hope of believing Abraham). That
   covenant produces slaves. The slave woman has her counterpart in present Jerusalem, the enslaved and doomed
   city. True sonship is that of Isaac, born "according to
   the promise" (by a graciously creative word of God),
   born of the free woman, who is typical of the covenant
   of freedom and corresponds to the Jerusalem above, the
   free redeemed people of God. The child of the free

woman was persecuted by the child of the slave woman;
the church is likewise persecuted by Israel. But that does
not change the destiny of either the one or the other.
Those who would be Abraham's sons must go the way
of the Gospel and freedom, not the way of enslavement
under the Law, 4:21-31.

III. Defense of the Gospel of Freedom in Its Practical Results,
5:1—6:10

A. What Freedom Under the Gospel Means, Basically and
in Principle, 5:1-24

1. Freedom and the Law are absolutely incompatible. Freedom is not a way which man has chosen, but the way
which God has established. No man may therefore compromise it; to return to the Law as the way of salvation,
in however slight a measure (such as submitting to circumcision), is to cancel the Gospel, is to lose the Christ
who has made us free. — Paul's opponents evidently ac-
cused him of compromising on circumcision on occasion;
his answer is simply to point to the fact that he is still
being persecuted; it was the stumbling block of the cross
that provoked persecution, and since circumcision and the
cross mutually exclude each other, acceptance of circumcision would have put an end to the offense and the persecution, 5:1-12.

2. Freedom does not mean license; it means being set free
by God from self to serve one's fellow man in love (which
is the essence of the will of God in the Law). The bitter
factionalism which the Judaizers have brought into the
church bids fair to destroy the people of God, 5:13-15.

3. Freedom means walking by the Spirit. It means entering
upon that struggle against the flesh and its desires which
a man can wage only in the power of the Spirit; it means
living a life led by the Spirit, a life which moves on a level
which the Law's threats and condemnation cannot touch;
it means that Christ's death to sin becomes a reality in
those who belong to Christ, 5:16-24.

B. What the Life of Freedom Under the Spirit Means Practically, 5:25—6:10

1. It means the end of all self-centered pride, the end of provocative self-assertion and of envy, 5:25, 26.

2. It means a life of meek and gentle ministry to the erring, performed in the consciousness of one's own frailty, 6:1-5.

3. It means a loving generosity toward those who teach in the church, 6:6. (This admonition was probably evoked by the fact that Paul's opponents misinterpreted his action in not accepting support for his preaching and used it as a pretext to cover callous neglect toward the teachers in the church.)

C. What a Life of Freedom Means in Terms of the Christian's Hope, 6:7-10

The freedom given to man in Christ does not absolve him of responsibility for his actions; rather, it heightens that responsibility. Man will sow what he has reaped. God will hold him accountable for what he has in his freedom done with the gift of the Spirit.

Conclusion, 6:11-18

The conclusion, written by Paul's own hand (the rest of the letter was dictated) sums up once more the chief thoughts of the letter, with special emphasis on the selfish motives of the Judaizers and the completely Christ-centered motivation of Paul. It closes with a plea that he, whom suffering for the Gospel has marked as Christ's own, may be spared further agony, and with a benediction on all who walk by the rule of his Gospel of freedom and are therefore the true Israel of God.

Result of the Letter

The letter achieved its purpose; the Galatians joined loyally in the gathering of gifts for the poor in Jerusalem (1 Cor. 16:1), an undertaking close to Paul's heart as an expression of the unity between Gentile and Judaic Christianity. A certain Gaius of Derbe (in Galatia) was among the representatives of the Gentile churches who accompanied Paul when he took the Gentile offerings to Jerusalem. (Acts 20:4)

Canonicity: Homologoumenon

A Historical Problem

The reconstruction of the historical situation given above has assumed that "Galatia" in Gal. 1:2 means the Roman province of Galatia, which comprehended not only the territory actually occupied by the old Galatian people but also other lands, including the territory in which lay the cities evangelized by Paul and Barnabas on the First Missionary Journey. This is known as the South Galatian Hypothesis. Others take "Galatia" to mean the actual Galatian territory, the land occupied by the Galatians in central Asia Minor, whose chief cities were Tavium, Pessinus, and Ancyra. This view, known as the North Galatian Hypothesis, would necessitate a later dating of the letter, since Paul did not touch this Galatian territory until the time of his Second and Third Missionary Journeys (A. D. 49—51 and 52—56). Neither hypothesis solves all the historical difficulties, and a decision between them is not easy. But the South Galatian Hypothesis has seemed preferable, in the main, for the following reasons:

1. On the North Galatian Hypothesis, why did the Judaizers in their campaign against Paul by-pass the South Galatian cities, readily accessible from Antioch, and go on into the wild, less civilized, and more remote regions of North Galatia?

2. If Paul's Letter to the Galatians was written after the Apostolic Council and its decision, why does Paul not refer to it? — Those who hold the North Galatian Hypothesis usually see in Gal. 2:1-10 a reference to the Apostolic Council. But it is difficult to see how a meeting which Paul there describes as a *private* meeting (Gal. 2:2) can be identified with the very public meeting described by Luke in Acts 15. And the question discussed in the meeting described by Paul in his letter, while no doubt related to the question up for discussion in the meeting of Acts 15, is hardly to be identified with it. Gal. 2:1-10 more naturally refers to the visit which Acts, too, makes Paul's second visit to Jerusalem after his conversion, the visit of A. D. 46 at the time of the famine.

3. If the proponents of the North Galatian Hypothesis raise the objection that the Roman province of Galatia had no fixed, official title (i. e., "Galatia") at the time of Paul's writing, that

Paul therefore could not with propriety call the churches at Antioch or Derbe churches of Galatia and address men of Pisidia and Lycaonia as "Galatians" just because they lived in a province popularly known as Galatia, one must answer that there was no other single term that Paul could have used to cover all the churches addressed in the letter.

Many other subtle and ingenious arguments have been advanced on both sides, but they are rarely conclusive arguments. Thus, for example, the fact that Paul can assume that the Galatians whom he addresses know Barnabas (Gal. 2:1) is used as evidence for the South Galatian Hypothesis, since Barnabas accompanied Paul only on the First Missionary Journey. But Paul assumes that the Corinthians, too, know Barnabas (1 Cor. 9:6), although there is no evidence that Barnabas was ever in Corinth. Apparently Barnabas was prominent enough in the early church to be known in North Galatia as well as in Antioch, Iconium, Lystra, and Derbe. Similarly the close affinity between the letter to the Galatians and the letter to the Romans seems to many scholars to be conclusive proof for the later dating. But is there anything conclusive in the fact that two letters, written by the same man, in the face of the same antithesis, within eight years of each other, should be similar in content and language?

Value of the Letter

The Letter to the Galatians is one of the most personal and autobiographical of the letters of Paul, invaluable for the historical appreciation of his Gospel and his work; it is therefore valuable for the understanding of the growth of the word of the Lord. We see here that the growth of that word is genuine human history; the chosen instruments of the Lord are anything but robots — they do their work and do the will of the Lord with the passionate intensity of personal involvement. The men who witness to the Christ are laid hold of by the Christ, and their mission becomes flesh of their flesh and bone of their bone.

Scarcely another epistle so emphasizes the "alone" of "by grace *alone,* through faith *alone"* as does this fighting exposition of the Gospel according to Paul, with its embattled stress on the fact that Law and Gospel confront man with an inescapable, not-to-be-compromised either-or. Paul's Letter to the Romans expounds the same theme more calmly and more fully and has a value of its own; but there is no presentation of the Gospel that can equal this letter in the force with which it presents the inexorable claim of the pure grace of God. Luther, who had to fight Paul's battle over again, said of the Letter to the Galatians: "The Epistle to the Galatians is my own little epistle. I have betrothed myself to it; it is my Catherine of Bora."

It should be remembered that the letter addresses itself to a very earnest, very pious, and very Christian sort of heresy and crushes it with an unqualified anathema. Our easy age, which discusses heresy with ecumenical calm over tea cups, can learn of this letter the terrible seriousness with which the all-inclusive Gospel of grace excludes all movements and all men who seek to qualify its grace.

CHAPTER IV: The Word of the Lord Grows in Europe: The Letters of Paul to the Church at Thessalonica

READINGS: ACTS 15:36–18:22; 1 and 2 THESSALONIANS

The Second Missionary Journey (A. D. 49—51)

The Letters to the Thessalonians are part of that history of the growth of the word of the Lord which we commonly designate as Paul's Second Missionary Journey. That journey took Paul, with his new companions Silas and Timothy, to Europe. The heart of the Second Missionary Journey was the apostle's 18 months' ministry in the great commercial center of Corinth. That ministry was preceded by a revisitation of the churches of Syria and Cilicia and of the Galatian churches founded on the First Missionary Journey; by missionary work in the European cities of Philippi, Thessalonica, and Berea, work again and again cut short by the malice of superstitious avarice or by the plottings of jealous Jews; and by missionary activity at Athens, the great cultural center of Greece. It was followed by a brief exploratory visit to Ephesus which prepared for Paul's long ministry there on his Third Missionary Journey.

The word of the Lord sped on and triumphed (2 Thess. 3:1) in Europe, but in its peculiarly divine way. It sped on surely but not without opposition; it triumphed with the inevitable triumph of a work of God, but its history is not the history of an easy and effortless triumph — it is a history marked, rather, by the persecution, suffering, and internal difficulties of the human bearers and the human recipients of the word. The history of the

Second Missionary Journey has left its mark on the Letters to the Thessalonians. Paul's companions on the journey, Silas (Paul calls him by his Roman name Silvanus) and Timothy, join in the sending of both letters. Paul's opening words in the first letter are a commentary on the history that brought him to Thessalonica: "We know, brethren beloved by God, *that He has chosen you,* for our Gospel came to you not only in word, but also in power and in the Holy Spirit and with full conviction" (1 Thess. 1:4, 5). Paul knew from his own experience that the existence of the church at Thessalonica was due not to human planning and devising, but to the elective love of God which had become history in Paul's mission to Europe. Paul would recall, as he wrote these words, how he and his companions had been led, uncomprehending but obedient, by God's own hand and by the Spirit of Jesus (Acts 16:7), past the province of Asia, which would have seemed the logical next step on their missionary way, past Mysia, away from Bithynia, to Troas, to receive there the vision which summoned them to Europe (Acts 16:9); he would recall, too, how persecution had pushed him on with illogical haste from Philippi to Thessalonica. When Paul spoke of the elective love of God to the Thessalonians, he was not uttering a theoretical tenet of his faith; he was uttering that which God had woven into the living texture of his faith by a history in which he, Paul, had himself acted and suffered.

Paul bore the badge of suffering which was the mark of his apostolate when he came to Thessalonica from Philippi. The Paul and Silvanus who took to "praying and singing hymns to God" in the jail at Philippi after being beaten by the magistrates (Acts 16:25) had learned to see in their sufferings not the defeat, but the triumph of the word of the Lord; and they spoke the word in Thessalonica with the robust and confident courage of men who know that they are bearers of the word of God (1 Thess. 2:13) — and they did not conceal from their Thessalonian hearers that their word would put the imprint of suffering upon the church of God in Thessalonica, too (1 Thess. 1:6; 2:14; 3:3, 4; 2 Thess. 1:4-7). No small part of that suffering was due to the rancor of unbelieving Jews; and this, too, finds expression in the letter. (1 Thess. 2:14-16)

Paul experienced anew on this journey the power and activity of Satan, who plants weeds where the Lord plants good seed. Forced to leave Thessalonica before his work there was really finished, he tried again and again to return to the young church — "but Satan hindered us," he writes (1 Thess. 2:18; cf. 3:5). He experienced also the power for order and discipline which God had set into the world in the form of the Roman government (cf. Rom. 13:1-7); his Roman citizenship had procured him an honorable release from prison at Philippi (Acts 16:37-39), and the power of Rome was to stand between him and Judaic malice again at Corinth (Acts 18:12-17), when the proconsul Gallio refused to entertain the ambiguous and invidious Jewish charges against him. When Paul spoke to the Thessalonians of the power that restrains the anti-Christian attack upon God and God's people (2 Thess. 2:6, 7), he was writing revelation which God had given him, to be sure; but God had written that revelation into the history and the experience of Paul the apostle, too.

The Founding of the Church at Thessalonica

Thessalonica was the kind of place that Paul usually chose for an intensive and prolonged ministry. It was the capital of the Roman province of Macedonia and the residence of the Roman proconsul, commercially important as a harbor town, and an important communications center, lying on the *Via Egnatia*, the road which connected Rome (by way of Dyrrachium) with Byzantium and the East. It was thus naturally fitted to become a missionary center, a point from which the word of the Lord, once established in men's hearts, might readily "sound forth." (1 Thess. 1:8)

Paul, with his companions Silas and Timothy (one representing the old Jerusalem church; the other, half Jew and half Greek, representing the young church in Galatia), arrived at Thessalonica in A. D. 50 and began his work, as usual, in the synagog. According to Luke (Acts 17:2), Paul's work in the synagog lasted "three sabbaths"; and Luke records no further activity in Thessalonica. But Paul's own account of his work as missionary and as pastor of the new church in Thessalonica (1 Thess. 2:1-12) suggests a more prolonged ministry among the Gentiles after the break with the synagog had taken place (Acts 17:5). This is confirmed by a notice in Paul's Letter to the Philippians, where Paul recalls that the Philippians *twice* sent money for his needs when he was at Thessalonica (Phil. 4:16). Luke's account in Acts is therefore a highly compressed one; he gives an impression of Paul's ministry at Thessalonica by indicating only the initial and the final stages of his work there.

The break with the synagog came early; the ministry among the Gentiles was perhaps prolonged for several months. The congregation at Thessalonica was therefore, as the letters to the Thessalonians also indicate, predominantly Gentile (1 Thess. 1:9; 2:14; cf. Acts 17:4). The life of that congregation was from the first a vigorous one, marked by the characteristically Christian joy which even severe trials cannot quench, an active faith which documented itself in a far-reaching missionary witness (1 Thess. 1:3, 7 f.), a brotherly love which Paul can speak of as taught them by God Himself (1 Thess. 4:9, 10), and an intense hope which longed for the return of "Jesus, who delivers us from the wrath to come" (1 Thess. 1:10; cf. 4:13 ff.). Paul says of them (and Paul's generous recognition of what God has wrought in men never degenerates into empty flattery) that they "became an example to all the believers in Macedonia and in Achaia," all Greece (1 Thess. 1:7). Only, they were still little children in Christ, good and gifted children, but not mature and stable men, when Paul was forced to leave them. (Acts 17:5-10; 1 Thess. 2:17)

THE FIRST LETTER TO THE THESSALONIANS

Occasion of the First Letter

Paul proceeded southwest from Thessalonica to Berea; and from there, when Jews from Thessalonica stirred up opposition to him in Berea also (Acts 17:10-13), to Athens; and after a brief ministry there, which brought him into contact with the philosophy of the Greeks, he went on to Corinth, where a vision of the Lord bade him remain and work in depth. And remain he did, for almost two years. Meanwhile the church at Thessalonica remained in his thoughts and his prayers, and he was filled with a deep and restless anxiety for the brethren of whom he was "bereft . . . in person, not in heart" (1 Thess. 2:17). Would they stand fast under the persecution which had come upon them?

Would they misunderstand his departure and his continued absence from them? In this connection it is well to remember that Paul and his companions were not the only propagandists and pleaders for a cause that traveled the Roman roads in those days; they were part of a numerous and motley troup of philosophers, rhetoricians, propagandists for various foreign and domestic cults, missionaries, charlatans, and quacks who went from town to town, all intent on getting a hearing, all eager for money or fame or both. These usually came and went, never to be heard from again. Paul would in the popular mind be classified with them. And Paul in Thessalonica, A. D. 51, was not yet the apostle Paul as the church has learned to see him since; he was simply a hitherto unknown little Jew who had come and gone, like hundreds of brilliant and persuasive men before him. The church of Thessalonica would of itself not be minded to classify Paul thus; but his enemies would, and they would thus undermine his apostolic authority and, with it, the faith in the Gospel with which he was identified as apostle.

Paul's anxieties and fears were well founded. And he could not return to Thessalonica, although he attempted to do so more than once, to relieve his anxieties and to do the work which would obviate the dangers which gave rise to them. Satan hindered him (1 Thess. 2:18); we can only guess as to what form this hindering took. Finally, when he could no longer endure the suspense, he sacrificed the aid and companionship of Timothy (a real sacrifice, for Paul's was a nature that needed the presence of friends and brethren) and sent him to Thessalonica, both to strengthen the faith of the church and to learn at first hand how they fared. (1 Thess. 3:1-5)

Neither the account in Acts nor Paul's account in his first letter makes it clear whether Timothy first joined Paul at Athens and was sent back to Thessalonica from there or whether Paul, alone at Athens, directed Timothy by letter to revisit Thessalonica before rejoining him at Corinth. At any rate, when Timothy returned from Thessalonica to Paul at Corinth with the good news of the Thessalonians' faith and love and fidelity to Paul (1 Thess. 3:6), it meant for Paul the release from a long and agonizing tension. He threw himself with new vigor into his work at Corinth

(Acts 18:5), and he wrote the letter which we call First Thessalonians. Paul's First Letter to the Thessalonians is Paul's response to Timothy's report, a long thanksgiving for the good news which Timothy had brought, a thanksgiving which looks back over the whole history of the Thessalonian church since its founding and is at the same time a vindication of the purity and sanctity of his motives as their apostle and pastor (chaps. 1—3). The thanksgiving is followed by a series of admonitions suggested by Timothy's report. Paul is doing by letter what he could not do face to face; he is supplying what is lacking in their faith. (Cf. 1 Thess. 3:10)

Timothy would have reported that these Christians in a Gentile environment, and in a Greek harbor town at that, where the idea of sexual purity was a complete novelty, were having difficulty in maintaining that chastity which a life of faith demands; that their past made it difficult for them to shed at once and altogether the unscrupulous craftiness which they had hitherto regarded as normal and prudent; that their fervent hope easily degenerated into an excited and irresponsible enthusiasm which led them to neglect the tasks and duties of daily life; that their imperfect grasp of the hope which the promised return of the Christ gave them made them despondent regarding their kin and brethren who had died before that return; that their hope was not content to be pure hope and leave the times and seasons of fulfillment in God's hands but sought to calculate and predict; that their life as a community bound together by faith and love and hope was not without its frictions and difficulties. To these difficulties Paul's warm and pastoral heart responded with a wisdom and a love that only the Spirit of God can bestow.

Content of the First Letter to the Thessalonians

I. Thanksgiving for the Word of God in Thessalonica, a Grateful Survey of the History of the Thessalonian Church, 1:1—3:13

   A. Looking Back to the Time of the Founding of the Church, 1:2—2:12

     1. The coming of the Gospel to the Thessalonians and their exemplary reception of the word, 1:2-10.

2. Paul's behavior as missionary: courageous, pure in motive, unselfish, and gentle, 2:1-8.

3. Paul's pastoral behavior toward the converted Christians of Thessalonica, his selfless devotion in supporting himself by the toil of his hands while he tended them with a father's care, 2:9-12.

B. Looking Back to the Time of Persecution, 2:13-16

The Thessalonians received the apostolic word as the very word of God which it is, and that divine word evinced its power in them when they endured persecutions comparable to those endured by the churches of Judea.

C. Looking Back to the Time of Paul's Separation from the Church, 2:17—3:5

1. Paul's longing to see them again, 2:17.

2. Paul's attempts to return to them, 2:18-20.

3. The sending of Timothy, 3:1-5.

D. Looking to the Thessalonians' Present State According to Timothy's Report, 3:6-10

Paul's joy at their steadfastness in the faith and their loyalty to himself.

Conclusion, 3:11-13

Intercessory prayer that God may direct Paul's way back to them and that he may establish their faith in perfect love and sure hope.

II. Exhortations (designed "to supply what is lacking in their faith"), 4:1—5:28

A. Moral Exhortation for Individuals, 4:1-12

1. to sexual purity, 4:1-5.

2. to honesty in business, 4:6-8.

3. to ever-increasing brotherly love, 4:9, 10.

4. to lives of quiet industry, 4:11, 12.

B. Two Exhortations Concerning Last Things, 4:13—5:11

1. Assurance concerning those who have fallen asleep in Jesus: They shall have full share in the joy and glory of Christ's return, 4:13-18.

2. Admonition to vigilance and sobriety in view of the coming of the day of the Lord. That coming is as incalculable as it is certain, 5:1-11.

C. Exhortations for Congregation Life, 5:12-22

1. to a due recognition of Christian leaders "because of their work," 5:12, 13.

2. to a life of loving and patient service to one another, 5:14, 15.

3. to a worship life of unbroken joy, prayer, and thanksgiving, 5:16-18.

4. to a full but discerning use of the gifts of the Spirit, 5:19-22.

D. Conclusion, 5:23-28

1. Intercessory prayer for the Christians of Thessalonica: May they be sanctified and kept by the faithful God of grace for the coming of the Lord Jesus Christ, 5:23, 24.

2. Request for the church's intercessions, greetings, instructions for the public reading of the letter (we see here the beginnings of the liturgical use of the apostolic word), 5:25-27.

3. Closing benediction, 5:28.

Time and Place of Writing: A. D. 50, at Corinth

Canonicity: Homologoumenon accepted as inspired right away

Peculiar Value of the Letter

The first three chapters give us a particularly vivid picture of Paul the missionary and pastor at work in a young Gentile church — how the word of the Lord grows on pagan soil.

The value of the hortatory *[advice, urge to good deeds]* section may be measured by the fact that these two brief chapters have furnished no less than three Epistles in the ancient church's pericopal *[section]* system, the Epistle for the second Sunday in Lent (1 Thess. 4:1-7), and for the twenty-fifth and twenty-seventh Sundays after Trinity (1 Thess. 4:13-18; 5:1-11).

Few letters offer more sustenance for the hope of God's people than this one; note, besides the two great sections on the lot of the dead in Christ (4:13-18) and on the times and seasons of the Lord's return (5:1-11), the fact that practically every major section in the letter ends on the note of the return of the Lord (1:10; 2:12; 2:16; 2:19; 3:13; 5:23).

THE SECOND LETTER TO THE THESSALONIANS

The Second Letter to the Thessalonians was evidently written not long after the First, perhaps a few months later, A. D. 50, at Corinth. According to reports which reached Paul at Corinth (we do not know how; perhaps the church wrote to Paul), the Christians of Thessalonica were still standing firm under persecution (2 Thess. 1:4), but false notions concerning the "coming of our Lord Jesus Christ and our assembling to meet Him" (2 Thess. 2:1) had gained currency in the church. Those who advocated these notions apparently appealed to some alleged prophetic utterance ("spirit") or teaching or writing of Paul's to support them (2 Thess. 2:2). The resultant excited, almost hysterical expectation (2 Thess. 2:2) had led some to abandon their regular occupation and to lead an idle and disorderly life in dependence upon the charity of the church (2 Thess. 3:6-12). Others, it would seem, struck by the high demands of the first letter (the demand that they be found "blameless" at the coming of the Lord, 1 Thess. 3:13; 5:23), had grown fearful and despondent concerning the coming of the Christ; for them, they felt, it would mean not deliverance, but judgment and destruction.

Paul's second letter is his answer to this situation in the church at Thessalonica. It therefore sounds two notes. For those who indulge in overheated eschatological fantasies there are sobering words which point to the events which must necessarily precede the coming of the Christ in glory (2 Thess. 2:1-12). For the despondent and the fearful there is an eloquent and reassuring recognition of the new life which God has worked in them and a comforting emphasis on the certainty of their election by God (2 Thess. 1:3-12; 2:13-15). Paul turns the church from both excitement and despondency to that sober and responsible activity which is the hallmark of the genuinely Christian hope: The hoping church turns from preoccupation with itself to God; the church must pray, pray "that the word of the Lord may speed on and triumph" (2 Thess. 3:1); and the hoping church must work — work for its living in sober industriousness and work for its own health as the church of God by disciplining and correcting all those whose life is a departure from the apostolic word and example and is therefore a denial of the real character of the church (3:6-15).

Content of the Second Letter to the Thessalonians

I. Thanksgiving and Prayer, 1:1-12

A. Thanksgiving for the faith and love of the Thessalonians and for their steadfastness amid persecutions. The fidelity and righteousness of God make their present suffering His pledge that they shall participate in the final deliverance, when those who do not obey the Gospel and oppress the church shall perish in the judgment of the Lord Jesus Christ, 1:3-10.

B. Prayer that God in His power and grace may sustain and perfect them, 1:11, 12.

II. Admonition Concerning the Coming of the Lord

A. That coming is not yet, for it must be preceded by the great apostasy and the coming of the Man of Lawlessness. That man is as yet being restrained. The present has in it the tokens of his coming in the working of the mystery of lawlessness, but his coming in the strength of the plausible religious lie is still in the future. Not until he has been revealed, will the end, which means his destruction, come, 2:1-12.

B. That coming spells salvation for God's elect, among whom the Thessalonians are numbered, 2:13-15. The Lord Jesus Christ and God the Father will preserve them until that day, 2:16, 17.

(This section is in form a prayer. Unlike the prayer in the first letter [1 Thess. 3:11-13], it contains no request that Paul may be enabled to return to the Thessalonians; he had meanwhile received the vision which told him to remain in Corinth, Acts 18:9-11.)

III. Exhortations, 3:1-14

A. To pray for the success of the word and the preservation of the apostle, 3:1-5.

B. To correct and discipline the idle and disorderly, 3:6-15.

Conclusion: Benediction, 3:16. Autograph conclusion as authentication of the letter, 3:17. Second benediction, 3:18

Canonicity: Homologoumenon

Authenticity of the Second Letter

The authenticity of the second letter has been seriously questioned. The chief arguments against Pauline authorship are the following:

1. The second letter, it is said, largely repeats the first, and this marks it as a forgery. The statement is an exaggeration; about one third of the second letter is parallel to the first, and even this does not give the impression of mechanical copying, such as might be expected from a forger, for the material occurs in a different order from that in the first letter.

2. The second letter, it is said, teaches a different eschatology from that of the first: the first letter stresses the fact that the coming of the Lord will be like that of a thief in the night, while the second points to certain events as signs which must precede and will therefore foretoken the Second Coming. It should be noted that this same double emphasis is found in Jesus' own teaching concerning His return (Matt. 24:6-8, 36). Paul does not abandon the teaching of the first letter in the second; he simply defines it more sharply by the statement that certain events must precede the Second Coming of Jesus. Neither Jesus' words nor Paul's provide a means of forecasting the end.

The strongest arguments for authenticity (besides the unanimous testimony of the ancient church) are the lack of any motive for a forgery, and the genuinely Pauline tone and character of the second letter; even some of the scholars who question the authenticity of the letter admit that there is nothing in it that could not have come from the pen of Paul.

Value of the Second Letter

The Second Letter to the Thessalonians is an outstanding example of the spiritual tact of the apostle, which enables him to quell the fevered excitement of a hope grown hysterical without quenching the fervor and the life-shaping force of that hope and to instill sobriety without robbing the Christian hope of its intensity, leaving both fear and faith to do their salutary work in man. His emphasis on working industry in this connection (an emphasis which he spelled out in his life too, by supporting himself) is a part of the apostolic recognition of the order established by God the Creator and remains one of the great safeguards of Christian sanity over against all falsely spiritual contempt for the gifts and claims of God's created world.

The eschatological teaching is an amplification and an enrichment of what Paul has given the church in the first letter, particularly in the second chapter, which is for the Lutheran Confessions the classic passage in support of their affirmation that the papacy is the Antichrist. The passage renews and explicates the warning of Jesus, who taught His disciples that wheat and weeds must ripen together till the harvest; it reminds the church that the satanic counterthrust is inevitable and constant wherever God's word grows and God's reign is established, that any shallow ecclesiastical optimism which bows the knee to the idol of Progress and any churchly piety which becomes comfortably at home in this world is a denial of the revelation on which the life of the church is built.

CHAPTER V: The Letters of Paul's Third Missionary Journey

READINGS: ACTS 18:23–21:17; 1 and 2 CORINTHIANS; ROMANS

"Fighting Without and Fear Within": The Letters to Corinth

Paul wrote his letters to Corinth during that strenuous, perilous, and exhilarating period of his life which is commonly known as his Third Missionary Journey (A. D. 52—56). The heart of that journey was the nearly three years' ministry in the great metropolis of Asia Minor, Ephesus; this ministry was preceded by a revisitation of the churches founded on the First Missionary Journey and was followed by a revisitation of the European churches of Macedonia and Achaea founded on the Second Journey.

Paul himself had prepared the way for his ministry in Ephesus by his visit to Ephesus on his return from Corinth to Palestine at the close of the Second Journey (Acts 18:19-21). The men of the synagog were so much moved by his words that they asked him to stay on. He promised to return to Ephesus and left Aquila and Priscilla there. As their contact with Apollos shows (Acts 18:24-26), they did not remain silent concerning the faith that was in them. The learned and eloquent Apollos became a full-fledged witness to the Christ through them (Acts 18:26) and thus further prepared the way for Paul. Perhaps the twelve "disciples" who knew only the baptism of John and had not heard of the outpouring of the Holy Spirit in the last days (Acts 19:1-7) had been won by Apollos. Paul baptized them and laid hands on them, that they might receive the Holy Spirit. Thus his work at Ephesus began. The beginning was slight, only twelve men, but the foundation was, as always, essentially his own (Rom. 15:20), and he built upon it with a will.

That will generated conflict. Luke's account of Paul's Ephesian ministry is anything but complete. He gives no chronicle of it, but presents it schematically, as a series of three conflicts, each of which results in a triumph for the cause of the apostle of Christ. The first conflict was with the synagog (Acts 19:8-10). Paul was here permitted to witness in the synagog for an unusually long period, for three months, and with considerable success. The Jews of the province of Asia were therefore particularly bitter against him, and it was they who later instigated the riot in Jerusalem which led to Paul's arrest and imprisonment (Acts 21:27, 28). The break with the synagog came, as it inevitably did: "Some were stubborn and disbelieved, speaking evil of the Way before the congregation" (Acts 19:9), and Paul withdrew from the synagog to continue his teaching in the school of Tyrannus. He continued there for two years, and the conflict with Judaism proved to be a triumph for the word of the Lord: "All the residents of Asia heard the word of the Lord, both Jews and Greeks." (Acts 19:10)

The second conflict generated by the Christ-centered will of Paul was the conflict with magic, for which Ephesus was notorious (Acts 19:11-20). The fact that "God did extraordinary miracles by the hands of Paul" (Acts 19:11) made the superstitious look upon Christianity as a new and more potent kind of magic; but the experience of the Jewish exorcists who sought to use the names of Jesus and Paul in their trade made it plain that Jesus is Lord in personal and august power, a Lord who can defend His name against misuse by those who deem Him a power which they can manipulate and employ. "The name of the Lord Jesus was extolled," and the conscience of believers was quickened — the line between magic and religion was sharply and critically drawn for them by this incident. They confessed their wrong and burned their infamous Ephesian books of charms and incantations, and "the word of the Lord grew and prevailed mightily" (Acts 19:20). The magical word by which men sought power grew impotent before the divine word.

The third and most dangerous conflict was the conflict with

the commercialized state religion of Ephesus (Acts 19:23-41). The zeal of the silversmith Demetrius and his guild was something less than a purely religious fervor; but the fury of the guild members and of the huge, shouting city mob which they aroused is nevertheless an illustration of the demonic power which Paul in his First Letter to the Corinthians describes as at work in the worship of gods that are no gods (1 Cor. 10:19, 20). The fury of that demonic power fell upon Paul and the Christians of Ephesus; but the conflict led to a vindication of Paul and his followers, so that Paul could leave Ephesus with an unsullied reputation and with the respect of men like the Asiarchs and the town clerk (the most important city official of Ephesus). This was something which Paul valued; it was soon after he left Ephesus that he wrote the words: "We aim at what is honorable not only in the Lord's sight but also in the sight of men." (2 Cor. 8:21; cf. Col. 4:5, 6)

Luke himself gives a hint that the Ephesian years were filled with difficulties and dangers beyond those noted by him in his account of those years. He records the words of Paul to the elders of Ephesus which speak of the trials which befell him through the plottings of the Jews (Acts 20:19), tells of the Jewish plot against Paul's life at Corinth a little later (Acts 20:3), and notes that the Jews of Asia were especially rancorous in their hatred of Paul (Acts 21:27). Paul's letters of this period further fill in the picture of this time as a period of perils. Paul speaks in his First Letter to the Corinthians of the fact that his great opportunity at Ephesus has as its cast shadow the presence of many adversaries (1 Cor. 16:9), and that he has "fought with beasts at Ephesus" (1 Cor. 15:32) — whether the expression is to be taken literally or, as is more probable, figuratively, it is a vivid expression of extreme peril. In the opening verses of his Second Letter to the Corinthians Paul gives thanks for an unlooked-for divine deliverance from desperate danger in the province of Asia (2 Cor. 1:8-10). And when he speaks in his Letter to the Romans of the fact that Aquila and Priscilla have risked their necks for him, he is probably referring to the Ephesian period also. (Rom. 16:4)

Paul is no bloodless saint on a gold background. He held

life dear, just because he had committed it wholly to the Christ, and he hoped to live to see his Lord when He returned in glory (1 Cor. 15:51; 2 Cor. 5:1-5). While he was ready to sacrifice his life (Acts 20:24), he was not ready to waste it. And so he suffered in a genuinely human way. He feared in the face of perils and was racked by his fears. But in his human frailty, which he never denied, but rather asserted (1 Cor. 2:3, 4), he held in faith to the fact that all things that are and that happen are from God the Father and are mediated by the Lord Jesus Christ, so that he saw in everything that befell him God's fatherly dealings with him and the Lordship of Christ exercised over him and through him (1 Cor. 8:6). He experienced again and again the truth of what his Lord had told him: "My grace is sufficient for you, for My power is made perfect in weakness" (2 Cor. 12:9). Thus a period singularly marked by perils was for Paul also an exhilarating one; we see him in the letters of this period exuberantly welcoming suffering as essential to the Christian life and a salutary part of it (Rom. 5:3-5; 8:35-39) and triumphantly boasting of his perils and afflictions as being the glory of his life as an apostle. He is employing high irony when he contrasts the assured complacency of the Corinthians with his own sorry and embattled existence (1 Cor. 4:8-13), and the only boast he really permits himself over against the boasting of his detractors in Corinth is a glorying in his sufferings (2 Cor. 11:23-33). He sees in the paradox of "dying, and behold we live" (2 Cor. 6:9) the apex of his apostolate. The three mighty letters from this period are the golden products of the alchemy of faith and suffering.

It was a perilous period; it was also a strenuous one. The evangelization of Ephesus was also the evangelization of the province of Asia. Whether men like Epaphras, who brought the Gospel to Colossae in the interior, worked under the direct supervision of Paul or not cannot be made out; certainly he and others like him must have consulted Paul frequently in the course of their work, as Epaphras did later on when heresy threatened the inland cities (Col. 1:7, 8; 4:12). The sending of Timothy and Erastus to Macedonia (Acts 19:22) indicates that the churches there, too, needed help. But Paul's dealings with his beloved, brilliant, and wayward child, the church of Corinth, give us the most vivid picture of what Paul meant when he spoke of the daily pressure of "anxiety for all the churches" (2 Cor. 11:28). If the growth of the word of the Lord in this period meant conflict, if it meant "fighting without," it also meant for Paul an intense personal and pastoral anxiety; it mean "fear within." (2 Cor. 7:5)

The church of Corinth was a brilliantly endowed church, "enriched . . . with all speech and all knowledge . . . not lacking in any spiritual gift" (1 Cor. 1:5, 7). Corinth had had the benefit of a much longer ministry by Paul than any of the other Greek cities. Paul was the "father" of the Corinthian Christians; their life in Christ had his unmistakable and ineradicable imprint upon it. We can gauge from Acts and from Paul's letters what it meant to have Paul for a father, how rich a heritage this father gave his children. (Cf. 2 Cor. 12:14)

They had also had the benefit of the ministry of Apollos, that eloquent and fervent Alexandrian, powerful in the Scriptures (Acts 18:24). His coming to Corinth with letters of recommendation from Ephesus (Acts 18:27, 28) apparently led to a renewed contact with the synagog in Corinth, which had previously broken with Paul (Acts 18:6-8): "He powerfully confuted the Jews *in public,* showing by the Scriptures that the Christ was Jesus" (Acts 18:28). Perhaps it was Apollos who won for Christ the ruler of the synagog, Sosthenes, whom the crowd had beaten before the tribunal of Gallio (Acts 18:17). Paul includes Sosthenes with himself in the sending of his First Letter to the Corinthians (1 Cor. 1:1). If this Sosthenes is a Corinthian, moreover, a Corinthian converted by Apollos, the fact that Paul thus singles him out is significant; Paul is telling the clique-ridden church of Corinth: Here is one who received the Gospel from Apollos and is one with me in all that I am telling you, just as Apollos himself is. (1 Cor. 3:5-9; 16:12)

At the time when Paul wrote his first letter, there were in the Corinthian church those who said, "I belong to Cephas" (1 Cor. 1:12). They professed a special allegiance to Simon Peter, and they used the original Aramaic form of his official name (Cephas). This would indicate that they were Jews who had come to Corinth from one of the eastern Judaic churches which Peter had evangelized. The presence of these Christians from the fields where

Peter had worked no doubt meant an enrichment for the church at Corinth; but it also created tensions. The various components of the young church — the original converts of Paul, the converts of Apollos, and the new arrivals from the east — could not as yet, or would not, unite in that free and richly various oneness which Paul described as essential to the life of the church (1 Cor. 12). Apollos himself had worked in complete harmony with Paul; no shadow of blame attached to him, as every mention of him in the first letter shows. But there were those, converts or admirers of Apollos, who compared this personable, energetic, and brilliant preacher with Paul and found him more to their liking than Paul, the bondservant of God who had come to Corinth "in weakness and in much fear and trembling" (1 Cor. 2:3), who candidly described himself as "unskilled in speaking" (2 Cor. 11:6), and preached the *crucified* Christ with an almost monomaniac insistence (1 Cor. 2:2). The new arrivals from the east, the Cephas people, quite naturally felt themselves to be the representatives of a maturer, more original kind of Christianity than that of the churches founded by Paul. They had received the word from Peter, the "first" of the apostles, who had seen the Lord Jesus and had lived with him; Paul was, in their eyes, an apostle of not quite equal rank with the Twelve, the child "untimely born" (1 Cor. 15:8), not really a full member of the apostolic brotherhood. They felt as charter members of an old, honorable club might feel toward newer members, who besides being new would not be members at all if *they* had not generously relaxed the rules a bit.

The church was full of tensions and ferment. And the church's outward situation did nothing to improve its inward state. This church lived in Corinth, where all the brilliance of the Greek mind and all the vagaries of the Greek will mingled with an influx of Oriental religiosity to produce a moral climate which even the Greeks found singularly vicious.

The Corinthian church had, moreover, never been tried, refined, and unified by persecution. The policy of noninterference which the Roman proconsul Gallio had enunciated to the Jews (Acts 18:14-16) apparently remained in force with his successors; and while the church no doubt had to endure the social pressures and animosities which any consistent opposition to the prevailing culture and religiosity evoked, it was safe from Jewish vindictiveness and from governmental coercion. The Christians of Corinth waited for the "revealing of our Lord Jesus Christ" (1 Cor. 1:7), but they were tempted more than other churches to make themselves comfortable and at home in the world while they waited. They enjoyed security, and they had leisure to speculate about the implications of the Gospel, since they were not called upon to affirm the Gospel in action in the face of persecution.

Such was the climate of the church life in Corinth. All that was potentially harmful and disruptive in it was crystallized and intensified by the emergence of a fourth group in the congregation. Since Paul never fully describes this group, it is difficult to get a clear picture of these people, and sometimes it is impossible to see where the line between them and the Cephas people, for instance, is being drawn. But the following would seem to be a fair characterization of them. They came from outside the Corinthian church. Paul distinguishes them from those who professed allegiance to himself or to Apollos, the men who had worked at Corinth (1 Cor. 1:12). His words in 2 Cor. 11:4 explicitly mark this group as new arrivals in Corinth: "If someone *comes* and preaches another Jesus than the one we preached. . . ." Paul's contemptuous reference in 2 Cor. 3:1 to "some" who need letters of recommendation makes it probable that they came with such letters from one of the eastern churches (which need not imply that any of the eastern churches was necessarily responsible for the teaching which they developed at Corinth). They were Judaic and proud of it, Hebrews, Israelites, descendants of Abraham (2 Cor. 11:22). But they were not Judaizers of the sort that had disturbed the churches of Galatia; we hear nothing of circumcision and the reimposition of the Mosaic Law in connection with these men. One can imagine that they claimed to be the inheritors of the true Judaic-Christian tradition and for that reason felt themselves uniquely qualified to lead the church beyond the first stages of that tradition into the full riches of knowledge and freedom in Christ.

What they brought into Corinth was a brilliant and persuasive kind of liberalism, which operated (as liberalism characteristically does) with genuinely Christian slogans and catchwords. If, according to Paul, they preached "another Jesus," *they* no doubt claimed that they were preaching the genuine Jesus; if they proclaimed a "different Gospel" and had and imparted a "different spirit," it was Paul who said so, not they; they claimed that their Gospel was the true Gospel and their spirit the true Spirit of God (2 Cor. 11:4). The slogan which they brought with them (or developed in the course of their activities at Corinth) was as Christian as a slogan can be: "I belong to Christ" (1 Cor. 1:12; 2 Cor. 10:7). Paul himself uses the phrase to designate the Christian. (1 Cor. 3:23; cf. Rom. 8:9)

They exalted the Christ and awaited His return; they treasured His gift of the Spirit and set great store by the gifts given by the Spirit (2 Cor. 11:4; cf. 1 Cor. 7:40). But they exalted the Christ as the Giver of knowledge and treasured the gifts of the Spirit primarily as a means to knowledge of God, as the way to wisdom (1 Cor. 3:18-20; 8:1-3, 10, 11; 13:9). And this knowledge, they claimed, made them free; the knowledge and wisdom which they possessed carried them beyond any previous revelation of God, beyond the Old Testament Scriptures, beyond anything contained in the apostolic word. Before this ultimate knowledge of God, which they claimed to possess, all previous standards became meaningless, all former ties were dissolved, all the old taboos were gone: "All things are lawful for me" — that was their boast (1 Cor. 6:12; 10:23). It was an intellectually appealing and an intoxicating message that they brought; it is not surprising that they attracted followers and deeply influenced the whole church.

Their influence on the life of the church went deep, and it was harmful in the extreme. We can trace its beginnings in Paul's reference to a letter (now lost) which he had written to the Corinthians before our present first letter (1 Cor. 5:9). In that earlier letter Paul had demanded of the Corinthians that they refuse to have fellowship with "immoral men." This demand of Paul's was questioned by the church, perhaps even rejected as being unclear and impracticable. (1 Cor. 5:9-11)

Perhaps it was "Chloe's people" (to whom Paul refers in 1 Cor. 1:11) who delivered Paul's earlier letter to Corinth; they would then have seen and could report to Paul how it was received, how the church broke up into factions over the issues involved (1 Cor. 1—4); it was probably they who reported to Paul the conditions which resulted from this new proclamation of absolute liberty at Corinth; they could tell Paul why his letter was questioned and contradicted: the new teachers were saying that the new knowledge set men free, and at least one Corinthian Christian had drastically used that liberty (1 Cor. 5:1): Why should not a man be free to "live with" his father's wife (probably his stepmother) after his father's death? What the Old Testament said no longer bound him (Deut. 22:30; 27:20), and the authority of Jesus and His apostles had been superseded by the new revelation of the Spirit. The Corinthian church as a whole not only tolerated this immorality, but was even "arrogant" about it (1 Cor. 5:2); these men felt that they were demonstrating their spiritual maturity in tolerating it. The people of Chloe could tell Paul, too, of the breakdown of discipline in the church, how differences between Christian brethren were no longer being settled within the church, but were being taken into pagan courts; the preachers of the new freedom had no interest in, and no taste for, the serious and painful business of keeping the church pure by calling erring brethren to repentance (1 Cor. 6:1-11). Paul has to hammer home the most elementary moral facts in his attempt to pierce the complacency of the people intoxicated by the new freedom. (1 Cor. 6:9-11)

The new liberty preached in Corinth conceded to the Christian man the freedom to associate with prostitutes. The Law which demanded sexual purity of them was being put on the same level with the law concerning clean and unclean foods (1 Cor. 6: 12-20) — or, at least, the satisfaction of sexual desire was being put on the same level with the satisfaction of hunger (1 Cor. 6:13). The fact that the Apostolic Council had expressly laid the abstaining from immorality on the consciences of the Gentile Christians made no impression in Corinth. (Acts 15:29)

Not everyone at Corinth was so completely swept away by the eloquent rationalism of the new teachers or so deeply intoxicated by the liberty which they offered that he asked no questions or raised no objections. Men like Stephanas (1 Cor. 16:15) and Fortunatus and Achaicus (1 Cor. 16:17) saw that it was high time that Paul be consulted explicitly and at length on the questions which were raised by the new theology of knowledge and freedom, and they saw to it that he was consulted. The congregation wrote Paul a letter (1 Cor. 7:1) and laid before him a series of questions on points where it was becoming evident that the teaching of the new teachers was not only different from Paul's, but was contradicting it.

The first question concerned marriage (1 Cor. 7). The form that Paul's answer to their question takes makes it tolerably clear what direction the new teachers were taking here. Pursuing their ideal of religious self-fulfillment, they saw in marriage merely an impediment to the religious life and were intent on making the church an association of celibates, without regard for the moral dangers involved in this mass imposition of celibacy, without regard for the authority of the Lord Jesus, who had blessed little children and had declared the bond which united man and woman to be inviolable (Matt. 19:3-9, 13-15) and made celibacy a gift reserved for those "to whom it is given" (Matt. 19:11). They were running counter to the thinking and practice of the apostles also, for the apostles saw in the family and all natural orders primarily vehicles which the grace of God might employ — "You will be saved, *you and your household,*" Paul told the jailer at Philippi (Acts 16:31). But the new teachers not only sought to keep men and women from marriage (the passage on the "unmarried" and the "betrothed" takes cognizance of this, 1 Cor. 7: 25-38); they also apparently permitted men and women to free themselves of their spouses, especially pagan spouses, in order to be "free for the Lord," again in contradiction to the express command of Jesus (1 Cor. 7:10, 11). Perhaps the license which they conceded with regard to association with harlots (1 Cor. 6:12-20) is connected with this attitude toward marriage: If a man could not be continent and yet wished to be free of the impediment of marriage, the association with the harlot would be a solution, since "all things are lawful for me." (1 Cor. 6:12)

To the question, "May a Christian eat food that has been offered as a sacrifice to idols?" (1 Cor. 8—10) the new teachers had a ready and simple answer: "All of us possess knowledge" (1 Cor. 8:1): which meant, since knowledge gives liberty, that "all things are lawful," including the sacrificial meats consecrated to idols. In their self-centered piety, puffed up as they were by knowledge, they did not consider what harm their freedom might do to the brother whose knowledge was not yet deep and firm enough to make him capable of exercising such freedom. In their complacent self-assurance they did not pause to consider that demonic powers are at work behind all false worship of false gods, though the gods themselves are nothing. They disregarded the warning example of Israel recorded for them in the Old Testament. They flouted the example of the apostles, whose knowledge was as great as theirs, whose wisdom was more profound and certainly more sober and realistic than theirs. Paul has to remind the Corinthians: "Be imitators of me, as I am of Christ." (1 Cor. 11:1)

But it was not only in the family and in private life that the intoxication of the new liberty was working mischief; it infected the worship life of the church too (1 Cor. 11—14). Women were asserting their new-found liberty by appearing at worship without the veil, which was the badge of their womanliness and their recognition of the place which God the Creator and Redeemer (1 Cor. 11:3, 8) had assigned to them (1 Cor. 11:2-16). They were also adding to the confusion of an already chaotic public worship by an unwomanly assumption of a teaching authority which neither Jesus nor the apostles had given them (1 Cor. 14: 33-36). But the voice of Jesus, the voice of His apostles, the practice of the churches of God (1 Cor. 11:16) did not deter the proponents and adherents of the new liberty; they were "disposed to be contentious" nevertheless.

This spirit of rampant individualism made the common fellowship meals of the church a scene of feasting and carousing, in which the rich disregarded the poor and made of the Lord's Supper, celebrated in connection with the common meal, anything but the *Lord's* supper. The supper which commemorated and made effectively present the utter self-giving and self-sacrifice of the Lord Jesus Christ and was designed to unite the Lord's people in the eating of the one loaf and the partaking of the one cup became the scene and the means of man's self-assertion and of division (1 Cor. 11:17-34). When knowledge is the capstone of the religious structure and love no longer rules (1 Cor. 13), decency and order are sacrificed, edification is no longer possible, the salutary commands of the apostle are disregarded (14:37, 38), and the example of the churches of God everywhere means nothing. (1 Cor. 14:36)

All that characterizes the "Christ-men" appears in a concentrated and a peculiarly clear form in their denial of the bodily resurrection of the dead (1 Cor. 15) — their false spirituality, which disregarded and degraded the body and all things natural; their false conception of knowledge, which made them manipulators of ideas who could disregard the central fact of all history, the bodily resurrection of Jesus Christ from the dead; their false conception of freedom, which moved them to oppose themselves and their ideas, not only to Paul but to all the apostles and to the Old Testament witness to Christ as well. In their intoxication of liberty (Paul has to tell them to come to their right mind, to sober up, 1 Cor. 15:34), they felt free to sacrifice the central fact of the apostolic proclamation to Greek prejudice — to the Greek the idea of a bodily resurrection was particularly offensive, as the reaction of the Stoics and Epicureans at Athens to Paul's preaching of the resurrection shows. (Acts 17:32)

It has become abundantly clear by now that when these men said, "We belong to Christ," they were saying it in an exclusive sense, as a fighting slogan. The liberty which their "knowledge" gave them, their "freedom" in the Spirit, necessarily involved a break with the authority of Paul, who had planted the word in Corinth; there is some evidence to indicate that they considered Paul superseded and unnecessary to the church at Corinth and claimed that he would not come to Corinth again; Paul's words in 1 Cor. 4:18, 19 hint as much: "Some are arrogant, as though I were not coming to you. But I will come to you soon if the Lord wills, and I will find out not the talk of these arrogant people, but their power." A break with Paul necessarily meant a break with Apollos, who had watered where Paul had planted; and it meant a break with all apostolic authority. Paul's words concerning their arrogance (1 Cor. 4:18, 19) and their contentiousness (1 Cor. 11:16; 14:38) seem to indicate that they were highly autocratic and contemptuous of any power but their own, a fact which is confirmed by the bitter irony of Paul's reproach to the Corinthians in 2 Cor. 11:20, 21: "You bear it if a man makes slaves of you, or preys upon you, or takes advantage of you, or puts on airs, or strikes you in the face." They and those who were most completely taken in by them thus constituted a clique in the church; and as a clique produces more cliques by way of reaction, there ensued that sorry and divided state of the church which Paul deals with so powerfully in the first four chapters of his First Letter to the Corinthians. At Corinth the line between the church (where Christ alone is Lord) and the world (where *men* head movements and command loyalties) was being perilously blurred.

THE FIRST LETTER TO THE CORINTHIANS

Our present first letter is Paul's response to this situation, as he had learned it from Chloe's people, from Stephanas, Fortunatus, and Achaicus, and from the letter of the Corinthian church. If all the problems at Corinth have a common root, all Paul's responses to the various derangements and sins in the church also have a common denominator. The first letter, for all its variety, is one unified answer, one brilliant demonstration of how a genuinely apostolic authority makes itself felt. And the common denominator, the unifying power, is the cross of Jesus Christ, seen in its full significance by the light of the resurrection.

Paul operates with the slogans of the new leaders, but by relating them all to the cross he gives them a radically different content. If they extolled the Christ as the giver of knowledge and freedom, Paul exalts Him as the Lord of glory who was crucified by the rulers of this world. If they empty the cross of its power (1 Cor. 1:17), he is resolved to know nothing but the cross (1 Cor. 2:2); and he sets the cross squarely in the center of the church again, the cross which, with its pure and all-inclusive grace, lays a total claim upon man, body and soul, for a life lived wholly to God (1 Cor. 6:19, 20). The cross, which pronounces an annihilating judgment on all human greatness and on all human pretenses to wisdom, cuts off all boasting of man, and marks as monstrous and unnatural any clustering about great men in schools and factions that give their loyalty to men.

If they boast of possessing the Spirit and foster a spirituality which disregards the body and feeds the religious ego, Paul interprets the Spirit by the cross, by that event in history in which the Son of God suffered in the flesh for men in the flesh, that event in which God spoke His unmistakable yea to the body which He had created. Paul proclaims a Spirit who dwells in the human body and lays a consecrating claim upon it (1 Cor. 6:19). He proclaims a Spirit who enables men to say that *Jesus* is Lord (that is, Jesus the Crucified whom the Jews call the Accursed because He hung upon the tree, 1 Cor. 12:3, cf. Gal. 3:13), a Spirit who gives gifts to the church "for the common good" (1 Cor. 12:7), whose highest gift is the love which does not seek its own (1 Cor. 13).

If they boast a knowledge which makes them "wise in this age" (1 Cor. 3:18), a knowledge which puffs men up (1 Cor. 8:1) and makes them boast of men and creates cliques clustered about men, Paul proclaims the offensive wisdom of the cross (1 Cor. 2:6-13) which brings man low, both Jew and Greek, and makes him glory in the Lord alone. Paul proclaims a whole and unabridged grace of God, the grace of the cross, and that grace gives a knowledge which is not primarily *man's* knowing at all, but man's being known by God; it means that a man has a knowledge that matters when God knows him (that is, loves, chooses, and calls him), and man is thus enabled to love God. (1 Cor. 8:1-3)

If they have and exercise a freedom which overrides all authority, exalts the self of man, and disregards the brother, Paul proclaims the freedom of the Christian man, who is lord of all things because he is the Christ's (1 Cor. 3:21, 22) and in this his freedom comes under the law of Christ and enslaves himself to all men in order that he may by all means save some (1 Cor. 9: 21, 22). Paul knows freedom as freedom from sin and self, a being set free for ministry to one's fellow man.

These are the basic convictions which underlie Paul's full and many-sided treatment of all the questions posed by the situation in Corinth. No outline of the letter can do justice to it. The following may suffice to indicate the scope of the letter.

Content of the First Letter to the Corinthians

I. Factions in the Church, 1—4

The Gospel of the Crucified is the absolute opposite of that wisdom of this world which fosters human greatness and creates factions which center in men. The cross of Christ destroys all human greatness. If the new teachers seek power and create a faction, Paul seeks unity and decries all parties, including the one that called itself after him.

II. Moral Problems, 5—6

A. Incest, 5:1-13

The cross has redeemed man and has claimed man, bodily man, wholly for a life lived to the glory of God, cf. 1 Cor. 6:20. The church, liberated from bondage by the Passover sacrifice of the Lamb of God, cannot tolerate the leaven of impurity, but must keep the new feast of unleavened bread in sincerity and truth.

B. Litigation, 6:1-11

The church has by the new Passover become the new, free people of God; as such it must take seriously its freedom, by disciplining itself and thus retaining its character as the pure people of God. The church cannot commit its task of dealing with brothers at variance with one another to the powers of this judged and dying world.

C. Immorality, 6:12-20

If the church dare not tolerate impurity, much less may the members of the church, whose bodies are members of Christ, practice impurity with harlots. "You are not your own; you were bought with a price. So glorify God in your body," 6:19, 20.

III. Celibacy and Marriage, 7

The cross has bought men with a price, 7:23, and has destined them for glory. Their life in the orders of this world (e. g., in marriage, slavery, commerce) has a preliminary, penultimate character, for "the form of this world is passing away," to give place to the new world of God,

7:31. As redeemed men they are to have a loose hold on the things of this world, 7:29-31, and are to aim always at an "undivided devotion to the Lord" who bought them, 7:35. That gives celibacy its value and its place in the church. But celibacy is a gift which only the free grace of God can give, 7:7; man cannot demand it or take it for himself. If life in this world has a preliminary character, it also has a preparatory character; men are to live their lives in the faith that God has placed them where they are and has called them to be His own where they are, 7:17-24. They may not, in blind enthusiasm, set out blithely and boldly to free themselves of the marriage bond which the word of their redeeming Lord has hallowed, 7:10; and they dare not attempt a self-chosen course of celibate devotion to their Lord which will plunge them into sin, 7:2-5, 9, 36, 38.

IV. The Eating of Meat Offered to Idols, 8—10

The cross has put men under the sole Lordship of the Christ, 8:6; they are free men — no idol has a claim upon them or power over them. But a man's weaker brother, the brother for whom Christ died, 8:11, has a claim upon him which calls for a self-sacrificing love, such as marked the ministry of Paul himself, chap. 9. The Christian man is, moreover, under the Lordship of the Christ in an alien world, where demonic powers lurk behind the facade of empty idolatry; the church is no more automatically secure than ancient Israel was, for all the blessings that Israel received; this calls for a life lived in sobriety and holy fear, lest the church, in attempting to divide her loyalty between her Lord and other lords, "provoke the Lord to jealousy," 10:22.

V. Disorders in the Worship Life of the Church, 11—14

A. Women in the Church, 11:2-16, cf. 14:33-36

God's act of redemption in the cross has not abrogated the order which He established in creation, 11:7-10; rather, the cross has affirmed and hallowed that primal order, 11:3. No woman in Christ will therefore rebel against that order either by laying aside the badge and token of her God-given womanliness, 11:2-16, or by assuming a function in the church beyond that which her Lord has assigned to her, 14:33-36.

B. The Lord's Supper, 11:17-34

The Lord's Supper is the *Lord's;* it is the gift of His cross effectually present in the church, to enrich and to unify the church. To make of it man's supper, a meal wherein the Lord's real and redeeming bodily presence is not recognized, to make of it the scene of man's carousing, the expression of his divisive and contemptuous self-will, is to invite the judgment of God upon the church.

C. The Use of Spiritual Gifts, 12—14

The Holy Spirit puts men under the Lordship of the Crucified; the gifts which the Spirit bestows are therefore to be the expression of the Lord's self-giving will and are to be used in mutual ministration for the furthering of the body of Christ, His church, a ministration in which no member can be solitary and all members are necessary, chap. 12. The highest gift of the Spirit is the gift of that indispensable and eternal love which sets man free for ministry, chap. 13. No gift of the Spirit is rightly used when it is used to foster individualism in worship and to create a confusion in worship which cannot edify. The God who gave His Son to be the Peace of the world is a God of peace and not of confusion. "All things should be done decently and in order," chap. 14.

VI. The Resurrection of the Dead, 15

A. The Significance of the Resurrection of Christ, 15:1-34

The resurrection of the dead stands or falls with the resurrection of the Christ who "died for our sins." So firmly established is the link between the two, between the resurrection of the Christ and the resurrection of those who are His, that the obverse is also true: The resurrection of the Christ stands or falls with the resurrection of the dead. And if the resurrection of the Christ falls, all is lost; the cross is "emptied of its power," for no mere martyr's death can assure the forgiveness of sins; what the apostles proclaim is nothing and worse than nothing, a lie; what the church believes is nothing; and the church's hope is nothing. Christian suffering and martyrdom have lost all point and purpose. And yet the Corinthians have listened to "some" who in their boasted wisdom have no knowledge of the God who raises the dead, 15:34; they have admitted into their midst "bad company" who will ruin them morally by tampering with the fact on which the whole Christian life is based, namely the resurrection, 15:33.

B. The Manner of the Resurrection of the Dead, 15:35-58

These same spiritual "some" are foolish enough to ask, "How are the dead raised?" They thereby reveal their ignorance of the creative possibilities of God, who gives each of His creatures its own fit kind of body and can therefore as certainly create a spiritual body for His new creature, the man in Christ, as He created a physical body for man in Adam. The Corinthians must be mad and drunk to listen to such "foolish men," men who in their ignorance of God cast to the winds the victory over death which God has given them through the Lord Jesus Christ, that triumphant certainty of life which makes men not theorists and debaters, but "steadfast, immovable, always abounding in the *work* of the Lord," 15:58.

VII. Practical and Personal Matters, 16

    A. The Collection for the Poor Saints at Jerusalem, 16:1-4

    B. Paul's Travel Plans, 16:5-9

    C. The Coming Visit of Timothy; Apollos' Plans, 16:10-12

    D. Commendations and Greetings, 16:15-20

    E. Autograph Conclusion: Anathema on all who have no love for the Lord; prayer for the coming of the Lord; and benediction, 16:21-24

Value of the Letter

Here is God's plenty; here in this severely functional, working theology of First Corinthians, a genuine letter, conditioned by history and directed to real-life situations from beginning to end, are inexhaustible riches for the church to live by. To begin with the most obvious and most important fact about the letter: The whole New Testament is a chorus of grateful praise for the cross, but this letter drives home the centrality of the cross in a peculiarly vital way; it proclaims the cross not as a tenet to be held or as an article to be believed, but as a power which makes possible, and demands, a life lived to God in all its parts and all its functions, a human life judged by the righteousness of God and a new life created and endowed by His grace.

The letter consequently draws the line between the church and the world, between human wisdom and the Gospel, between the wisdom of this age and the "foolish," paradoxical wisdom of God, in a way which should have quashed once for all all attempts to make Christianity a rich and interesting blend of the two. The legacy of the First Letter to the Corinthians is a perpetual reminder to the church that she must dare to be "other" if she is to be the apostolic church of God, that she must dare to cut athwart the axioms and standards of this world if she is to do her divine work in the world. In a way, the first four chapters of the letter are a practical commentary on those words of our Lord in which He inverts the standards of this world, and does so by pointing to His cross: "You know that the rulers of the Gentiles lord it over them, and their great men exercise authority over them. It shall not be so among you; but whoever would be great among you must be your servant, and whoever would be first among you must be your slave; even as the Son of man came not to be served but to serve, and to give His life as a ransom for many." (Matt. 20:25-28).

"Whoever would be great among you *must be your servant"* — the First Letter to the Corinthians is a rich explication of that word of Jesus. Jesus spoke these words to His disciples, to men who had received His promise that they should share royally in the enthronement of the Son of man (Matt. 19:28). Paul tells the men of Corinth, "All things are yours . . . the world or life or death or the present or the future, all are yours" (1 Cor. 3: 21, 22); but he tells them in the same breath, "And you are Christ's" (1 Cor. 3:23). He tells them that they belong to the Crucified, who gave Himself for men. And so all their liberty in Christ and all the riches given them by the Spirit are theirs for ministry; they are enriched in all things in order that they may enrich their brethren.

The First Letter to the Corinthians has also impressed upon the church the religious significance and the sanctity of the human body, the body as God's creation, as the abode of the Spirit, destined for glory, the expressive instrument of man's will in the service of God. His words on the bodily worship of the Christian man in this letter are his practical application of the broad imperative in his Letter to the Romans: "Present your bodies as a living sacrifice, holy and acceptable to God, which is your spiritual worship" (Rom. 12:1). These are the words of a man who worked with his hands to the glory of his Lord. Closely related to this religious appreciation of the body is Paul's sense of history as the vehicle of divine revelation: The "mighty acts of God," the cross, the resurrection, the hard, nonmalleable fact, the act of God that man cannot manipulate — these are for him the very essence of theology. The Gospel is not ideas and principles about which man may theorize and speculate; the Gospel is news of that culminating act of God which has transformed the relationship between God and man and will transfigure all creation.

This emphasis on the body and on history gives Paul that sober sense of reality which makes him the enemy of all enthusiasm and enables him to see both sides of a question, like the question of celibacy and marriage, and to deal fairly with both; it enables him to give a full and evangelical answer to a question like that concerning meat offered to idols instead of a doctrinaire oversimplification; it enables him to do both, to give sober, down-to-earth directions for the worship of the church, and to carry his readers aloft in a hymn on the divinely given love which gives all gifts of the Spirit their value, spends itself in a reckless splendor of self-giving, and is a piece of the new world of God transplanted to this dying world even now.

THE COMING OF TIMOTHY

Paul had in his first letter prepared the church of Corinth for a coming visit by Timothy. That visit was designed by Paul to reinforce and to carry further the work which his letter was designed to do, namely, to bring the Corinthians back from their flight out of Christian reality and into an intoxicated and enthusiastic individualism, back to the cross, back to where Paul stood: "I urge you . . . be imitators of me. Therefore I sent you Timothy . . . to remind you of my ways in Christ, as I teach them . . . in every church" (1 Cor. 4:16, 17). What those "ways in Christ" were, the immediately preceding context makes plain: Paul ironically contrasts the blissful state of the Corinthians, who have become kings, who are rich and reign, are wise and strong and held in honor, with the apostles' wretched and unfinished state under the cross, men sentenced to death, a spectacle for angels and men to gaze on, fools, weak, in disrepute, hungry, thirsty, ill-clad, homeless, the meekly enduring, toilworn refuse of the world (1 Cor. 4:8-13). Paul anticipates that Timothy's task will not be a pleasant one and that the reception he will get may be less than amiable (1 Cor. 16:10, 11). Timothy's stay was brief, and since the Second Letter to the Corinthians says nothing of it, we know nothing of its results except what we can infer from the events that followed.

PAUL'S INTERMEDIATE VISIT TO CORINTH

Timothy soon returned to Paul, who thus quickly learned how his letter had been received and how things stood at Corinth. What he heard moved him to interrupt his work at Ephesus and to proceed to Corinth at once. This is the second visit which is implied by 2 Cor. 13:1, 2; 12:21, the "painful visit" to which Paul alludes in 2 Cor. 2:1. Timothy's report had made clear to Paul that the influence of the new teachers had spread farther and gone deeper than he had realized. There were not only "some" who were arrogant (1 Cor. 4:18), "some" who denied the central content of the apostolic proclamation (1 Cor. 15:12); the whole church was infected and endangered — the very existence of the "temple of God" (1 Cor. 3:17) was being threatened. Immediate action was necessary, drastic action which had to be taken personally. The visit therefore proved to be a painful one for the Corinthians, who were rudely shaken out of their dreaming self-assurance by the home truths which their apostle had to tell them (2 Cor. 2:2; 13:2); but it was a painful visit for Paul too, for the opposition to him, under the leadership of the men who claimed to be Christ's, proved strong. They must have been bold, intellectually vigorous, and capable men — they were able to face Paul and to keep a sizable part of the congregation with them. Just what form Paul's dealings with the church took cannot be clearly made out, but this much is plain: Paul was convinced that fellowship with the new leaders was no longer possible, that a break had to be made (2 Cor. 13:2); he left Corinth, however, without immediately forcing the issue. He still trusted that the church would come to see the necessity for the break as clearly as he himself saw it and left with the promise that he would return to Corinth when his work in Ephesus was done and would pay the church a double visit, both before and after the proposed revisitation of the Macedonian churches (2 Cor. 1:15, 16). This was, of course, a change from the travel plans which Paul had announced in 1 Cor. 16:5, 6.

The Severe Letter

What follows now is the obscurest part of an obscure history. Paul's trust that the church would see the light and would walk in that light was, apparently, disappointed. There occurred an incident which strained still further the already strained relations between Paul and the church. Paul speaks of one who did an injury which caused him pain (2 Cor. 2:5), an injury not directly to Paul himself but affecting him. Since Paul does not indicate the nature of the wrong done him, we can only conjecture what it may have been. Perhaps one of the men loyal to Paul suffered violence at the hands of an opponent in the heat of party strife. At any rate, the offense was so flagrant and involved the authority of Paul so immediately that the church could not ignore it and still be in any sense "his" church, still esteem him as apostle and father in Christ. Paul therefore changed his plans once more; instead of going directly to Corinth from Ephesus, he first proceeded northward toward Macedonia by way of Troas. Before leaving Asia he wrote a letter (now lost) to which he refers as a "severe" letter, a letter written "with many tears" (2 Cor. 2:4). This letter summoned the church to repentance in no uncertain terms: The wrongdoer must be dealt with and disciplined, and the church must return in obedience to its apostle. Paul dispatched the letter by the hand of Titus and instructed Titus to rejoin him at Troas and report on its effect.

THE REPORT OF TITUS

Titus had not yet returned to Troas when Paul arrived there (2 Cor. 2:12); and so Paul, in an agony of doubt concerning the outcome of Titus' mission, left Troas and proceeded to Macedonia (2 Cor. 2:13). And God, who comforts the downcast, comforted him by the coming of Titus (2 Cor. 7:5, 6). For Titus brought good news. The church at Corinth had heeded Paul's summons to repentance, had bowed to his authority, had disciplined the offender, who had also repented and asked for forgiveness. The church was ready to forgive him and only awaited Paul's assent to such a course before granting forgiveness. The church thus cleansed and restored by repentance longed to see Paul again, in order that the ties so long strained and endangered might be confirmed and strengthened once more. (2 Cor. 2:6; 7:7-16)

That was the positive side of Titus' report, and Paul welcomed it with that exuberant gratitude with which he received every good gift of God; he did not let the fact that there was another side to the report, a negative one, dampen his joy. Titus' news was not all good. The offender at Corinth had been punished by the "majority" of the congregation only, not by all (2 Cor. 2:6). There were still those at Corinth who held to the new teachers. Neither Paul's visit nor his severe letter had silenced the men who maliciously misinterpreted his every word and action, for example, his change in his travel plans (2 Cor. 1:17) or his letters (2 Cor. 1:13), and sought always to undermine his apostolic authority. It was probably their influence that had brought to a standstill a project which Paul had promoted with such energy and with such good initial success: the collection for the poor saints at Jerusalem.

THE SECOND LETTER TO THE CORINTHIANS

Occasion of Paul's Second Letter to the Corinthians

The unfinished task of the collection for the saints of Jerusalem was the occasion of Paul's fourth letter to the church at

Corinth, our present Second Letter to the Corinthians. But only the occasion; dear as the success of that undertaking was to Paul's heart and much as he valued the collection as an expression of the unity between the Gentile and the Judaic church, it is not the central concern of his letter. That is rather the re-establishment of a full and pure understanding of his authority as "apostle of Jesus Christ by the will of God." His desire to make clear forever to the Corinthians wherein the glory and power of his ministry lay is the dominant impulse in his writing. This concern dominates the first section (chaps. 1—7), which looks to the past, wherein Paul welcomes the penitent advances of the majority of the church, forgives the disciplined wrongdoer and bespeaks the love of the church for him, and appeals for a renewal of the full communion of love which had been characteristic of his association with the church of Corinth from of old. It dominates the last section of the letter also, where Paul looks forward to his coming visit to Corinth and deals rigorously and definitively with his detractors and their hangers-on (chaps. 10—13). And that concern has left its marks also on the chapters (8—9) which deal with the collection; here we see in action that peculiarly divine apostolic authority which seeks nothing for itself, but all for Christ, which will not autocratically lord it over men's faith, but works with men for their joy in Christ (2 Cor. 1:24). This authority is essentially the vehicle of the potent claim of the grace of the Lord Jesus Christ; therefore it will not command, but need only advise (8:8, 10). It is an expression of the Lordship of Christ (8:5), which can expect and claim obedience only because it is centered wholly in God the Father of the Lord Jesus Christ, in His power (8:5), His gifts and goodness (8:16; 9:7, 8, 11, 12, 15), and has His glory for its goal (9:13).

Content of the Second Letter to the Corinthians

I. Retrospect: Paul's Apostolic Authority with Special Reference to His Ministry in Corinth, chaps. 1—7

This whole first section is actually the thanksgiving with which Paul regularly opens his letters; but it is here, as in the First Letter to the Thessalonians, executed on a monumental scale, as an awed and grateful retrospective survey of the ministry which the grace of God has assigned to him.

A. 1:1-11. That ministry is pure grace, and the grace of God sustains him in it. He designates himself "apostle . . . by the will of God" in the salutation, and opens with a thanksgiving to the Father of the Lord Jesus Christ who has delivered him from desperate danger in Asia, giving him comfort in order that he might be able to comfort others in the strength thus given him, the strength, namely, to rely solely "on God who raises the dead," 1:9.

B. 1:12—2:17. The grace of his apostolic ministry makes his life a life full of agonizing stress; Paul has had to endure the malice of men who misinterpreted his letters, 1:12-14, who used his change of plans (he had delayed his coming to Corinth in order to *spare* the church, 1:23) to charge him with vacillation and unreliability, 1:15—2:4. But God has helped him, now as always; he stands vindicated as the proclaimer of the Christ who is God's great Yes to all His promises. The church over which he travailed has repented; the offending brother is restored in love. "Thanks be to God," Paul breaks out even before he has told of his meeting with Titus, who brought him the comforting news, "Thanks be to God, who in Christ always leads us in triumph," 2:14.

C. 3:1-3. Since his sufficiency is from God, he needs no letters of men to recommend him in his ministry (as the "Christ-men" apparently did); the church which his apostolic ministry has by God's grace created stands as his letter of commendation, "a letter from Christ . . . written . . . with the Spirit of the living God," 3:3.

D. 3:4—4:6. God has given him his ability as minister of God's New Covenant, to carry out a ministry not of the letter of the Law which condemns and kills, but a ministry of the Spirit which justifies and gives eternal life, a ministry not of transient and fading glory (such as Moses' was), but of surpassing and enduring glory, which gives him a "boldness" which Moses could not have and which Israel cannot know until she turns to the Lord, a boldness in the Lord whose Spirit gives freedom and carries the apostle and all who receive his liberating word "from one degree of glory to another," 3:18. This boldness brings with it a pure and candid honesty, for the apostle proclaims not himself, but Christ; he proclaims the miracle of the new creation, the dawn of a new first day, "the light of the knowledge of the glory of God in the face of Christ," 4:6.

E. 4:7—5:10. The glory of this apostolic ministry is solely God's, not man's; therefore the frailty and sufferings of the men who exercise this ministry, as men who are afflicted, perplexed, persecuted, and struck down, take nothing from its glory, for it is just in their weakness that the transcending power of God is manifested; in their defeat and dying the new life of Jesus is released for men, 4:7-12. And so suffering and the prospect of dying do not discourage the ministers of God; they work in the faith that the God who raised Jesus from the dead will raise them with Jesus, in the courageous certitude that the as yet unseen glory of the new creation will enfold them in an eternal splendor which outweighs by far their present momentary affliction, in the knowledge that the Spirit given them by God is His pledge of a new and eternal bodily life, 4:13—5:5. They long to be at home with their Lord, clothed with the new body which God will give them; but this longing does not make them weak and inert dreamers; it makes them strong and courageous workers who "make it their aim to please Him," Christ, before whose judgment seat they must appear to give an account of their working, 5:6-10.

F. 5:11—6:10. The apostle works to win men, but with a high independence over against the praise or blame of men. Whether men esteem him mad or sane is of small moment to him; his madness and his sanity are both in the service of his apostolic ministry, which moves between the two poles of the fear of the Lord who will judge all men and the impulse of the all-controlling love of the Christ who died that all men might live for Him, 5:11-15. Human standards do not apply to this ministry, for it is nothing less than the ministry of the divine reconciliation; it gets its content and its authority from that act of God's

by which God's new creation has broken victoriously into
the present evil world and has made the old world irrelevant and obsolete. The apostle is nothing less than the
ambassador for the Christ, who knew no sin, whom God
made to be sin for sinful man, in order that man may
become the righteousness of God in Him; God Himself
makes His appeal to man through the apostle, 5:16-21.

G. 6:1—7:4. The church lives by perpetual repentance. The
church at Corinth can be a real church, can be an apostolic
church, can be "the church *of God* at Corinth" only by
heeding the appeal of God through the apostle. Reconciliation with Paul can only take place as a piece of the
church's reconciliation with God. And so Paul renews
once more his ambassadorial plea of "Be reconciled to
God" in the form that the present situation of the Corinthian church calls for: "We entreat you not to accept the
grace of God in vain," 6:1. They have been in danger
of squandering the grace which they had once accepted;
there is still time for reconciliation, but that time is now,
6:2. And as he renews his appeal, Paul sums up once
more the whole glory of this apostolic ministry as the
pure and free channel of the reconciling grace of God,
6:3-10. And Paul reminds the Corinthians that the appeal
of God the Reconciler is an exclusive appeal; the reconciliation with God calls for a radical break with all that
opposes God. He reminds them that if God is their Father
and they His sons and daughters, they must come out from
the world around them and touch nothing unclean, must
cleanse themselves "from every defilement of body and
soul and make holiness perfect in the fear of God" — the
secularized Christianity with which Paul dealt in his first
letter is being touched on once more here, 6:11—7:1.
Then, when they have opened their hearts to God and
made their hearts His alone, then they can open their
hearts to their apostle, who loves them with the forgiving
love of God: "You are in our hearts, to die together and
to live together."

H. 7:5-16. Now at last Paul tells what he had been on the

verge of telling at 2:13, but could not tell until he had
given thanks to God for His gift; now he tells of his meeting with Titus and of Titus' report of their repentance.
And now the note of thanksgiving with which Paul began
and which has been the constant undertone in all his
description of his apostolate, is heard once more full and
clear. Paul "rejoices" and is "comforted"; he cannot say
it often enough.

II. The Present: The Collection for the Saints of Jerusalem,
chaps. 8 and 9

Paul closed his account concerning Titus' report with the
words, "I rejoice, because I have perfect confidence in you,"
7:16. The two chapters in which Paul gives directions concerning the collection for the saints are an expression of that
confidence, tactful and gentle though his directions are.

A. 8:1-7. Paul holds before them the example of the Macedonian churches, who in their poverty and affliction gave
beyond their means — because the grace of God moved
them to give *themselves* to the Lord and the Lord's apostle;
when men give themselves, their money is given too.
(Paul characteristically never speaks of money, in so
many words, at all in this section.)

B. 8:8-15. He will not command them; he reminds them,
instead, of what they already know — of the grace of the
Lord Jesus Christ who became poor for the enrichment
of men. And he reminds them of what they have already
done; they had set about the gathering of the collection
as early as the previous year.

C. 8:16—9:5. Paul is sending Titus and two other brothers
to aid them in the task which will prove their love and
make good Paul's boast concerning them, lest Paul (and
they themselves too) be put to shame when he comes
to Corinth with the representatives of the Macedonian
churches and find the Corinthians not ready.

D. 9:6-15. He reminds them that generous giving reaps a great
harvest: not only will the God who loves a cheerful giver
reward such giving; God will also be glorified in the

thanksgiving of the recipients of the gift. As in the description of his apostolic ministry, so here also in the exercise of it, Paul's first and last word is in praise of the grace of God: That Gentiles are bound to Jews in such communion that Jewish need provokes a Gentile gift, that this gift is the fire which sends up clouds of grateful incense in Jerusalem, to the glory of the God who is Lord of Jews and Gentiles both, that is grace, a grace greater than man's words can tell. "Thanks be to God for His inexpressible gift!" 9:15.

III. Prospect: Paul's Coming Visit to Corinth. Personal Vindication in the Face of the Charges Brought Against Him by His Opponents, chaps. 10—13

Paul has spoken the word of conciliation to the full; he has set before the eyes of the Corinthians all the wondrous grace of God which had united him with them in the past. He has enlarged upon the task which unites them in a common effort in the present as an "inexpressible gift" of God. But between Paul and the Corinthians there still falls the shadow of the men who say, "We belong to Christ," in their peculiar and exclusive sense. They stand in the way of full and perfect conciliation. And there is no possibility of conciliation with them; they have given no indication of change. Being what they are, they *must* oppose Paul, for Paul is the opponent of all human greatness, including his own. He is opposed to all factions and all parties in the church, the Pauline party included. Paul upholds and affirms all that they sought to override and supersede — the Old Testament Scriptures, the commands of Jesus, the apostolate as the vehicle of the power and presence of the Christ, an earthen vessel perhaps, but the vessel which God Himself has chosen and therefore the only vessel. Paul interprets all the terms which they used as slogans (freedom, knowledge, Spirit, the Lordship of Christ) in a sense radically different from theirs. There is no possibility of compromise here, no prospect of conciliation; and so the message of conciliation must show the hard edge of its exclusiveness — Paul must unmask them for what they are, the satanic messengers who destroy the work of God, and bid the Corinthians come out from them and be separate from them.

Paul had touched on the attitudes, methods, and accusations of his opponents as early as his first letter, 1 Cor. 4:18-21; 7:40; 14:37, and the anathema upon those who have no love for the Lord in 1 Cor. 16:22 is no doubt intended primarily for them. There are indications in the first section of the second letter too that Paul is seeking conciliation in an atmosphere charged with calumny and controversy, cf., e. g., 2 Cor. 1:12ff.; 2:6; 3:1ff.; 4:2, 5; 5:11f.; 6:3. But it is not until now, when the word of conciliation has been fully spoken, that he meets his adversaries and their charges head on.

A. 10:1-18. Paul's Defense Against the Charges of His Opponents

1. The Charges of His Opponents, with Paul's Comment, 10:1-12

Their charges, as Paul enumerates them here, are: Paul is humble when face to face with the Corinthians and bold only when absent, 10:1; he terrifies them with his letters, but his bodily presence is weak and his speech is of no account, 10:9, 10; he "acts in worldly fashion," 10:2, blustering when he can and stepping softly when he must. This proves that he is not one who "belongs to Christ" in the sense and to the degree that they, his bold and brilliantly persuasive opponents, do, 10:7.

Paul's answer is simply this: Do not force me to demonstrate the authority divinely given me, an authority given me for building up the church, not for destruction, an authority which therefore has the patience to wait for repentance and its fruits before it performs the necessary but painful task of destruction by judgment, 10:4-6, an authority which my opponents cannot even understand, for they know nothing but themselves, 10:12.

2. Paul's Authority as Apostle, 10:13-18

Over against the self-commendation of his detractors Paul sets the fact that the Lord has "commended" him by building the church at Corinth through him. Paul has built the church, and he has not thrust himself into another man's field of labor either, as his opponents have done. That is the solid and factual vindication of his authority, one that permits him to boast only in the Lord and allows him to hope that he will be further vindicated by greater work in a wider field, as the Corinthians' faith increases — Paul is here looking, as the Letter to the Romans makes plain, to the West, to Rome and beyond Rome to Spain.

B. Paul's Foolish Boasting, 11:1—12:21

To defend the church which he has betrothed to Christ and to protect her from the satanic influence of those who preach "another Jesus," Paul will play the fool and boast; a holy jealousy for the church impels him to it, 11:1-4.

1. 11:5, 6. Though he makes no pretense of rivaling these "superlative apostles" in skilled speech, he will boast of his knowledge.

2. 11:7-15. He will boast, ironically, of that which has been made a reproach against him, of the fact that he worked without pay. He will not let the insinuations of the "false apostles" (who evidently interpreted his refusal to accept remuneration as an admission that he lacked full apostolic stature) drive him from this policy, which his love for the Corinthians dictates.

3. 11:16-33. Though he is too "weak" to assume the arrogant and selfish demeanor of his opponents, he will boast of all that they dare boast of — and more. If they are Hebrews, Israelites, descendants of Abraham, he is all that, *and* a better servant of the Christ than they, marked by toil, suffering, and persecution, worn by the daily pressure of his anxious care for all the churches. He "will boast of the things that show his weakness," to the glory of the Lord.

4. 12:1-10. He will boast of the visions and revelations of the Lord which have been vouchsafed him; but he again ends by boasting of his weakness, of the affliction which his Lord would not take from him, in order that the Lord's power might be made perfect in the apostle's weakness.

5. 12:11-18. But though he be in his person nothing, Paul

is not at all inferior to these superlative apostles; he can boast of the signs of the true apostle which were performed by him at Corinth, signs, wonders, and mighty works. In the light of this, the Corinthians cannot give ear to those who interpret his refusal to accept pay as a sign that they were less favored than churches founded by other apostles. Neither can they lend credence to the charge that he refused to take pay directly in order to gain it indirectly, through his helpers and associates. Selfless men like Titus are the sufficient refutation of that charge. This practice was dictated by his fatherly love for them, and he will not depart from it now.

6. 12:19-21. Paul's "boasting" has not been a defense of himself to the Corinthians; he has been speaking in the sight of God for their edification, that they might repent before Paul's impending visit and spare him and themselves the grief of another "painful" visitation.

C. Paul's Impending Visit, 13:1-10

Paul will come and deal unsparingly with those who do not repent; they shall have full proof of the power of his apostolic authority, 13:1-4. But, characteristically, the apostle who is strong when he is weak implores the Corinthians not to put his authority to the test; he bids them do what is right, in order that *he* "may seem to have failed," that he may not have to demonstrate the power given him by the exalted Christ who speaks in him. (Nowhere, perhaps, does the complete selflessness of Paul's apostolic will and the purity of his apostolic love appear in clearer light than here.)

Conclusion, 13:11-14

Concluding admonition: "Mend your ways, heed my appeal, agree with one another, live in peace!" 13:11
Greetings, 13:12, 13
Closing benediction, 13:14

Effect of the Letter

Paul spent the three winter months A. D. 55—56 in Greece, shortly after the second letter was dispatched to Corinth (Acts

20:2, 3), and he there wrote his Letter to the Romans, most likely at Corinth itself. In the Letter to the Romans he looks back over his work in the eastern Mediterranean area as finished and looks westward with serenity and confidence (Rom. 15:14-33). No doubt the second letter had done the work it was intended to do, and the reconciliation with Corinth was complete.

Integrity of the Letter

(The question of the integrity of a work is the question whether the work has come down to us in its original form, whether parts may have been lost, whether sections may have been added, either by a later hand or from another work by the same author.)

In the case of the Second Letter to the Corinthians the question of integrity has been posed by the following considerations: The transition from 6:13 to 6:14 is so abrupt, and the change of mood at the beginning of chapter 10 is so violent that some scholars have conjectured that the second letter is not a single letter, but a conglomeration of three letters, all of them admittedly by Paul. The section 6:14—7:1 is thought to be a fragment of the Previous Letter referred to in 1 Cor. 5:9, and the last four chapters of the second letter are thought to be a part of the Intermediate Letter (or the Severe Letter) referred to in 2 Cor. 2:3f.; 7:8.

These conjectures have a certain surface plausibility, but in the last analysis such critical constructions are neither convincing nor necessary:

a. All the ancient manuscripts and versions give us the second letter as we have it today.

b. The abruptness of transition and the change of mood are more readily understandable on the assumption that Paul wrote the letter as it stands. An editor patching up a number of letters into a unity would presumably avoid such harshnesses in the interest of obtaining a smoothly unified whole, whereas the apostle writing in the heat and passion of the situation would not be too much concerned about smooth transitions. And there remains always the unanswerable question: Why were just these fragments of the letters preserved and not the complete letters?

c. Chapters 10—13 do not in fact fit into the situation presupposed for the so-called Intermediate Letter. There is no refer-

ence to the person who committed the injury which so deeply
affected Paul nor to the sending of Titus.

d. Most important of all, the letter, as it stands, does have
a natural sequence and an understandable order. As the outline
given above has indicated, Paul passes from the past with its
tensions and conflicts to the present with its concern for the work
of charity that unites apostle and church, and then on to the future
with its unavoidable decision. The situation in Corinth as Paul
pictures it in the first section of the letter calls for a section such
as we have in the last four chapters: The success of Titus' mission
had, after all, been only partial; and Paul must still deal with the
opposition and disobedience which remain to muddy the relationship between him and his church. That there should be a change
of mood and tone corresponding to the change in topic is completely understandable.

Value of the Letter

The Second Letter to the Corinthians is certainly one of the
most difficult of Paul's letters — which is not to say that it was
difficult or obscure for its first readers; they lived in the situation
which we must laboriously reconstruct. Since the hints given by
the letter itself are not always full enough to permit a complete
and accurate reconstruction of the situation, the letter is for us
difficult, an angel to be wrestled with if we would receive a blessing.
But the blessing is a rich one and worth the wrestling.

The letter resembles the Letter to the Galatians in being richly
autobiographical; we here see Paul the man in all the human
frailty and the human agony, which he never attempts to conceal.
But Paul the man cannot be separated from Paul the apostle of
Jesus Christ by the will of God. And the letter reveals the apostle
with a fullness that even *Galatians* cannot rival. As in *Galatians,*
we see the apostle engaged in battle, here a battle for his very
existence as apostle to the Corinthians; and a man shows what
he truly is in battle. The battle which Paul wages in this letter
reveals him down to the very roots and bases of his apostolic
existence. We learn from this revelation that battle must be, and
why it must be, within the church of the God and the Prince of
Peace, that lines must be drawn and where they must be drawn;
we learn that Satan is at work even in that which passes for an

advanced and superior form of Christianity, that his weapon is always the plausible lie which imitates the truth — one must never forget how very "nice" and very "Christian" the men of the Christ-party must have appeared to be. We learn that battle is necessary in the life of the church and can be salutary for the life of the church.

We learn also that the necessity of battle need not harden the battler; the church that fights for truth need not lose the love it had at first, as the church at Ephesus did (Rev. 2:4); the first seven chapters of this letter are a witness to the fact that the love which "does not rejoice at wrong but rejoices in the right" (1 Cor. 13:6) is the only genuine love. Luther had these chapters especially in mind when he wrote of the Second Letter to the Corinthians: "In his first epistle St. Paul dealt severely with the Corinthians on many points and poured sharp wine into their wounds and terrified them; therefore he now . . . also pours oil into their wounds and is wondrously gracious to them. . . ."

As an apostle Paul is a "man in Christ," a man whose whole existence and activity is shaped and formed by the single fact of Him in whom God reconciled the world to Himself. There is hardly a more vivid documentation of this lived Christianity than the Second Letter to the Corinthians. No aspect of Paul's life is exempt from Christ; if he says, "Yes, I will come," or "No, I shall not come," he can say it only in the light of the great yes which God has spoken to all His promises in Christ (1:20). He can speak of Christian giving only in terms of the grace of our Lord Jesus Christ (8:9). His suffering is the mark of the Christ imprinted upon his life, the sign manual of Him whose strength is made perfect in weakness.

As apostle, Paul is a man in whom Christ speaks; he is the earthen vessel that conveys the treasure of the Christ. Paul is here fighting for his apostolate; that means, he is fighting for the Christ, for the apostolate is nothing less than the power and the presence of Christ among men. Men will find the treasure in this earthen vessel or they will not find it at all; they will behold the light of the knowledge of the glory of God in the face of Christ in the apostolate or they will not behold it at all. There is nothing like this letter to bind the church to the apostolic word of the New

Testament. The Reformation's embattled emphasis on *Sola Scriptura* finds powerful justification in this embattled epistle.

Through conflict to triumph — the Second Letter to the Corinthians was born of conflict; and the triumph which Christ worked through it is not limited to the restoration of the Corinthian church of the first century. By it the church can triumph still.

"TO THE END OF THE EARTH": THE LETTER OF PAUL TO THE ROMANS

Occasion and Purpose of the Letter

The historical situation out of which the Corinthian letters grew is in many points unclear, and we are forced to grope our way through it as best we can. The historical situation of the Letter to the Romans is clear in outline and presents relatively few problems. Paul had been looking Romeward and westward for some years before he wrote his letter to the church (or churches) at Rome (Rom. 15:23). He had met Aquila and Priscilla as early as the year 50, when the edict of Claudius banishing all Jews from Rome brought that couple, destined to be so dear and so valuable to him, to Corinth (Acts 18:1-3). They could tell him of the church in that capital and key city of the empire, its problems and possibilities, especially its possibilities as a missionary center for the western half of the Roman Empire.

When Paul was in the act of concluding his work at Ephesus in the late summer of A. D. 55 and was about to return to Jerusalem by way of Macedonia and Achaia, he gave expression to a long-cherished hope, saying: "After I have been there, I must also see Rome" (Acts 19:21). The same hope finds expression in the letter which he wrote to the Corinthians from Macedonia soon afterwards: "Our hope is that as your faith increases, our field among you may be greatly enlarged, so that we may preach the Gospel in lands beyond you" (2 Cor. 10:15, 16). "Lands beyond you," coming from the pen of men who had lived and worked in the eastern Mediterranean area, points westward.

The close of the Third Missionary Journey would seem to be the fitting time for the writing of the Letter to the Romans, and the notices in the letter itself confirm this. According to the letter itself, Paul is about to conclude his work in the East; he has fully preached the Gospel of Christ "from Jerusalem and as far round as Illyricum" (Rom. 15:19). He is about to go to Jerusalem with a collection gathered in Macedonia and Achaia (Rom. 15:25-27; cf. 2 Cor. 8 and 9). All this points to the end of the Third Missionary Journey in the winter of A. D. 55—56.

Paul probably wrote the letter in Corinth, during his three months' stay in southern Greece, referred to in Acts 20:2, 3. In Rom. 16:23 he sends greetings to the Romans from "Erastus, the city treasurer"; this Erastus is associated with Corinth in 2 Tim. 4:20, and an inscription has been found in Corinth which mentions an Erastus as a city official there. Furthermore, Paul in Rom. 16:1 commends to the Roman church a woman named Phoebe, a deaconess of the church at Cenchreae, the eastern harbor town of Corinth. Paul is at the time of writing the guest of a man named Gaius (Rom. 16:23), and we know of a Gaius who was a member, and apparently a prominent one, of the church at Corinth (1 Cor. 1:14). Gaius is, of course, a very common Roman name, and one should not make too much of the coincidence; but it does serve as cumulative evidence.

Paul, then, wrote to Rome from Corinth during the winter of A. D. 55—56. To what end did he write? His aim in writing is delicately but clearly stated in the letter itself. His lettter is to prepare for his visit to Rome. But Rome is not the ultimate goal of his travels. It cannot be, for Paul has made it his ambition as apostle to the Gentiles "to preach the Gospel, not where Christ has already been named," lest he build on another man's foundation (Rom. 15:20). The apostle's task is to lay foundations, not to build on foundations already laid by others (1 Cor. 3:10). And the foundation has long since been laid in Rome; Paul's words in his Letter to the Romans indicate that the church there had been in existence for a considerable time ("Your faith is proclaimed in all the world," Rom. 1:8. "Your obedience is known to all," Rom. 16:19. "I have longed *for many years* to come to you," Rom. 15:23). Non-Christian sources indicate that there was a church in Rome at least as early as A. D. 49 and probably considerably earlier. Since neither Paul nor any other early source points to any single outstanding personality as the founder of the Roman church, we may assume that the word of the Lord grew and produced a church in Rome through the agency of a number of nameless men, men like the "visitors from Rome" who were present in Jerusalem at Pentecost (Acts 2:10) and later returned to Rome, probably at the time when Saul persecuted the churches of Judea.

Paul plans to spend some time in Rome and to proclaim the Gospel there, to enrich and to be enriched by his association with the Roman Christians (Rom. 1:11-13; 15:24). But he is looking beyond Rome to Spain (Rom. 15:24, 28); Paul hopes to be sped on his way thither by the Romans (15:24). The expression "to be sped on one's way" may cover anything from a simple "God speed!" to something more concrete and material in the way of support for a journey. The word seems to have become almost technical for the support, both moral and material, given to missionaries by established churches or individual Christians (Acts 20:38; 21:5; 1 Cor. 16:6, 11; 2 Cor. 1:16; Titus 3:13; 3 John 6). Paul evidently hopes that Rome may become his missionary base in the West, what Syrian Antioch had been for him in the East. The Letter to the Romans, the most elaborate and most systematic exposition of the Gospel as Paul proclaimed it, is written in the interests of Paul's missionary work.

Some scholars have seen something of a problem in this fact that the treatment of the Gospel in the letter is of such unparalleled breadth and depth. Why should just this letter, written merely to *prepare* for a visit to Rome and work in the West, deal so searchingly and so comprehensively with the Gospel? The answer is not far to seek. Everything that we know of Paul's missionary preaching and his missionary methods (e. g., his practice of revisiting already established churches and his continued contact with them by letter and by means of personal emissaries) makes it clear that he did not aim at creating a vague, emotional, and enthusiastic movement but rather the firmly rooted, grounded, and established church of God, in which the word of Christ dwelt richly. What he sought therefore in a church which was to be his base in the West was a full and complete common understanding of the Gospel and a common obedience to the Gospel. At his former base in the East, this common understanding was something he could presuppose and rely on. Antioch had been deeply influenced by Barnabas, and Paul himself had preached and taught at Antioch for a full year before the Holy Spirit sent him forth from Antioch (Acts 11:26). What a year's ministry had accomplished in the East, a single letter had to accomplish in the West. That letter had of necessity to be a full and rich one.

Another problem is constituted by the fact that Paul expounds the Gospel in the Letter to the Romans so largely by way of setting it in antithesis to Judaism (the works of the Law, circumcision, descent from Abraham, etc.). Why should Paul choose to expound his Gospel in just this form to the Roman church? Why should just this letter deal at length (chaps. 9—11) with the tragic fate of Israel, the people of God who have rejected the righteousness of God which the Gospel reveals? We do not know the situation at Rome so well that we can be positive in our answers here. But two reasons may be suggested as probable. One reason would be Paul's personal experience. Paul had become a Christian by way of a radical and total break with Judaism. It would be natural for him to make clear to others the absolutely free grace of God's acquittal of guilty man in the Gospel by showing how that grace had come home to him, as the absolute antithesis to a religion of human performance and merit. He was, of course, not giving the Gospel a new or alien form by so portraying it, for the Gospel is always, whether set in a Judaic framework or not, God's great Nevertheless to God's condemnation of man and man's performance in the Law.

The other reason is to be found in Paul's experience as missionary. Paul had seen, with sorrow and indignation, how the Judaizers had sought to make Christianity a compromise between legalistic Judaism and the Gospel of free grace in Christ; this was for him the classic form of man's rebellion against the free grace of God freely given, without condition and without price. If Judaism is exposed for what it is, the Judaizers are refuted; if the Judaizers are refuted, that is the refutation of every attempt, in whatever form, to make man as man somehow count in the relationship between God and man — and the air is cleared for the proclamation of the true Gospel of grace.

Possibly the situation in Rome also made this emphasis necessary; the church at Rome had come out of the synagog and seems to have been, to begin with, predominantly Judaic — although at the time when Paul wrote, it had become a predominantly Gentile church, as Paul's letter makes clear (1:13-15; cf. 1:5, 6; 11:13, 28-31). As members of an originally Judaic church, the Roman Christians had probably heard slanderous misinterpretations of Paul's preaching and needed to be disabused of false notions concerning it.

Content of the Letter to the Romans

Introductory: Greeting, thanksgiving, prayer, 1:1-15

Theme: The Gospel is the power of God for salvation because it is the revelation of the righteousness of God through faith, 1:16, 17

I. The Wrath of God upon the Universal Unrighteousness of Man, 1:18—3:20

II. The Righteousness of God for All Mankind, 3:21—5:21

III. The Believer's Life in Righteousness, chaps. 6, 7, 8

IV. The Righteousness of God in History: The Enigma of Unbelieving Israel, chaps. 9, 10, 11

V. The New Life in Love, the Fruits of the Righteousness of God, 12:1—15:13

VI. Paul's Plans for Missionary Work in the West, 15:14-33

VII. Commendation of Phoebe, Greetings, Warning Against Makers of Divisions and Offenses, Concluding Doxology, chap. 16

The Effect of the Letter

Paul never reached Rome in the way he had hoped and intended; but the Lord who comforted him when he was taken prisoner in Jerusalem and told him, "Take courage, for as you have testified about Me at Jerusalem, so you must bear witness also at Rome" (Acts 23:11), made good His promise. Paul did reach Rome, years later than he had hoped, and not as a free missionary, but as a prisoner. But the Letter to the Romans had not been written in vain; as Paul approached Rome, the brethren there, having heard of his coming, came out 30 and 40 miles to meet him at Three Taverns and the Forum of Appius. "On seeing them, Paul thanked God and took courage," Luke writes (Acts 28:15). Whatever Rome might hold for Paul, whatever the future might bring — death or work in Rome and beyond Rome — Paul knew that the church of Rome was one with him in the Gospel; and for that he thanked God.

Canonicity of the Letter: Homologoumenon

Integrity of the Letter

The one really debatable question concerning the integrity of the letter is the question whether the sixteenth chapter was originally a part of the Letter to the Romans or not. The arguments used in questioning the integrity of the letter in this respect are chiefly the following:

a. The letter seems to come to a close at 15:33, with a benediction such as is common at the conclusion of Pauline letters.

b. The closing doxology (16:25-27) is placed at various points in the ancient manuscripts. Some put it after 14:23; some after 15:33; some after 16:23; and some do not have the doxology at all. This would seem to indicate that the sixteenth chapter was not a fixed part of the letter in the manuscript tradition.

c. It seems unlikely that Paul would have so many acquaintances in Rome (26 names!) as the greetings of this chapter would indicate.

d. It seems unlikely that Aquila and Priscilla (16:3) would change their place of residence as often as this chapter would require: They have moved from Rome to Corinth, from Corinth to Ephesus, are at the time of writing at Rome, and a few years later we find them once more at Ephesus (2 Tim. 4:19).

e. The content of 16:17-20, a warning against men who create dissensions and divisions, is not prepared for by anything in the first fifteen chapters; and the tone of these verses, it is argued, is too brusque and authoritative for Paul to have used in addressing a church which he had not founded and does not know personally.

As for arguments (a) and (b), it should be noted that, while 15:33 does seem to be the closing benediction, a lengthy post-script is not improbable or impossible. The variant position of the doxology in the manuscripts would point to variations in the liturgical usage of the churches — the last chapters were prob-ably not everywhere used in public reading in the services of the churches. It really says nothing about the length of the letter as preserved in various quarters of the church, for even the manu-scripts which place the doxology early contain all the chapters of the letter as we have them today.

Regarding (c) (the number of Paul's friends and acquaintances in Rome), we have no way of determining whether Paul could have had some two dozen acquaintances in the Roman church or not. The edict of Claudius (A. D. 49 or 50) banning Jews from Rome affected Jewish Christians too; it brought Aquila and Pris-cilla to Corinth, and it may have brought others into contact with Paul as he worked in Greece and Asia Minor or visited Antioch and Jerusalem.

The movements of Aquila and Priscilla (d) are likewise no decisive argument against the integrity of the Letter to the Romans. They had moved from Corinth to Ephesus to be of assistance to Paul in his new field of labor; and a couple whose devotion to the missionary cause Paul could praise with such high words as those of Rom. 16:4 might surely have preceded Paul to Rome as they had preceded him to Ephesus. What took them back to Ephesus later we do not know; perhaps they could be of service to Timothy there. (2 Tim. 4:19)

As for the content and tone of the warning against the dis-turbers of the church (e), we do not know the historical situation well enough to judge whether such a warning would be out of place or improbable in a letter to Rome or not. And is the tone of the warning, after all, any more brusque and authoritative than the many imperatives of chaps. 12 through 15? It should be noted, moreover, that in both sections (Rom. 12—15 and Rom. 16: 17-20) Paul qualifies the brusqueness of his imperatives, in the first case by recognizing his readers' Christian maturity and their capacity for mutual correction and admonition (15:14), in the second case by gratefully acknowledging their exemplary obedience to the Gospel (16:19).

The chief argument for the integrity of the letter in the form in which it has come down to us will always be the difficulty of explaining how a letter (or fragment of a letter) commending Phoebe to a church (Ephesus is usually taken to be the church addressed) should have become so firmly attached to the first 15 chapters that there is no single outright witness for its omission in all the manuscripts and versions that have been preserved.

Whether the closing doxology (16:25-27) was originally a part of the letter is a separate question. It is obviously more probable that a doxology should have been added to, or inserted in, the letter for liturgical use than that a fragment of a whole letter should have somehow become attached to it. But there is really nothing un-Pauline about the doxology; it fits the whole content of the letter; and there is only very slight evidence that the letter ever existed anywhere without it.

Value of the Letter

Pointing up the value of this letter is like commenting on the depth of the Grand Canyon. But perhaps a word or two on the letter as a missionary document (an aspect of the letter not always sufficiently appreciated) may be in place. The breadth and depth of this exposition of the Gospel of Christ is a perpetual warning against the temptation, which the church has not always resisted, to make of its missionary endeavors a vague and sentimental humanitarian activity, in which penicillin becomes a substitute for the power of God, the Gospel. It is the most obvious and natural thing in the world that the Gospel should march through the world with steps of mercy, that faith should document itself in a love which comprehends all man's need and agony; but the temptation to "give up preaching the word of God to serve tables" (Acts 6:2) is particularly strong in missionary work, and the Letter to the Romans is the church's salutary monitor concerning the primacy of the word. The letter is therefore a reminder too that the content of missionary preaching is of critical importance, that a perversion or dilution of the divine word is no more permissible here than anywhere else in the life of the church, that co-operation in mission work on the basis of an ill-defined or undefined minimum of agreement on the substance of the missionary proclamation is a perilous and unpardonable procedure, that the confessional question is an acute question just in missionary work.

On the Letter to the Romans as a setting-forth of the Gospel there is hardly a better comment than that of Martin Luther, the man for whom this letter became a key to all God's revelation and the voice of God that summoned him to the task of the Reformation. He begins his Preface to the Epistle to the Romans with these words: "This epistle is the very heart and center of the New Testament and the purest and clearest Gospel. It well deserves to be memorized word for word by every Christian man; and not only that: A man ought to live with it day by day, for it is the daily bread of souls. One cannot read it too often or too thoroughly or consider it too often or too well; and the more one deals with it, the dearer it becomes and the sweeter it grows upon the tongue. . . ." And he closes his Preface thus: "Thus we find in the epistle all that a Christian ought to know, and that in great abundance, namely, what the Law is, what the Gospel is, what sin and punishment are, what grace, faith, righteousness, Christ, God, good works, love, hope, and the cross are, and what our attitude toward all men ought to be, toward saints and sinners, the strong and the weak, friend and foe, and toward ourselves. And all this excellently supported by Scripture and proved by examples, some of them Paul's own and some taken from the prophets, so that there is nothing left to be desired here. Wherefore it would seem that Paul intended this epistle to give a kind of summary of the whole Christian Gospel, and to open up for us the Old Testament. For there is no doubt that if a man has well learned this epistle by heart, he has the light and the power of the Old Testament for his own. Therefore every Christian should be familiar with this epistle and practice its teachings constantly. May God grant His grace to that end."

CHAPTER VI: "But the word is not bound": The Captivity Letters of Paul

READINGS: ACTS 20:1–28:31; COLOSSIANS, PHILEMON, EPHESIANS, PHILIPPIANS

Paul Goes to Jerusalem, Spring A.D. 56

Paul went from Corinth to Jerusalem. It was a Christlike way that he went; it was a way of love, for he went bringing gifts. "I came to bring to my nation alms and offerings," he says at his trial before Felix (Acts 24:17). He attached great importance to these alms and offerings, for he saw in them the concrete expression of what he had written to the Corinthians concerning the members of the body of Christ: "If one suffers, all suffer together" (1 Cor. 12:26); in these gifts from Gentile to Jew he saw the miracle of the unity of the church being enacted (Rom. 15:25-29; cf. 15:7-9). And so he requested the prayers of the Roman church for a safe journey and a successful mission, "so that by God's will I may come to you *with joy*." (Rom. 15:32)

Paul knew that the way he was going was a dangerous one (Rom. 15:31). He knew how much his unbelieving fellow countrymen hated him and how desperately they wanted him out of the way; he had been in "danger from his own people" more than once before (2 Cor. 11:26; cf. 11:24). His fears were confirmed at the very outset of his journey to Jerusalem, at Corinth, where a "plot was made against him by the Jews as he was about to set sail for Syria" (Acts 20:3) and Paul was forced to change his itinerary to avoid death. And as he journeyed toward Jerusalem, the Spirit warned Paul, directly and through the voice of prophecy, that "imprisonment and afflictions" awaited him. (Acts 20:22-24; cf. 21:4, 10, 11)

And yet he went willingly and resolutely to Jerusalem, "ready . . . to die at Jerusalem for the name of the Lord Jesus" (Acts 21:13) if need be, for he saw in this bringing of gifts to Jerusalem a piece of the ministry which he had received from the Lord Jesus, "to testify to the Gospel of the grace of God" (Acts 20:24). To whom did Paul want to testify? Certainly to his Jewish Christian brethren; the gift of the Gentiles would speak unmistakably to them of the universal grace of God. But also surely to his Jewish "kinsmen by race" who had not yet obeyed the Gospel. Their hatred of him had not engendered hatred in his heart; his mission to the Gentiles did not mean the end of his love for his kinsmen or the cessation of his efforts on their behalf (Rom. 9:1-5; 10:1; 11:13, 14). "I came to bring *to my nation* alms and offerings," Paul said pointedly at his trial (Acts 24:17); he evidently hoped that the sight of gifts pouring into Jerusalem from Gentile lands, lands to which the Jew had hitherto looked in vain for kindness, might open the eyes of at least some to the grace of God, to the "inexpressible gift" of God.

Luke marks this way of Paul's as a Christlike way, a way of giving, a way of suffering, a way of love for his people, the Jews. Even externally the life of Paul has on it the imprint of his Lord's life: the time of travels is followed by a time of imprisonment and suffering. "A disciple is not above his teacher, nor a servant above his master" (Matt. 10:24). That parallelism between the Lord and His apostle is apparent in what follows also, in the arrest and imprisonment of Paul. Like Jesus, he is tried before the Sanhedrin (Acts 22:30—23:10), before the Roman procurator (Acts 24:1-23; 25:6-12), and before a Jewish king, Herod Agrippa II (Acts 25:23—26:32). And, one might add, he resembles Jesus in this too that he tries to the last to bring the men of Jerusalem under the wings of the Christ who can save them (cf. Matt. 23:37); even when the Jerusalem mob had all but killed him and was screaming for his blood, he once more addressed them, in their own tongue, and sought even then to gain a hearing by stressing all that he and they had in common by the grace of God (Acts 22:1-21).

Paul's Imprisonment at Caesarea, A. D. 56—58

He appealed to his people in vain. He was imprisoned at Jerusalem, removed to Caesarea when the fury of his people again threatened his life (Acts 23:12-35), and imprisoned there for two years under the weak and vicious procurator Felix. When even the fair and conscientious procurator Festus wanted to prolong his already long-drawn trial by transferring him for trial to Jerusalem, as a conciliatory gesture toward the Jews, Paul made use of his privilege as a Roman citizen and appealed to Caesar. (Acts 25:11)

Paul's Roman Imprisonment, A. D. 59—61

"You have appealed to Caesar; to Caesar you shall go," the Roman procurator said (Acts 25:12). Paul was sent to Rome. The long voyage to Rome (winter, A. D. 58—59) with its dangers and disasters, through which Paul was led safely to his goal in Rome, is, as it were, an epitome of his whole career as an apostle; again the strength of the Lord was made perfect in His apostle's human weakness. He remained a prisoner in Rome for two years, but the terms of his imprisonment were not such that he was reduced to absolute idleness. He had his own dwelling, and his friends, the emissaries of the churches, and his co-workers had free access to him (Acts 28:30); they could aid and comfort him, and the matured wisdom and the ageless love of the aging apostle were available to them. Jesus' promise that Paul would testify to him at Rome also was fulfilled; Paul is seen, at the close of Acts, "preaching the kingdom of God and teaching about the Lord Jesus Christ quite openly and unhindered." (Acts 28:31)

What Luke has pointed up by the shaping of the narrative in Acts is also expressed by Paul in the letters which issue from his captivity. Just as he viewed his journey to Jerusalem as an apostolic undertaking, undertaken on behalf of the Gospel of the grace of God, so he considers his imprisonment and suffering as apostolic, as dominated by the Lordship of Jesus Christ and an essential part of his ministry for Christ. He speaks of his sufferings as, virtually, an extension of "Christ's afflictions" (Col. 1:24), for the sake of Christ's church. He is a "prisoner for Christ Jesus" on behalf of the Gentiles; his afflictions are a ministry to them (Eph. 3:1). He is a "prisoner for the Lord" (Eph. 4:1; cf. Philemon 9; Phil. 1:13). His imprisonment is therefore an imprisonment for the Gospel, for the word of the Lord (Philemon 13); he is an "ambassador in chains" for the Gospel (Eph. 6:19, 20). As his imprisonment is for the Christ and the Gospel, so his trial too is for the "defense and confirmation of the Gospel" (Phil. 1:7). His sufferings remain sufferings, and he feels them strongly. There is a deep pathos in his closing words in the Letter to the Colossians: "Remember my fetters" (Col. 4:18). But his sufferings are part of the grace bestowed on him in the gift of his ministry, and he rejoices in them too. (Col. 1:24; Phil. 2:17)

Paul's imprisonment was therefore not an interruption of his apostolic ministry, but a fruitful exercise of that ministry. Not least among the fruits that grew on that tree of adversity are the Captivity Letters, in which we have Paul's fullest and profoundest proclamation of the all-embracing significance of the Christ (Letter to the Colossians) and of the nature of the church (Letter to the Ephesians), a small but impressive record of how the Gospel can transfigure even the dark and sordid aspects of human life (Letter to Philemon), and a letter whose dominant note of hopeful and expectant joy in the midst of suffering has kept the church the hoping Advent church through the ages (Letter to the Philippians).

THE LETTER TO THE COLOSSIANS

Occasion of the Letter

Among those who came to Paul and were welcomed by him during his Roman imprisonment was Epaphras. He came from Colossae, a city in Asia Minor some 125 miles east of Ephesus. He brought Paul news of the Gentile church that had been founded there, probably by Epaphras himself (Col. 1:5-8), working under the direction of Paul or at least with Paul's full approval (Col. 1:7). He had good news to bring. He could speak warmly of the Colossians' faith and of their love; the Gospel had grown and borne fruit in Colossae as everywhere (Col. 1:6). But what had brought Epaphras to Rome was his anxiety for the church at Colossae, not his pride in it. The Christians of Colossae and of neighboring Laodicea were still holding to the Gospel which they had received; but that pure loyalty was being threatened and undermined. The church was threatened by a new teaching which was in many ways strikingly similar to the Gospel which Epaphras had preached there. Both the new teaching and the Gospel originally preached in Colossae proclaimed a non-national, universal religion. Both recognized the great gulf which exists between God and natural man. And both proffered a redemption which would bridge that gulf. But the new teaching was in the last analysis an utter distortion of the Gospel which Epaphras had proclaimed. Epaphras sensed the difference, but could not, perhaps, analyze and define it well enough to be able to oppose it vigorously and effectively. He therefore appealed to Paul, wise in the ways of Greek and Jew alike, keen in insight, and ready to do battle for the truth. Would Paul help him?

It is difficult to get a clear and consistent picture of the heresy which threatened Colossae, for Paul in his letter to the Colossians does not so much oppose it argumentatively as overwhelm it by confronting it with the whole riches of the true Gospel of Christ. It seems to have been a religion of self-redemption of the "gnostic" type. Built upon a Jewish or Jewish-Christian basis, it was a fusion of Greek and Oriental ideas and combined at least three elements. One of these elements was theosophic, that is, the new teaching claimed to have and to impart an occult, profound knowledge derived from God; Paul speaks contemptuously of a "tradition" and a "philosophy" (Col. 2:8). Another element was ritualistic; stress was laid on circumcision (Col. 2:11); questions of food and drink, festivals, new moons, and sabbaths were deemed important (Col. 2:16). A third element was ascetic; Paul speaks of prescriptions of abstinence ("Do not handle, Do not taste, Do not touch," Col. 2:21) and of a "rigor of devotion," of "self-abasement," and of "severity to the body" (Col. 2:23). We are left to conjecture how these elements were combined into a system.

Paul's references to the "worship of angels" (Col. 2:18) and to "elemental spirits of the universe" (2:8, 20) indicate what was the heart of the danger present in this teaching. Other powers besides the Christ were being proclaimed and invoked as mediators between God and man; the ritual and ascetic aspects of this religion probably represent means of placating or of obtaining contact and communion with these powers. What Epaphras, with a sound Christian instinct, surely sensed and what Paul clearly saw was this: *the new teaching called into question and obscured the unique greatness of the Christ and the complete sufficiency of His atonement.* What made this heresy all the more dangerous was the fact that it claimed not to supplant, but to supplement, the Gospel which the Colossians had received. The new teaching would, so the new teachers claimed, carry the Colossian Christians beyond their rudimentary Christianity to fullness and perfection; hence Paul's repeated emphasis on the fact that the Colossians are complete and full in the Gospel which they have received, that in the Christ whom they know they can find all the treasures of divine wisdom. (2:2, 3, 9, 10; cf. 1:28)

Content of the Letter to the Colossians

Introductory: Greetings, Thanksgiving, and Prayer, 1:1-14

I. The Completeness and All-Sufficiency of Christ and the Gospel, 1:15—2:23

A. The Full Glory of the Christ, the Son of God, 1:15-23

1. His Person, 1:15-18

a. in relation to God: He is God's perfect manifestation, 15a.

b. in relation to the universe: He is antecedent to, and Lord over, all created beings, including the angelic powers, 15b-17.

c. in relation to the church: He is Head of the church, which is His body, 18.

2. His Work, 1:19-23

a. In Him dwells the fullness of the Godhead, to reconcile *all* things to God, 19, 20.

b. You Colossians too are included in this reconciliation, if you abide in the Gospel which you have heard, of which I, Paul, am a servant, 21-23.

B. The Full Glory of the Gospel Which Proclaims the Christ, 1:24—2:5

1. It is precious: Paul rejoices to suffer in its behalf, 1:24, 25.

2. It is universal: Its content is the revealed "mystery" of "Christ in you," Christ the hope of glory for all men, 1:26, 27.

3. It is complete and sufficient: In Christ all the treasures of wisdom and knowledge are to be found, 2:1-5.

C. The Refutation of the Colossian Heresy: The insignificance of theosophy, angel worship, and ritual asceticism when confronted with the glory and the fullness of Christ and His Gospel, 2:6-23

1. Introductory admonition: In this Christ (whom you have learned), in this Gospel, walk, rooted and confirmed in the faith, 2:6, 7.

2. Do not let "philosophy" or human tradition or any talk of "elemental spirits of the universe" lead you astray from Christ, 2:8-15.

a. Christ, in whom you are complete, for in Him there is the fullness of the deity (He is above every angelic power);

b. Christ, in whom you have the true circumcision, Baptism, and with it new life, forgiveness of sins, and sure victory over all evil powers.

3. In Christ the ritual shadows of the Old Testament have found their substance and fulfillment, so that they can have no real meaning for you now; neither can any mystical angel worship. Christ is the Head, the source of all true strength and growth for His body, the church, 2:16-19.

4. In Christ you have died to the "elemental spirits of the universe"; they cannot have any significance for you now. The wisdom of those who promote such teachings is mere human teaching, not divine wisdom; and the asceticism which they foster is mere self-indulgence of the fleshly mind, 2:20-23.

II. Life in the All-Sufficient Christ, 3:1—4:6

A. Since you have been raised from the dead with Christ,

your life is hidden with Christ in God. Therefore look heavenward, lead the new life, a life in which Christ is all in all, where all the old divisions which once cleft mankind are lost in Christ. This means a life of love and peace, a life in which the word of Christ dwells richly, a life lived in the name of the Lord, that is, a life of such a quality that His name may be invoked over every part of it, that He is the ultimate source of all of it, 3:1-17.

B. Let this new life find its expression in all social relationships, in the relationship between man and wife, between parents and children, between servants and masters, 3:18 to 4:1.

C. Let this new life be characterized by constant prayer and thanksgiving, and by wisdom toward outsiders, 4:2-6.

Conclusion: Personal matters: the sending of Tychicus and the coming of Onesimus, greetings, directions for an exchange of letters with the neighboring church of Laodicea, 4:7-17. Autograph conclusion: Request for intercessions and benediction, 4:18

Canonicity: Homologoumenon

Authenticity: The authenticity of the Letter to the Colossians, once seriously questioned by many scholars, is today accepted by the great majority of scholars.

Value of the Letter

"As for you," Joseph told his brothers, "you meant evil against me; but God meant it for good" (Gen. 50:20). The new movement at Colossae meant evil, for it was an attack, all the more vicious because it was not a frontal attack, upon the fact that dominates the whole New Testament, the sole Lordship of the Lord Jesus Christ. But God meant it for good; He gave us in Paul's Letter to the Colossians a proclamation of the Lord Jesus Christ in unparalleled fullness and depth. The church that in its *Credo* intones, "God of God, Light of Light, very God of very God, begotten not made, being of one substance with the Father," is indebted not least to this letter.

The Letter to the Colossians is also a striking fulfillment of the promise of Jesus to His disciples, "Every scribe who has been trained for the kingdom of heaven is like a householder who brings out of his treasure what is new and what is old" (Matt. 13:52). The apostles of Jesus are not merely disciples of a rabbi, whose sacred duty it is to pass on their master's words unchanged. They are witnesses to Him who has all authority in heaven and on earth, and they have the Spirit as His gift, the Spirit who leads them into all truth and thus glorifies the Christ. At the time of the church's need the Spirit opened up to Paul dimensions of the glory of the Christ which the new people of God had not apprehended so fully before.

THE LETTER TO PHILEMON

Epaphras was not Paul's only visitor from Colossae; there was another visitor of quite another kind, a slave named Onesimus (badly misnamed, as it turned out; Onesimus means "useful"). Onesimus had run away from his master Philemon, lining his pockets for the journey with his master's goods, as was the usual practice of runaway slaves (Philemon 18). Somehow he reached Rome, and somehow he came into contact with Paul. Paul converted him and grew very fond of the young slave who now earned the name "useful" in his ready service to Paul (Philemon 11). He would gladly have kept Onesimus with him; and since the master, Philemon, was also a convert of his, he might have made bold to do so. But Paul honored all natural ties, including the tie which bound a slave to his master, as hallowed in Christ (Col. 3:22 ff.; Eph. 6:5 ff.). He therefore sent Onesimus back to Colossae with Tychicus, the bearer of his Letter to the Colossians (Col. 4:7-9), and wrote a letter to his master in which he bespoke for the runaway a kindly and forgiving reception. We can measure the strength of the bond between the apostle and his converts by the confidence with which Paul makes his request, a request all the more remarkable in the light of the fact that captured runaways were usually very harshly dealt with. Paul goes even farther; he hints that he would like to have Onesimus back for his own service. (Philemon 13, 14; 20, 21)

Content of the Letter to Philemon

1-3. Greetings to Philemon, his wife Apphia, and Archippus, probably Philemon's son, and the church in Philemon's house.

4-7. Thanksgiving for Philemon's faith and love, and a prayer for their continued effectual working. (Philemon had evidently distinguished himself by some work of love which "refreshed the hearts of the saints," v. 7.)

8-21. Paul's plea for Onesimus, his child in Christ. Paul appeals to Philemon to receive Onesimus again, now more than a slave to him, a beloved brother forever. Paul lets Philemon know how greatly he cherishes this child of his imprisonment and more than hints that he would like to have him back — after all, Philemon owes him more than a slave; as Paul's convert, he owes his very life and self to Paul. (19)

22-25. Paul bespeaks a guestroom in Philemon's house, against the time of his visit there, transmits the greetings of his fellow workers, and closes with a benediction.

Canonicity: Homologoumenon

Significance of the Letter

The Letter to Philemon is, besides the Second Letter to Timothy, the only personal letter from Paul that we have — the First Letter to Timothy and the Letter to Titus are official letters. One of the valuable insights that it affords is that there is no line of cleavage between the official Paul and the person Paul; for both, life has one content and one meaning: "For me to live is Christ." Luther portrays Paul in this letter as being a "Christ" to Onesimus, pleading his cause with his master as if he had no rights; "even as Christ did for us with God the Father, thus also does St. Paul for Onesimus, with Philemon. For Christ also has put Himself out of His rights and with humility has prevailed with His Father that He should lay aside His wrath and His rights and receive us to grace, for Christ's sake. . . . For we are all His Onesimi, if we believe it." All men the runaway slaves of God! A man who has come back to God as God's runaway slave and has been welcomed like a son, only such a man, only a man like Paul, can write a letter like the Letter to Philemon.

Personal letter though it is, the Letter to Philemon is an important document to illustrate the early Christian attitude toward social problems. It is noteworthy that Paul does not plead for Onesimus' liberation; whether he stays with Philemon or returns to Paul, Onesimus is to remain a slave. There is nothing like a movement to free slaves, even Christian slaves of Christian masters, either here or elsewhere in the New Testament. But a Gospel which can say to the master of a runaway slave that he is to receive him back "forever, no longer as a slave, but more than a slave, as a beloved brother" (15, 16) has overcome slavery from within and has therefore already rung the knell of slavery.

Paul's Letter to the Ephesians

The Letter to the Ephesians is linked by the evidence in the letter itself to the Letter to the Colossians and the Letter to Philemon. Tychicus is the bearer of the letter (Eph. 6:21) and will give the readers fuller information concerning the imprisoned apostle (Eph. 6:22). Since Tychicus is also the bearer of the Letter to the Colossians, and since Onesimus is returning to Colossae with Tychicus (Col. 4:7-9), the three letters (to the Ephesians, to the Colossians, and to Philemon) have a common historical background; they proceed from Paul's Roman captivity and are to be dated somewhere within the two years of that captivity (A. D. 59—61), perhaps in the earlier part of it.

But was the letter really addressed to the church in Ephesus? The earliest manuscripts do not have the words "in Ephesus" in the salutation (1:1), and their witness is confirmed by that of the early church fathers; the Revised Standard Version translators had good reason for omitting the words from their revision of the text. Moreover, the letter itself nowhere indicates that Paul and the readers whom he is addressing are personally acquainted with one another; there are passages which indicate the very opposite (Eph. 1:15; 3:2). When we consider how long Paul ministered in Ephesus and what close ties that ministry established (Acts 20:36-38), the absence of any personal touches in the letter is very striking. Similarly the letter gives no hint that Paul is personally acquainted with the life of the church — there are no concrete details, no reminiscences of former personal contact. Paul's letters to the Corinthians, written to a church in which he had worked and with which he was intimately acquainted, present a striking contrast to the Letter to the Ephesians in this respect. One can hardly avoid the conclusion that the letter known as the Letter to the Ephesians was not originally addressed to Ephesus, at least not to Ephesus alone.

The best explanation of the historical background of the letter would seem to be the one suggested as early as the sixteenth century by Beza, Grotius, and Ussher: When Paul sent Tychicus to Colossae, he at the same time sent a general letter designed especially for a group of churches in Asia Minor which had been evangelized under his supervision during his Ephesian ministry, but had for the most part never been personally visited by him, places like Colossae, Hierapolis, and Laodicea. Tychicus would leave a copy with each church in the towns through which he passed on his way to Colossae, and possibly he transmitted copies to towns which did not lie on his route. In the latter case Paul's promise that Tychicus would inform the churches of his estate (Eph. 6:21) would be fulfilled when Tychicus visited these churches after having completed his mission to Colossae. Each copy would bear the name of the church addressed. When Paul's letters were later collected and published, probably at Ephesus, the letter naturally came to bear the title "To the Ephesians," since Ephesus was no doubt included in the number of the churches addressed and was the most prominent among them. Some later copyist then probably inserted the words "in Ephesus" in the salutation, in order to bring the text of the letter into harmony with its title. Some scholars are inclined to see in the letter "from Laodicea" referred to in Col. 4:16 the letter which we know as the Letter to the Ephesians. It may be; copying was an onerous task in antiquity, and it would be natural and sensible to make one copy do for the two churches, since Colossae and Laodicea lay only thirteen miles apart.

The sending of Tychicus to Colossae thus provided the external occasion for the writing of the circular letter now called the Letter to the Ephesians. What Paul's motives in sending such a letter were, we can infer from the apostolic church's missionary practice and from a statement made by Paul toward the end of the letter itself. The apostolic church always sought contact with newly founded churches. John and Peter were sent to Samaria after the evangelist Philip had founded a church there (Acts 8:14). Barnabas was sent to the young church at Antioch (Acts 11:22). Paul took representatives of the Jerusalem church with him on his first two missionary journeys (Barnabas, Mark, Silas); he maintained contact with Jerusalem and Judaic Christianity and sought to express and to maintain the unity of the Spirit in the bond of peace by means of the Gentile collection for the Jerusalem saints; and he regularly revisited the churches which he had founded. As Paul surveyed his work in the East from the vantage point of his position in Rome, and saw from the reports of his co-workers the temptations and the dangers to which the young churches were exposed, he might well be moved to do by letter what he could not do in person, to go through his territory once more, "strengthening the churches" (Acts 15:41). That would be one motive for writing to the churches in the East.

The other motive was provided by Paul's peculiar situation. Paul in Rome knew himself to be an ambassador for the Gospel, albeit an ambassador in chains (Eph. 6:20). Again the strength of the Lord was being made perfect in weakness. The Gentile churches saw the human weakness of the imprisoned Apostle to the Gentiles more clearly than they saw the divine strength which worked through him; they had grown dispirited at the news of his imprisonment (Eph. 3:13). Moreover, Paul was facing a crisis in his ambassadorship, one which would ask of him all the boldness he could muster (Eph. 6:18-20). Paul therefore did two things in his letter. He asked for the intercessions of the churches, thus removing them from the role of lamenting spectators and making them active participants in his great ambassadorial task. And he held up before them the greatness of that task, the greatness of the church which the mighty divine word proclaimed by him had created and was sustaining. He had just written to the Colossians how God's act in the cross of Christ has made a peace which embraces the universe in all its parts and in all its powers (Col. 1:20); he had just written to Philemon and had seen, in applying the power of the Gospel to heal the breach between master and runaway slave, how that peace heals all man's life and removes its ugly rancors. He now spoke of "Christ our peace" (Eph. 2:14) to all the scattered and troubled churches and held before them the greatness of the new people of God which God has created by uniting Jew and Gentile, once enemies, in one church; he held up before them the glory of that one, holy church, thus keeping the churches conscious of their high privilege of unity in Christ and of the obligation which the high privilege of membership in the one church involves. If the Letter to the Colossians is the Letter of Christ the Head of the Church, the Letter to the Ephesians is the Letter of the Church, the Body of Christ. Its purpose and outreach are as universal as its destination is general.

Content of the Letter

The Letter to the Ephesians consists of two portions, the first being an exposition of what the church is, the second an exhortation concerning all that membership in the church involves. We can sum up the message of the letter in the words of the tenth verse of chapter 2: "We are His workmanship, created in Christ Jesus for good works."

I. The Church Is God's Workmanship, Created in Christ Jesus, 1—3

1:1, 2, *Salutation*

A. 1:3-14. A *doxology* which surveys the whole range of God's redemptive blessings: the eternal purpose of God which chose and predestined men to be His own through Christ, to the praise of His glorious grace, 3-5; the bestowal of His grace in the cross of Christ and in the proclamation of the cross, for the praise of His glory, 6-12; the ultimate fulfillment of His redemption, the final inheritance which the gift of the Holy Spirit guarantees to the church, to the praise of His glory, 13, 14. The church comes into being by God's will, in Christ. Note the constant recurrence of words denoting God's plan and purpose and the red thread of "in Christ" which runs through the whole doxology.

B. 1:15-23. *Thanksgiving* for the faith and love of the readers, 15, 16, and a *prayer* that they may be enabled by the Spirit of God to comprehend all that God has wrought for them: the hope that God's call has given them, the certainty of the inheritance which God's call has promised them, the assurance that the power of God will carry the believer safely through the dark present into future glory, that power which God has supremely manifested in raising Jesus Christ from the dead and manifesting Him as Lord of all and Head over all for the church, the body of Christ, 17-23.

C. 2:1-22. The Gentiles' Participation in the Redemptive Blessings.

1. They have part in the *redemption* which God has provided, 2:1-10.

a. God has delivered them from death and the dominion of of Satan and has raised them to life and glory with Christ, 2:1-7.

b. All this is unmerited grace, the gift of God received by faith. The church is solely and wholly God's creation, in Christ, created for good works, 2:8-10.

2. They have part in the redeemed community, the church, 2:11-22. Christ has by His cross abolished the Law which divided mankind into Jew and Gentile and has created and proclaimed peace, that is, the end of the ancient hostility between Israel and the Gentiles and the union of Jew and Gentile in one reconciled people of God. The Gentiles are incorporated into the people of God, into the family of God, into the living temple of God.

D. 3:1-19. *Prayer to the Father* that the Gentiles may comprehend the full measure of the blessings bestowed upon them, that they may know to the full the incomprehensible love of the Christ who has redeemed them, and may thus be filled with all the fullness of the God who has blessed them. (In a long parenthesis, 2-13, Paul dwells on the grace bestowed upon him as Apostle to the Gentiles, the high privilege of proclaiming to them their inclusion in the church, their sharing in the unsearchable riches of Christ. This grace gloriously transfigures the suffering which his apostolic task entails.)

3:20, 21. *Concluding Doxology:* Glory to God *in the church* and in Christ Jesus. (This is the only place in the New Testament where the church is thus emphasized in a doxology.)

II. The Church Is Created for Good Works, 4—6

A. 4:1-16. God's call is a call to unity, a call to the denial of self in the zealous pursuit of unity, to the utilization of the divine gifts bestowed by the exalted Christ for the full realization of this unity, that the church may be the mature and perfectly functioning body of Christ, its Head.

B. 4:17-24. God's call to unity in the church demands of the Gentiles a radical break with their pagan past and their pagan surroundings; it means putting on the "new nature, created after the likeness of God in true righteousness and holiness" and putting off the old nature which is corrupted by deceitful lust.

C. 4:25—5:20. God's call into the church shapes the Christians' every relationship, their relationship to one another in the church and their relationship to the world. Lying, thievery, anger and bitterness, immorality, covetousness, filthiness, silly talk — all these have become impossible for them as children of the light. They are to know that the wrath of God looms over all these transgressions still. They cannot participate in the works of darkness; they cannot even simply ignore them. They must expose them, in order to bring the sons of darkness to repentance and into the light. They must walk wisely in this evil world and make the most of the time which God yet gives them. The only intoxication in their lives must be the intoxication of inspired song, which edifies the church and gives thanks to God.

D. 5:21—6:9. Their reverence for Christ will mold their conduct in the relationships of this age and make of them all channels for the love of Christ. The relationship between wife and husband, between child and parent, between slave and master will all have upon them the mark of the Christ who is Lord of all.

E. 6:10-18. God's call makes the church God's outpost in an

alien and still hostile world. The Christian's life is therefore a life of battle with the powers of Satan, a battle
for which God gives them strength and equips them with
divine weapons; these weapons they must take up and use
with constant and vigilant prayer.

6:19-23. *Conclusion*

6:19, 20. Paul's request for the intercessions of the church

6:21, 22. The sending of Tychicus with news of the apostle

6:23, 24. Closing benediction

Authenticity of the Letter

The authenticity of the Letter to the Ephesians is seriously
questioned by many scholars. The case against authenticity is
often supported by ingenious and elaborately worked out arguments. Many of these appear at first glance to be conclusive
against authenticity; but a careful examination of all the data
(including the ancient tradition which unanimously attributes the
letter to Paul) will result in the realization that the arguments
against authenticity are, after all, far from decisive.

Among the more important of the arguments advanced against
the authenticity of the letter are: the peculiarities of its vocabulary
and style, alleged differences in teaching between the letter and
undoubtedly authentic letters of Paul, the peculiarly close relationship between the letter and the Letter to the Colossians (some
70 per cent of the Colossian letter has parallels in the Letter to
the Ephesians), and the generally derivative character of the
Letter to the Ephesians (that is, the fact that it gives the impression of being a rehash or summary of teaching given by Paul
in other letters). These and other arguments of less weight are
said to make Pauline authorship impossible and to make it probable that the letter is the work of a disciple of Paul's, some man
who was thoroughly familiar with his master's writings and was
restating their teaching in terms of the needs and questions of
his own day, probably in the last years of the first century. One
American scholar even names the author, Onesimus, and conjectures that he wrote the letter as a sort of preface to his edition
of the collected letters of Paul, by way of expressing his own great

indebtedness to Paul and in order to introduce later generations
to the thought of the great apostle.

There is no room for a full discussion of these arguments here.
In general it may be said that the arguments have often been
overstated in the eagerness of debate; that the differences in
vocabulary and style are in themselves far from being conclusive
proof that the letter is not authentic, as is being increasingly
recognized by most scholars; that the alleged differences in teaching tend to disappear upon closer examination and that the novelties supposedly introduced by the imitator are seen to be fresh
and original restatements of genuinely Pauline themes; that the
connection between the Letter to the Colossians and the Letter
to the Ephesians is so intricate and deep-rooted that the most
natural explanation is that both letters were written by one man,
Paul, at approximately the same time — that a later imitator
should have so thoroughly assimilated the material of the Colossian letter and have distributed it so completely and haphazardly
throughout the Ephesian letter remains historically very improbable. The argument concerning this imitation is, often enough,
both confused and confusing: Where the Ephesian letter is too
much like the other letters of Paul, that is proof of its derivative
character and therefore proof that an imitator wrote it; when it
is unlike the other letters of Paul, that too is proof that an imitator
wrote it. To sum up, all the arguments which have any validity
at all point up the fact that the Letter to the Ephesians occupies
a unique place among the Pauline letters; they cannot be said to
prove that the Letter to the Ephesians does not belong among the
Pauline letters.

Canonicity: Homologoumenon

Value of the Letter

Paul is here singing hymns in prison, as he once did at
Philippi. It is a hymn rich in content, a hymn which sings of
the "manifold wisdom of God" and "the unsearchable riches of
Christ." One very perceptive modern interpreter has compared
the letter with the Letter to the Romans; in both letters, he points
out, Paul elaborates the theme stated in 1 Cor. 1:24, "Christ the
power of God and the wisdom of God." Whereas the Letter to

the Romans stresses the element of power (Rom. 1:16), the Letter
to the Ephesians emphasizes the wisdom of God. The church
that is always prone to forget that it is God's creation and likes
to think of itself as a structure of strength which man in *his*
wisdom has reared and can in his wisdom control will do well
to immerse itself again and again in this hymn from prison and
to learn from the ambassador in chains an awed humility in the
presence of that awful, divine wisdom.

THE LETTER TO THE PHILIPPIANS

Occasion of the Letter

The Captivity Letters tell of still another visitor who came
from Paul's churches in the East to see Paul in Rome. His name
was Epaphroditus, and he came from Philippi in Macedonia, the
first church founded by Paul in Europe (Acts 16:11-40). Paul,
Silas, Timothy, and Luke had arrived in Philippi early in the
Second Missionary Journey (A. D. 49—51). Philippi was a Roman "colony," that is, a settlement of Roman soldiers, enjoying
Roman citizenship, settled at a strategic point in the system of
Roman roads for the security of the empire. There were, apparently, not many Jews there; there was no regular synagog, only
a "place of prayer" (Acts 16:13), probably in the open air,
at a river's side. It was there that Paul had begun his work.
The Lord opened the ear of a proselyte named Lydia to his
words, and we may suppose that the house of this wealthy and
generous woman became the meeting place of the church (Acts
16:14, 15). Paul knew "conflict" (Phil. 1:30) and suffering in
Philippi; he had been beaten and imprisoned without the due
process of law to which his Roman citizenship entitled him.
He had known not only conflict, but also that joy in the midst
of conflict and suffering which is the characteristic token of the
apostolic and Christian existence (Acts 16:25). And he had experienced triumph in conflict and suffering, the triumph of the
Lord whose strength is made perfect in weakness and defeat; he
was released from prison and vindicated, and he gained the jailer
and his household for the Lord. (Acts 16:25-40)

The church which grew, as the word of the Lord grew, in
Philippi was predominantly Gentile. And it was a church which

remained peculiarly near and dear to Paul. It was Paul's first-born in Europe; the faithful and consecrated Luke remained there when Paul continued on his journey and provided spiritual leadership of a high order; the impetuous generosity of Lydia in the first days evidently set the tone of the church's life for the years that followed. We recall how she viewed her baptism as an initiation into a life of giving; she told Paul and his companions, "If you have judged me to be faithful . . . come to my house and stay," and "prevailed" on them to comply with her wish (Acts 16:15). The generosity of the Philippians was so genuinely rooted in Christ and His Gospel that Paul felt free to accept gifts from them; he can call them his "partners" in the proclamation of the Gospel (Phil. 1:5; 4:15). They supplied his wants in Thessalonica (Phil. 4:16) and again in Corinth (2 Cor. 11:9), and that too at some sacrifice to themselves; Paul told the Corinthians, "I robbed other churches by accepting support from them in order to serve you" (2 Cor. 11:8). This same actively generous partnership in the Gospel had moved the Philippians (and the other churches of Macedonia), to contribute to the collection for the Jerusalem saints "beyond their means," even in the midst of a "severe test of affliction" and in the depths of poverty. (2 Cor. 8:1-5)

The coming of Epaphroditus was another link in the golden chain of Philippi's gracious generosity. Still suffering persecution (Phil. 1:29), still poor (Phil. 4:19), the men and women of Philippi had nevertheless gathered a gift for Paul, probably under the direction of their "bishops and deacons," whom Paul singles out in the salutation of his Letter to the Philippians (and only in this letter, Phil. 1:1). They had sent the gift to Paul by the hand of one of their number, Epaphroditus, and had instructed him to remain in Rome with Paul as a minister to his need (Phil. 2:25). Epaphroditus had delivered the gift and had performed his task of ministry with such self-forgetting devotion that "he nearly died for the work of Christ, risking his life" to complete the service of the Philippian Christians to their apostle. (Phil. 2:30)

Date of Writing

These events help fix the date of Paul's Letter to the Philippians more exactly within the limits of his two years' imprisonment at Rome (A. D. 59—61). There has been time for a series of communications between Rome and Philippi: News of Paul's imprisonment has reached distant Philippi; the Philippians' gift has been gathered, sent, and received; news of Epaphroditus' illness has reached Philippi and has caused great concern there; and news of this concern has again come to Paul and Epaphroditus at Rome. It has been calculated that this series of communications would require a total of five or six months at a minimum; they probably took considerably longer. Moreover, the letter itself indicates that Paul's long-deferred trial is at last in progress (Phil. 1:7), that it has proceeded so far that Paul can with some confidence hope for an early release from imprisonment (Phil. 1:25; 2:24), though there is still real danger of an adverse verdict and death. All this points to a date toward the close of the two years' imprisonment, probably to the early months of A. D. 61.

Paul is about to return Epaphroditus to Philippi (Phil. 2: 25-30); he sends with him a letter in which he gives his partners in the Gospel news of himself, his trial, and his prospects of release; thanks them for their gift; and excuses and commends their messenger Epaphroditus, who through no fault of his own has been unable to carry out fully the ministry entrusted to him. He notices too with pastoral concern and with kindly evangelical tact their internal troubles, a tendency to self-assertion on the part of some, with its consequent tendency to disunity. He encourages them in the persecution which presses on them from without; and he warns them, with passionate sternness, of the dangers which threaten them, alerting them to the threat posed by Judaistic and libertine perverters of the Gospel.

Content of the Letter to the Philippians

I. Introduction, 1:1-11

Salutation, 1:1, 2. (The special mention of the bishops and deacons is probably to be explained by the fact that they were the prime movers and leaders in the gathering of the gifts for Paul.)

Thanksgiving, 1:3-8. Paul gives thanks for the Philippians' "partnership in the Gospel from the first day until now" and emphasizes the personal character of the bond

which this partnership has established between himself
and them.

Prayer, 1:9-11. Paul prays that the love which they
have demonstrated by their gift may grow and increase and
that their knowledge and discernment may keep pace with
their love.

II. News from Prison, 1:12-26

    A. The news is good: Paul's trial has made it clear that he
is not what his accusers have charged, a seditious dis-
turber of the Roman peace, but what he himself has
always claimed, "a prisoner for Christ." Thus the cause
of the Gospel has been advanced through his imprisonment and trial, 1:12, 13.

    B. The turn which Paul's case has taken has emboldened
his brethren to speak the word of God more fearlessly
than before, and in this Paul rejoices, even though some
of these preachers are motivated by selfish and partisan
zeal in their preaching, 1:14-18.

    C. Paul is convinced that, whatever may befall him, Christ
will be glorified through him; his desire is to depart and
be with Christ forever; but the duty which he gladly
takes upon himself is that he remain in the service of
his Lord on earth; and so he looks forward to being
released and rejoining his church at Philippi.

III. Admonition, 1:27—2:18. "Let your manner of life be
worthy of the Gospel," 1:27. If they are partners in the
Gospel, their life must correspond to that Gospel; this will
show itself

    A. In *unity of spirit,* 1:27—2:2, especially in the face of
the persecution which it is their privilege to endure for
Christ. No enemies from without can destroy them; God
will destroy their enemies. But they can destroy themselves by disunity.

    B. In the *humility and self-effacement* which make true unity
possible, 2:3-11; this self-effacing and self-giving humility is theirs in Christ Jesus, who went a way that was

the divine way because it was the very opposite of the will of Satan (to be "like God"), the Servant-Messiah's way of self-giving, the way that took Him to the cross and thus to universal Lordship to the glory of God the Father. (These words of Paul concerning Christ are poetry, both in form and content; perhaps he is quoting an early hymn which both he and the Philippians knew and sang.)

C. In their *attitude as servants of God,* 2:12-18. The servant of God, eager to please and fearful of failure, works with "fear and trembling" at the work of salvation which God does in and through him and thus shows himself as the light of the world (by his glad acceptance of his hard lot, by the innocence of his life as a child of God in the midst of a world in revolt against God, by his unbroken hold upon the word of God). Paul will rejoice in them on the day of Christ, and he is now ready to be sacrificed for their sake; he rejoices and calls on them to share his joy.

IV. The Apostle's Actions on the Philippians' Behalf, 2:19—3:1

A. Paul is sending Timothy to them; he will cheer Paul by a fresh and firsthand report of them, and will be genuinely concerned for their welfare, 2:19-23.

B. Paul himself hopes to come to Philippi soon, 2:24.

C. Paul is sending Epaphroditus back to Philippi, with thanks to God for sparing his life, with high commendation of the work which he has done, and with the request that the Philippians receive him and honor him "in the Lord," 2:25-30.

Concluding call to joy, 3:1.

V. Apostolic Warning, 3:2-21

A. Warning against Judaizers, 3:2-11. With a vehemence which is in startling contrast to the cheerful serenity of the rest of the letter, Paul warns against his old and persistent enemies, the Judaizers, who had created such havoc in Galatia and elsewhere and were still at work. He turns against them every boast and every claim with which they sought to bolster their position. They who call the uncircumcised heathen unclean "dogs" are themselves "dogs" and unclean; they who shout "works" are themselves "evil-workers." Paul bitterly terms their vaunted circumcision a meaningless mutilation of the flesh; what circumcision once signified, namely membership in God's people, is no longer to be found in circumcision, but in Christ, 3:3. Paul then uses himself as an example of how all the old prerogatives and privileges of Israel have become meaningless in the presence of the Christ and the righteousness which man can find only in him. (Paul here gives his sharpest and most eloquent definition of the "righteousness of God," which has been the theme of his Letter to the Romans.)

B. Paul's "Maturity" and "Perfection" as an Example, 3:12-16. In a passage which provides the link between his warning against the Judaizers and his warning against the "enemies of the cross of Christ," 3:17-21, both of them people who had "arrived" and talked of "perfection," Paul gives a remarkable description of the Christian life as a constant and never-finished straining forward toward that which God has bestowed upon the believer: "I press on to make it my own, because Christ Jesus has made me His own," 3:12. Paul sees Christian perfection and Christian maturity in the ever imperfect and ever renewed appropriation of the gift of God in Christ.

C. Warning Against the Enemies of the Cross of Christ, 3:17—4:1. Since Paul describes this group of false teachers only sufficiently to condemn them, we cannot be sure of their identity. He had spoken of them to the Philippians before, often, 3:18, and they could readily identify them. Perhaps Paul is pointing to men of the kind whom he had had to combat at Corinth, the proud, secular, superspiritual, knowledgeable men who said, "We belong to Christ" and yet emptied the cross of Christ of its content, who on the basis of their higher "knowledge" came to terms with sin and made the church at home in the world. Paul had put an end to their influence at Corinth, but they no doubt continued their activities elsewhere, and not without success. Paul reminds the Philippians (for whom, as Roman "colonists" citizenship meant citizenship in the distant and splendid city of Rome) where their true home lay and where their heart should be: "Our commonwealth is in heaven, and from it we await a Savior, the Lord Jesus Christ," Phil. 3:20. They cannot boast in the flesh, in things of this world, like the Judaizers, or make this world their real home, like the enemies of the cross. In the pure hope of the Gospel they "stand firm . . . *in the Lord,*" Phil. 4:1.

VI. Concluding Admonitions, 4:2-9

    A. Settle your quarrels, 4:2, 3.

    B. Rejoice in the Lord, whose advent is near. Let your high hope give you a blithe and princely generosity toward all men; let your grateful prayer to God be the cure for all anxiety and care. Thus the peace of God will guard your hearts and minds more surely and securely than the Roman garrisons keep the Roman peace at Philippi, 4:4-7.

    C. Fill your hearts and minds with all that is true, honorable, just, pure, lovely, gracious, excellent, and praiseworthy. Do all that you have learned and received from your apostle and have witnessed in your apostle, 4:8, 9.

VII. Thanks for the Gift, 4:10-20

    A. Paul's pleasure at their concern for him, 4:10-13.

    B. Paul's thanks for their gift, in which he sees "a fragrant offering, a sacrifice acceptable and pleasing to God," 4:14-18.

    C. Paul's promise that his God will supply their every need, 4:19, 20.

    Conclusion: Greetings to all the saints from Paul, from all the brethren who are with him (his associates and co-

workers) and from all the saints (the church at Rome),
4:21, 22.

Canonicity: Homologoumenon

Integrity of the Letter

The sudden change of mood at 3:2 has led some scholars to
conjecture that this portion of the letter (3:2—4:1) is a fragment
of another Pauline letter. This conjecture receives some support
from the fact that Polycarp in writing to the Philippians in the
second century refers to "letter*s*" which they have received from
Paul. We do not know the situation well enough to decide
whether an abrupt change here (as in the Second Letter to the
Corinthians, beginning at the tenth chapter) is so improbable as
to demand a conjectural partition of the letter. As for the reference of Polycarp, even if he is referring to a number of letters
written by Paul to the church of Philippi (which is not certain),
this does not yet prove that our present Letter to the Philippians
is made up of two of them. All the ancient manuscripts and
versions give the letter as we have it today.

Value of the Letter

Among the Captivity Letters, the letters to the Colossians and
to the Ephesians show us Paul the fighter for the truth, the
thinker and theologian, the great strategist of church unity; the
Letter to Philemon shows us Paul the man whose whole life is
irradiated by the grace and glory of the Gospel. The Letter to
the Philippians, with its many and various facets, is harder to
classify; one modern scholar has brilliantly used this letter as an
introduction to the whole thought-world of Paul; he sees in it the
characteristic union of Paul the believer, Paul the missionary, and
Paul the theologian. Perhaps one might best use the bold joy of
faith as the common denominator of its multiplicity, faith as
Luther once described it: "Faith is a living, resolute total confidence in God's grace, a trust so certain that it is willing to die
a thousand deaths for its belief. And such a trust in God's grace
and such knowledge of God's grace make a man joyous, resolute,
and robustly cheerful over against God and all God's creatures."
An imprisoned apostle writes to a persecuted church, and the

keynote of his letter is: "I rejoice. Do you rejoice!" Where under the sun is anything like this possible except where faith is, where the Holy Spirit breathes His wholesome and creative breath? The whole letter is a good illustration of a word Paul uses in Phil. 4:5, a word which we are obliged to translate with some such term as "forbearance." But "forbearance" expresses only a part of Paul's meaning; the Greek word which he uses points to a princely quality in man, to that largeness of heart, that spacious generosity, that freedom from the cruelly competitive scrabble of this world which only he possesses whose "commonwealth is in heaven," who is heir to all that is Christ's, heir to the new world of God, in which he shall reign with Christ.

WHERE WERE THE CAPTIVITY LETTERS WRITTEN?

The historical setting of the Captivity Letters given above has assumed that they all issued from the Roman captivity of Paul (A. D. 59—61). A considerable number of scholars, however, favor other points of origin for all of them or for some of them. Some are inclined to place at least the Letter to the Philippians into the Caesarean captivity of Paul (A. D. 56—58; cf. Acts 23:33; 24:27). But this hypothesis really has very little to commend it. It is not likely that the runaway slave Onesimus would take refuge in a town like Caesarea, where he could hardly hope to escape detection. So far as we know, Paul never had any prospect of being released while at Caesarea, and he certainly never was in danger of being condemned and executed while there, something which Paul views as a distinct possibility in his Letter to the Philippians. Neither is it likely that Paul planned to visit his churches in Asia and Macedonia at this date; he was still turned Romeward and westward A. D. 56—58.

In the last fifty years a much larger number of scholars have argued for Ephesus; and their arguments have considerably more force. The following is a condensed survey of the most important arguments used to support the so-called Ephesian hypothesis; for reasons of brevity and convenience, the counterarguments will be given in parentheses after each argument.

1. *The Ephesian Imprisonment of Paul.*

The Book of Acts records no imprisonment of Paul during

his ministry at Ephesus. But, it is argued, Luke's account makes no pretense to completeness; and the following considerations make an imprisonment during this period at least possible if not probable: the whole period of Paul's activity at Ephesus was troubled by the machinations of his inveterate enemies, the Jews (Acts 19:9, 33; 20:19; 21:27; 1 Cor. 16:9); it was obviously a time of desperate dangers for Paul (1 Cor. 15:30 ff.; 2 Cor. 1:8-10; Rom. 16:4, 7). That is all the New Testament evidence. Later sources tell us that Paul once fought with a lion at Ephesus. A building in Ephesus was later pointed out as "Paul's prison." A set of introductory notes found in some ancient Latin manuscripts and dating from the third or fourth century (the so-called Monarchian Prologues) say of the Letter to the Colossians: "The apostle wrote it from Ephesus while already in prison."

(The direct evidence for an imprisonment is admittedly slight; no New Testament document mentions an imprisonment at Ephesus. The references in later sources to Paul's fight with a lion at Ephesus seem to be simply inferences from Paul's figurative language in 1 Cor. 15:32. The evidence of the Monarchian Prologue is made doubtful by the fact that this same source assigns the Letter to Philemon to Rome, and the Letter to Philemon cannot be separated from the Letter to the Colossians. Paul may possibly have been imprisoned at Ephesus; but it seems precarious to build a hypothesis on so shaky a foundation. It should be noted also that the events presupposed by the Letter to the Philippians demand an *extended* imprisonment; and the longer the imprisonment, the less likely it is that it should be wrapped in silence.

2. *The Flight of Onesimus.*

Onesimus is more likely to have fled to Ephesus, only 125 miles from his home in Colossae and large enough to enable him to remain undetected, than to have undertaken the long, difficult, and (especially for runaway slaves) dangerous voyage to Rome.

(We have no way of deciding whether Onesimus would have fled to Ephesus because it was near or to Rome because it was far. If he had lined his pockets with his master Philemon's money, the voyage to Rome would not have been so difficult as is often supposed. And Rome was notoriously the cesspool into which all the refuse of the Roman Empire flowed.)

3. *Paul's Request for a Lodging at Colossae,* Philemon 22

Paul is more likely to have planned a visit to Colossae from Ephesus A. D. 52—55 than from Rome A. D. 59—61.

(One may reasonably doubt whether Paul's words, "Prepare a guestroom for me," are to be taken quite so literally as many interpreters seem inclined to do. In a letter as easy and informal in tone as the Letter to Philemon the words may be no more than a strong expression of the good hope of release from prison which animates Paul as he writes. As for the revisitation of the eastern provinces and churches, it is much more probable on the Roman hypothesis. By the time of Paul's imprisonment in Rome almost five years had elapsed since Paul had left his work in the East and turned to the West. He may have found it advisable, in the light of developments such as had arisen in Colossae and Laodicea, to revisit Asia and Macedonia once more — or it may have simply been the will of the Lord. The Pastoral Letters indicate that he did revisit the East.)

4. *The Companions of Paul During His Imprisonment*

The large number of co-workers mentioned by Paul as being with him during his imprisonment seems unlikely for Rome but would be natural for the extended and intensive ministry at Ephesus.

(The place where Paul was would naturally be headquarters for his co-workers; and all calculations as to how many companions might or might not have been with Paul at Rome or at Ephesus, or which companions might more naturally be with him at either place, are bound to be highly speculative.)

5. *The Frequency of Communication Between Paul and Philippi*

The communications between Philippi and Paul in prison have been sketched above (see *The Date of Writing*). It is argued that such frequent communication is much more probable between Ephesus and Philippi than between Rome and Philippi.

(This is no doubt the strongest argument for the Ephesian hypothesis. But this too is not an overwhelming argument. It has been conservatively estimated that the communications which had taken place between Paul and Philippi by the time of the writing of the Letter to the Philippians need not have consumed more than six or seven months. They can be easily fitted into the two years of the Roman imprisonment. The journey between Philippi and Ephesus would require six or seven days, so that an imprisonment of considerable length would be necessary for the Ephesian hypothesis also.)

To sum up: The arguments (typical examples only have been given here) for the Ephesian imprisonment of Paul and for the dating of the Captivity Letters from that imprisonment range from the plausible and ingenious to the merely clever; but all are inconclusive. And until it can be shown that the Ephesian hypothesis better explains *all* the known facts concerning the Captivity Letters better than the Roman hypothesis, we are on safer ground in assigning the letters to the known and verifiable Roman imprisonment of A. D. 59—61. Two arguments *for* the Roman provenance of the letters deserve mention in closing: (a) According to the evidence of the letters themselves, Luke was with Paul during his imprisonment (Col. 4:14; Philemon 24); according to Acts, he was with Paul in Rome, but not in Ephesus; (b) in the Letter to the Philippians Paul faces the possibility of an adverse verdict and death as a consequence (Phil. 1:20). This could happen only in Rome; in any provincial court Paul could always appeal to the decision of the Emperor, as he did at Caesarea under Festus. (Acts 25:11, 12)

CHAPTER VII: Teacher of the Gentiles in Faith and Truth: The Pastoral Letters of Paul

READINGS: 1 and 2 TIMOTHY; TITUS

Historical Background of the Pastoral Letters

Since we do not have the help of the Book of Acts for the period in which the writing of the Pastoral Letters falls and must reconstruct the history of this period entirely from hints given in the letters themselves, the order of events must remain somewhat doubtful; even an approximate dating of them is difficult. The following is a probable, but only probable, reconstruction of the course of events:

1. That Paul was released at the end of the two years' imprisonment recorded in Acts 28:30 (A. D. 61) seems certain; there is really no evidence at all that his first Roman imprisonment ended in martyrdom. Paul apparently did not remain long in Rome after his release; the jealousies and frictions to which he alludes in his Letter to the Philippians (Phil. 1:15-17) would make it advisable for him to leave soon.

2. Whether Paul ever carried out his intention of going to Spain (Rom. 15:28) must remain doubtful. The Captivity Letters say nothing of an anticipated Spanish voyage, and the Pastoral Letters likewise say nothing of that undertaking. Neither did the Spanish church preserve any tradition which attributed its origin to the missionary work of Paul. On the other hand, Paul's journey to Spain is attested by early and reliable Roman sources like the Letter of Clement of Rome to the Corinthians (I. v. 5-7), written within a generation after the events (A. D. 96), and Mura-

torian Canon (about A. D. 175). The apocryphal Acts of Peter (written about A. D. 200) also refers to the Spanish voyage of Paul; and no one in antiquity seems to have questioned it. If Paul did make the voyage, it was probably soon after his release from imprisonment A. D. 61.

3. Paul intended to revisit his former mission fields in Asia and Macedonia (Philemon 22; Phil. 2:24); the Pastoral Letters indicate that he carried out this intention. He returned to the East by way of Crete, where he remained for a time as missionary. He left Titus in charge of the task of consolidating the church there when he himself proceeded eastward. (Titus 1:5)

4. Paul may have touched at Ephesus; if he did, he could not have remained there long. The instructions which he gave Timothy, whom he left in charge at Ephesus, indicate that much work still remained to be done there. (1 Tim. 1:3)

5. Paul himself proceeded from Ephesus to Macedonia, and from there wrote the First Letter to Timothy. (1 Tim. 1:3)

6. Paul wrote the Letter to Titus, either from Macedonia just before his departure for Nicopolis or during the journey to Nicopolis, where he planned to spend the winter. There were several prominent cities called Nicopolis; the one referred to in the Letter to Titus is probably Nicopolis in Epirus. Titus was to join Paul in Nicopolis when relieved in Crete by Artemas or Tychicus. (Titus 3:12)

7. During the interval between the writing of the Letter to Titus and the Second Letter to Timothy Paul visited Troas, Corinth, and Miletus. (2 Tim. 4:13, 20)

8. Paul was again arrested (whether in the East or at Rome can hardly be made out) and imprisoned at Rome. This time his imprisonment was much more severe than A. D. 59—61, and he saw no hope of an acquittal. In his Second Letter to Timothy he summons his "beloved child" to him once more before the end.

9. This second imprisonment in Rome ended in the martyrdom of Paul. It took place under Nero, certainly; but hardly during the great Neronian persecution A. D. 64. Paul would hardly have summoned Timothy, the man to whom he looked for

the faithful continuation of his work, to a certain death in Rome; neither would it be like Paul to lament that none of the Roman Christians had stood by him at his first hearing if those Christians were at that time dying for their faith. The writing of the Second Letter to Timothy and Paul's death must be dated either before the great persecution under Nero, perhaps A. D. 63; or later, perhaps even so late as A. D. 67, the last year of Nero's reign.

The Name "Pastoral"

The name "Pastoral" has been applied to the letters addressed to Timothy and Titus since the eighteenth century; the title had been applied to First Timothy alone as early as the thirteenth century, by Thomas Aquinas. This designation marks the letters as directed to "pastors" or shepherds of the church and as dealing with the office of the pastor. It is more properly applied to the First Letter to Timothy and to the Letter to Titus than to the Second Letter to Timothy. The Second Letter to Timothy has pastoral elements in it, but is basically a personal letter and in a class by itself. The First Letter to Timothy and the Letter to Titus are official letters, addressed not only to the recipient in each case, but also to the churches to which these men were being sent, and they cover the whole range of church life: offices in the church, the worship life of the church, the care of souls, and especially the combating of error which threatens the health of the church. The official character of the letters is seen in their form also; the usual Pauline thanksgiving at the beginning is replaced by words which indicate that the content of the letter is a repetition in writing of oral instructions already given — a common feature in official letters (1 Tim. 1:3; Titus 1:5). The personal communications usually found at the close of Pauline letters are either absent entirely, as in the Letter to Timothy, or kept extremely brief, as in the Letter to Titus. The style of the letters likewise reflects this "official" character: We have here terse and pointed directions delivered with apostolic authority; the doctrinal background and basis of the directions are given in pointed and pregnant formulations, designed to be readily grasped and remembered; some of them are "sure sayings," probably already familiar to the churches. (1 Tim. 1:15; 3:1; 4:9; Titus 3:8)

THE FIRST LETTER TO TIMOTHY

The Situation

Paul, on his way to Macedonia, has left Timothy at Ephesus with instructions to "charge certain persons not to teach any different doctrine" (1 Tim. 1:3); Paul does not describe this "different doctrine" systematically; but from his attacks upon it in 1:3-7; 4:1-3, 7; 6:3-5,20, 21 and from the tenor of his instructions for the regulation of the life of the church, it is clear that Timothy must do battle with a form of "Gnosticism," an early stage of that heresy which was to become in its fully developed form the most serious threat to the church in succeeding generations. Gnosticism is not so much a system as a trend or current of thought which produced a great variety of systems, often by combining with some already existing religion. It was therefore present and active as a corrupting force long before the great Christian-gnostic systems of the second century appeared; we have already seen one example of it in the heresy which threatened the church at Colossae.

Basic to all forms of Gnosticism is a dualistic conception of reality, that is, the view that what is spiritual, nonmaterial, is of itself good and what is material or physical, is of itself bad. This view affects man's whole attitude toward the world of created things. The dreary details of gnostic speculations on the *origin* of the material universe need not concern us here. It may suffice to note

a. that the world is no longer viewed as God's good creation, as the Scriptures view it (that is, a world which God created, fallen with fallen man but redeemed with man and destined to be transfigured with him, Rom. 8:19-22); rather, the created world is viewed as in itself alien and hostile to God because it is matter and not spirit;

b. that man's desperate predicament, his alienation from God, is no longer seen as being due to his sinful rebellion against God, but to the fact that he is entangled in the world of matter;

c. that redemption consists in being freed from the material world in which man dwells and is entangled. This liberation can come about only by knowledge (Greek, *gnosis,* hence the name of the heresy); this knowledge must be imparted to man by revelation from a higher world;

d. the mission of the Savior-God is to impart this knowledge not to all men, but to a select few who will pass it on to those who are "worthy";

e. that those who have knowledge, the "gnostics," must free themselves from the influence of matter by abstaining from certain foods and from marriage. (Sometimes the negative attitude toward things physical and material had the opposite effect and led to a supreme indifference to things physical and material, so that, for instance, the sexual life of man was considered to be morally indifferent.)

Such a trend of thought would lead inevitably to an utter distortion of all that "the glorious Gospel of the blessed God" (1 Tim. 1:11) proclaimed. God the Creator disappears — all the good gifts of food and drink which He gives are suspected and feared; all the salutary orders which He has established in this world (marriage, family, government) are despised and ignored. The Old Testament, which rings with glad adoration of the God who made the heavens and the earth and blesses man within the orders of this world, must either be ignored or have its obvious sense interpreted away by allegorizing "myths and endless genealogies." The Law becomes the arena of speculation and vain discussions, not the voice of God which calls the sinner to account and condemns him. In terms of this kind of thought, there can be no real incarnation of the Son of God; for how can the divine, which is spiritual, enter into union with matter, which is of itself evil? And when sin is not recognized as man's guilt, there can be no real redemption either. Where knowledge is made central in the religious life of man and self-redemption by way of ascetic exercise is made the way of salvation, there is no possibility of that pure Christian love which "issues from a pure heart and a good conscience and sincere faith" (1 Tim. 1:5). A narrow and sectarian pride takes its place (1 Tim. 6:4, 20; cf. 1:3-7). Where the teaching office becomes a wordy, speculative, disputatious purveying of "knowledge" to a select coterie of initiates, it is bound to become corrupted; it appeals to the pride, the selfishness, and the mercenary instincts of men, and the teacher becomes that ghastly, demon-ridden caricature of the true teacher which Paul has described in 1 Tim. 4:1, 2.

Timothy's task will be to let the fresh and wholesome winds of "sound doctrine" into the house of God, whose air has been infected by the morbid and infectious mists of this *gnosis*. To the demonic denial of God the Creator and the rejection of His good gifts he must oppose the glorious Gospel of the blessed God "who gives life to all things" (1 Tim. 6:13), the God whose every creation still has upon it the mark of His primeval "Very Good!" (Gen. 1:31) and is even in its fallen state "consecrated by the word of God and prayer" (1 Tim. 4:5). To "godless and silly myths" he is to oppose the grateful adoration of the Creator. To the gnostic misuse of the Law he must oppose the right and lawful use and let the sinner hear the fearful verdict of God in order that he may give ear to God's acquittal in His Gospel. (1:8-11)

To the rarefied and unreal Christ of gnostic speculation he must oppose "the *man* Christ Jesus" (1 Tim. 2:5), the Christ Jesus who really entered into history under Pontius Pilate (1 Tim. 6:13) and died a real death upon the cross for the sins of all men (1 Tim. 2:6). He must present this Christ as the whole content of the truth which the church upholds and guards, the mystery of God "manifested *in the flesh*" (1 Tim. 3:16). To gnostic self-redemption by means of knowledge and ascetic self-manipulation he must oppose redemption as the sole act of the Christ who came into the world, not to impart higher knowledge but "to save sinners" (1 Tim. 1:15), the Christ "who gave Himself as a ransom for all" (1 Tim. 2:6). To gnostic exclusiveness he must oppose the all-embracing grace of God, and to their narrow sectarian pride he must oppose the Gospel of universal grace (1 Tim. 2:4), and thus make of the church a church which can pray wholeheartedly for *all* men (1 Tim. 2:1), a church which lives in the "love that issues from a pure heart and a good conscience and sincere faith" (1 Tim. 1:5).

To the imposing picture of the gnostic teachers, these brilliant, speculative, disputatious, and mercenary men, he must oppose the picture of the true teacher. He must, first of all, himself *be* that picture; he dare not let himself be drawn down to the level of his opponents and fight demonic fire with fire; he must do battle, "holding faith and a good conscience" (1 Tim. 1:19); he must, as a good minister of Jesus Christ, not allow himself to be infected by what he opposes but must continue to be "nourished on the words of faith" (not knowledge) "and of the good doctrine" which he has followed hitherto. He must train himself, athlete-like, in godliness (1 Tim. 4:6, 7). Thus he will be able to fight the good fight of faith as a "man of God," standing in the succession of Moses and the prophets, singly devoted to God's cause (1 Tim. 6:11, 12; cf. 6:3-10), laying hold even now of that eternal life which shall be his in fullness at the appearing of the Lord Jesus Christ (1 Tim. 6:11-15). He must himself be all that the gnostic teachers are not; and he is to see to it that the men who oversee the church's life and administer the church's charity, the bishops and deacons, are men of like character. They need not be brilliant men; they must be good men. It is enough if a bishop be "an apt teacher" (1 Tim. 3:2); he need not be a brilliant speaker or a captivating personality. The qualifications which Paul sets up for bishops and deacons are singularly sober and down to earth; but the moral standards which he sets up for them are awesomely high (1 Tim. 3:1-13). Paul wants men whom the grace of God has "trained," as he puts it in his Letter to Titus (Titus 2:11, 12), seasoned, selfless, wise, and gracious men whose faith has borne fruit in their homes, in their marital fidelity, and in the training of their children (1 Tim. 3:2, 4, 12).

Timothy had a great piece of work assigned to him. And he was a good man for the task. He was both Jew and Greek (Acts 16:1). He had lived with the Old Testament from childhood (2 Tim. 3:15). Prophetic voices had assigned him to this "good warfare" (1 Tim. 1:18). God had given him the requisite gifts for it (1 Tim. 4:14), and his whole history had been one that fostered those gifts. He had been Paul's almost constant companion for a dozen years (Acts 16:1 ff.). The apostolic "pattern of sound words" (2 Tim. 1:13) had become a part of his make-up, and the apostolic example had been constantly before him (2 Tim. 3:10, 11, 14). Paul had employed him as his emissary before this, though never for so extended and difficult a mission as this one. When Paul was prevented from returning to Thessalonica,

he sent Timothy to the young and troubled church to establish
the believers in their faith and to exhort them (1 Thess. 3:1, 2).
He had sent Timothy to Corinth during that troubled period when
the Corinthians were becoming drunk on the heady wine of the
new teaching, to remind them of the apostle's "ways in Christ"
(1 Cor. 4:17; 16:10). He had sent him to Philippi from Rome
during the time of his imprisonment and had commended him to
the Philippians with the finest tribute that can be paid to a servant
of God in the Gospel: "I have no one like him, who will be
genuinely anxious for your welfare. They all look after their own
interests, not those of Jesus Christ. But Timothy's worth you
know, how as a son with a father he has served with me in the
Gospel." (Phil. 2:20-22)

If Paul was a fond father to Timothy, he was not a blind one.
He knew his beloved child's weaknesses: Timothy was still young
and apparently conscious of it as a handicap (1 Tim. 4:12). He
was inclined to be timid (cf. 1 Cor. 16:10, 11; 2 Tim. 1:7).
Besides, his health was not of the best; his stomach troubled him,
an ailment not uncommon among sensitive and conscientious
young men of God. (1 Tim. 5:23)

Therefore Paul writes Timothy a letter which sums up once
more the oral instructions already given him (1 Tim. 1:3). This
letter will give his work the sanction and authority of Paul, "an
apostle of Christ Jesus by command of God our Savior and of
Christ Jesus our Hope" (1 Tim. 1:1). Paul is in effect telling the
church of Ephesus what he had once told the Corinthians: *"He is
doing the work of the Lord, as I am.* So let no one despise him."
(1 Cor. 16:10, 11)

Content of the First Letter to Timothy

The letter falls into three sections, each of which is introduced
by an attack upon the gnostic false teaching. Each attack introduces, negatively, the theme of the section.

Salutation, 1:1, 2

I. 1:3—3:16. First Attack, 1:3-7. The gnostic heresy corrupts
   the teaching of the church, both Law, v. 7, and Gospel,
   vv. 4, 5; cf. v. 11.

A. Timothy is to oppose this corrupting influence,

1. By recognizing the true function of the Law, 1:8-11;

2. By seeing in the Gospel of pure grace the only power that can re-create rebellious man and make him a doer of the will of God, as Paul's own example has demonstrated, 1:12-17;

3. By waging this good warfare in the conviction that God Himself has called him to this task through the utterance of His prophets, 1:18-20.

B. Timothy is to oppose this corrupting influence,

1. By so ordering the worship of the church that its prayers may be an expression of the all-embracing grace of God and a recognition of government as a good and wholesome ordinance of God, 2:1-7;

2. By so ordering the worship of the church that its prayers may be said in the peacable and forgiving spirit of the Fifth Petition, 2:8, and the conduct of the worshipers may be a recognition of the sanctity of the position which God the Creator has assigned to woman, 2:9-15;

3. By providing for the church bishops and deacons whose conduct, example, and influence shall be the living embodiment of the fact that the church is the "pillar and bulwark of the truth," the truth, namely, of the Gospel which proclaims the Christ as the Savior of man by a real incarnation which ties Him to the flesh, to the nations, to the world — not the Christ of gnostic speculation who has no real contact with man. The church's true Gospel proclaims both His complete manhood and His total Godhead, His utter humiliation and His absolute exaltation, 3:1-16.

II. 4:1—6:2. Second Attack, 4:1-5. The gnostic heresy corrupts the daily life of the church. This false teaching is, for all its pretentions to rigorous piety, a demonic denial of the goodness of God's creation. The appearance of these false teachers is a first fulfillment of the Spirit's warning for the last days, cf. Acts 20:29, 30; 1 John 4:3.

Timothy is to oppose this corrupting influence,

A. By a sober, scrupulous, and strenuous performance of his duties: by avoiding the godless and silly myths which obscure the good doctrine of the Gospel, by training himself in godliness, by fixing his hope in the living God who is the Savior of all men, by using to the full the gift which God has given him — thus he will set an "example in speech and conduct, in love, in faith, in purity," 4:6-16;

B. By his treatment of the various age groups and classes in the church: He is to deal with young and old as with his kinfolk in the household of God, 5:1, 2. His treatment of widows who receive support from the church is to be both respectful and realistic, 5:3-16. He is to honor the elders who do their work faithfully; he is to deal soberly and conscientiously with those who fail in their duties, 5:17-25. He is to remind slaves that their relationship to their masters, particularly Christian masters, is not abrogated by their freedom in Christ, but is hallowed by it; they are to serve all the better for serving freely, 6:1-2.

III. 6:3-21. Third Attack, 6:3-10. The gnostic false teaching corrupts its teachers. Men who have broken with the "sound words of our Lord Jesus Christ" and have wandered away from the faith become conceited, contentious, and mercenary. Their love of gain especially proves their ruin: They have lost the faith and the peace of a good conscience.

Timothy is to oppose this corrupting influence,

A. By being a true "man of God," combining a militant zeal for the cause of God with love and gentleness, having his whole riches in the eternal life to which he has been called, 6:11, 12;

B. By keeping pure the "commandment" which he received with the call of the Gospel at his baptism, in a career of obedient and selfless ministry until the return of the Lord Jesus Christ, 6:13-16. (6:17-19: Not only the teacher is exposed to the temptation of avarice; the rich in this world are to be admonished to find their true riches in God, in generous deeds, and in the life to come which is life indeed.)

C. By faithfully guarding the truth which has been entrusted to him, remembering that the key to it is not "knowledge," but "faith," 6:20, 21.

Time and Place of Writing: A. D. 62 or 63, probably in Macedonia.

Canonicity: Homologoumenon

THE LETTER OF PAUL TO TITUS

The Letter to Titus is quite similar to the First Letter to Timothy in its occasion, purpose, and content and can therefore be treated rather briefly here. Paul had worked for a while as missionary on the island of Crete together with Titus, the prudent, able, and tactful Gentile companion who had rendered him such valuable services at the time when the relationship between the Corinthian church and Paul had been strained to the breaking point (2 Cor. 2:13; 7:6ff.; 8:6; 12:18). At his departure from Crete Paul left Titus in charge of the task of consolidating and organizing the newly created Christian communities. His task resembled that of Timothy at Ephesus in that the faith and life of the church were being endangered by the rise of false teachers of a gnostic type, more pronouncedly Judaic in their teaching than those at Ephesus (Titus 1:14; 3:9). The situation was further complicated in Crete, however, by the fact that in these newly founded Christian communities solid organization was lacking and the pagan environment was particularly vicious (1:5, 12, 13). Whereas Timothy was to restore order in established churches, Titus had to *establish* order in young churches. It was a task which called for all his courage, wisdom, and tact. Paul wrote to Titus to encourage him in this difficult assignment, to aid him in combating the threatening heresy, to advise him in his task of organizing and edifying the churches and, not least, to give Titus' presence and work in Crete the sanction and support of his own apostolic authority. This last intention of the letter is evident in the salutation of the letter, which dwells on Paul's apostolate (1:1-3) and in the closing greeting, "Grace be with you *all*" (3:15), which shows that the letter addressed to Titus is intended for the ear of the churches also.

Time and Place of Writing: about A. D. 63, in Macedonia or en route to Nicopolis.

Content of the Letter to Titus

Salutation, 1:1-4

Titus' Task in Crete

I. 1:5-9. To appoint elders, men of unimpeachable character, firmly grounded in sound doctrine, able to instruct the faithful and to confute the contradictor.

II. 1:10-16. To expose the pernicious teaching of men who "profess to *know* God" *(gnosis)* but "deny Him by their deeds," 1:16, those insubordinate, loquacious, deceitful, mercenary men who purvey "Jewish myths" and impose human commands of abstinence in the name of higher knowledge and higher purity. Their teaching reveals their ignorance of God and the impurity of their minds.

III. 2:1—3:8. To edify the church

    A. By instructing men of all ages and classes, by word and by example, in that high conduct of life which the grace of God, manifested to all men in Christ, has made possible. The life of the redeemed people of God is to be a living preachment of that enabling grace — even the life of a slave may "adorn the doctrine of God our Savior," 2:1-15;

    B. By instructing the believers to be obedient to governmental authority and to show to all men that perfect and winning Christian courtesy which has been engendered in them by the "goodness and loving-kindness of God our Savior," 3:1-7;

    C. By impressing upon all who have come to faith that they have but one profession which they must pursue, namely, good works, 3:8.

IV. 3:9-11. To exclude from the church those who persist in their false teachings.

Conclusion, 3:12-15. Instruction and Greetings

Titus is to rejoin Paul in Nicopolis when Artemas or Tychicus comes to relieve him, 3:12. Titus is to speed Zenas and Apollos, the bearers of this letter, on their way. The Cretan Christians, too, are to do their part in supporting these missionaries, 3:13, 14.

Greetings from Paul and his co-workers to Titus and all believers.

Closing benediction, 3:15

Canonicity: Homologoumenon

THE SECOND LETTER OF PAUL TO TIMOTHY

The Situation

Paul writes from prison in Rome. He has been a prisoner for some time: Onesiphorus, a Christian of Ephesus, has already sought him out and visited him in Rome (2 Tim. 1:16, 17). There has already been one hearing, at which Paul was deserted by all men and yet, with the Lord's help, so successfully defended himself that he "was rescued from the lion's mouth" (2 Tim. 4:16, 17). But Paul has no hope of ultimate acquittal; he is at the end of his course. And he is virtually alone; only Luke is with him. He longs to see "his beloved child" Timothy once more and bids him come to Rome before the winter makes travel by sea impossible (2 Tim. 1:4; 4:9, 21). But he must reckon with the possibility that Timothy may not reach Rome in time; and so he must put in writing all that he hopes to tell Timothy in person if and when he arrives. The letter is thus, as Bengel has put it, Paul's "last will and testament," in which he bids Timothy preserve the apostolic Gospel pure and unchanged, guard it against the increasingly vicious attacks of false teachers, train men to transmit it faithfully, and be ready to take his own share of suffering in the propagation and defense of it. The most personal of the Pastoral Letters is therefore in a sense "official" too; for Paul cannot separate his person from his office. The man who has been "set apart for the Gospel of God" (Rom. 1:1) remains one with that Gospel in life and in death.

Date of Writing: A. D. 65—67

Content of the Second Letter to Timothy

Salutation, 1:1, 2

Thanksgiving, 1:3-5. Paul gives thanks for the bond of affection which has united him and Timothy, expresses his strong desire to see him again, and gratefully recalls the sincere faith that dwells in him. This introduces

I. 1:6-18. *Paul's Appeal to Timothy* to rekindle the gift of God that is within him, to make full proof of that "Spirit of power and love and self-control," 1:6, 7, which will enable him

A. to remain loyal to the imprisoned apostle and be ready to take his own share of suffering for the Gospel, in the conviction that the power of God which has in Christ Jesus overcome death and has sustained Paul in the faithful discharge of his appointed task will empower and enable him too, 1:8-12;

B. to hold fast and to guard the truth which Paul has communicated to him, by the power of the Spirit that dwells in him as it dwells in Paul, 1:13, 14.

Paul concludes his appeal by pointing to the warning example of "all those of Asia" who have deserted him, and to the heartening example of the kind and courageous Onesiphorus, 1:15-18.

II. 2:1—4:5. *Paul's Charge to Timothy*

A. To entrust the truth to faithful men, 2:1-13.

1. Timothy can train and inspire faithful men only if he is himself faithful, ready to endure hardships and toil with a soldier's single loyalty, an athlete's rigorous self-discipline, and a farmer's strenuous industry, 2:1-7.

2. This he can do by the strength which is to be found in Christ Jesus, the risen Christ who has given Paul the courage to suffer disgrace and imprisonment for the sake of God's elect. Timothy must work and suffer in the faith that union with Christ in suffering and death is the promise of union with Him in life and glory, 2:8-13.

B. To train these faithful men in the defense of the truth against the attacks of false teachers, 2:14—4:5.

1. Timothy must warn them against sinking to the level of their opponents with their disputes about words — the teacher of the church is not to be a debater, 2:14. Again, Timothy can accomplish this only

a. if he himself is an honest workman of the Lord, the very opposite of men like Hymenaeus and Philetus with their godless and cancerous teaching, which is upsetting the faith of some, 2:15-18;

b. if he does his work in the believing confidence that God's truth cannot be overcome. God knows His own; He has chosen them, loves them, and will protect and vindicate them, 2:19;

c. if he obeys the command to holiness (given by God's elective grace) and becomes a pure vessel fit for God's noblest uses — as such he will rise above stupid controversies and be able to create faithful men in his own image, 2:20-23.

2. Timothy must train servants of the Lord who will overcome error with apt teaching, with kindly, forbearing, and gentle correction, in the faith and hope that God can grant their opponents repentance and deliver them from the devilish lie which ensnares them, 2:24-26.

C. To do his work in the sobering conviction that times and men will grow worse and that opposition to the truth will increase, 3:1-8.

D. To do his work in the encouraging conviction

1. that the folly of those who oppose the truth will expose itself, 3:9;

2. that he has sufficient equipment for his difficult and dangerous task in the apostolic example which he has witnessed, in the apostolic teaching which he has received, and in the inspired Scriptures which he has known from childhood, 3:10-17.

E. To fulfill his ministry strenuously, insistently, courageously in the face of men's indifference to sound teaching and in spite of their itching lust for false teaching; the Christ will return to judge all men, to be manifested in glory, and to reign, 4:1-5.

It is Timothy who must now do the work of the evangelist; Paul's course is run, his fight finished, 4:6-8.

III. 4:9-22. *Paul's Request to Timothy*

"Come to me soon," 4:9; "Come before winter," 4:21. Paul's longing for his beloved child, a longing intensified by the fact that he is alone in prison, and his desire to impress on him once more, face to face, the greatness and the glory

of the task which is now his to carry on break forth into the
urgent request that Timothy come to him in Rome, 4:9-18.

Greetings and Benediction, 4:19-22

Canonicity: Homologoumenon

VALUE OF THE PASTORAL LETTERS

Among the letters of Paul there are none which connect Paul
the writer so closely with Paul the worker who is portrayed in the
Book of Acts as the Pastoral Letters. This is Paul the worker,
consumed in the white heat of ministry, the missionary, the
organizer, and the discipliner at work. Missionaries have always
found these letters indispensable and have often understood them
better than the armchair interpreters back home. Consecrated
pastors and teachers have found in them their own New Testament within the New Testament and have lived of them and by
them, soberly and successfully in the daily round of their duties.
These letters hold before the church and the church's teachers
an ideal of a ministry and a teaching which have on them the
imprint of godliness and sublimity just because they are down
to earth; they walk on the ground, where men are, where the
Son of God, the descendant of David, walked and worked for the
salvation of men. Indeed, not the least of the services rendered
to the church by the Pastoral Letters is the instilling of a healthy
contempt for all brilliant and speculative theologies that fail
to edify.

The Pastoral Letters are Pauline barley bread, honest workman's food, rough and plain. They do not have the great sustained
flights of letters like those to the Romans, or Ephesians, or
Colossians; neither do they have the transfixing impact of letters
like that to the Galatians. But if they usually walk, they never
crawl; and the worker is bidden again and again to lift up his
eyes and to walk by the light of the glory of God that shines
from above. These letters abound in clear and trenchant formulations of the truth that we live and work by, the sort that deserve
and demand to be "gotten by heart." Paul's thanksgiving to
Jesus Christ, who came into the world to save sinners and made
Paul the copy-book example in which all sinners might see spelled
out the grace of God (1 Tim. 1:12-17); the proclamation of the

grace of God which has burst upon all men like a sunrise for their deliverance and remains their trainer in sobriety, righteousness, and godliness (Titus 2:11-14); the sure saying which comforts all who endure and die with Christ with the assurance that they shall live and reign with Him (2 Tim. 2:11-13); the great words on the inspired usefulness of Scripture (2 Tim. 3:16, 17) — it is hard to imagine the holy Christian church living without these words.

THE AUTHENTICITY OF THE PASTORAL LETTERS

The authenticity of the Pastoral Letters has been called into question on a number of counts; chief among them are the following five: (1) the historical setting of the letters; (2) the type of church organization presupposed by the Letters; (3) the nature of the heresy combated in the letters; (4) the doctrinal substance of the letters; (5) the style and language of the letters.

a. *The historical setting:* It is argued that the journeys and acitivities presupposed by the Pastoral Letters cannot be fitted into the life of Paul as known from his undoubted epistles and from the Book of Acts. It is usually assumed that the Roman imprisonment of A. D. 59—61 ended in Paul's death.

Over against this, one may urge that there is good reason to believe that Paul's imprisonment ended in his release; both Festus and Agrippa deemed him innocent, and no ancient source actually says that Paul was executed after his two years' imprisonment in Rome A. D. 61. Assuming, then, that Paul was released from prison A. D. 61, the years between that date and the death of Paul (which may have occurred as late as A. D. 67) leave ample room for the activities presupposed by the Pastoral Letters, even if we cannot reconstruct the history of this period with absolute accuracy. It should be noted, on the positive side, that the personal notices in these letters are so true to the life and character of Paul that even many of the convinced opponents of the authenticity of the letters are inclined to believe that a later forger has made use of fragments of genuine Pauline correspondence.

b. *Church organization:* The church organization presupposed by the letters, it is urged, is too far advanced and too well established for the first century. It is assumed, therefore, that a writer of the late first or early second century wrote the letters in Paul's name in order to get apostolic sanction for contemporary arrangements in the church.

It may be said in reply that we hear of the appointment of elders in the churches as early as the First Missionary Journey (Acts 14:23). Paul speaks of "pastors" and "teachers" in his Letter to the Ephesians (Eph. 4:11) and addresses the bishops and deacons of Philippi in his Letter to the Philippians (1:1). Moreover, the organization presupposed in the letters is not elaborate and is not fixed with legal precision. The terms "elder" and "bishop" (which were later distinguished) are still used interchangeably (Titus 1:5, 7), and the concern of the letters is always for the *function* of the office as a power to edify the church, not for an exact definition of its rights and powers.

c. *The nature of the heresy combated in the letters:* It is asserted that the false teaching attacked by the author can only be the great second-century gnostic systems.

It is true that the false teachers and teachings attacked in the Pastoral Letters have some of the characteristic marks of second-century Gnosticism. But it should be noted also that Gnosticism existed as a tendency or trend long before the second century. The heresy combated by the Pastoral Letters has a strongly Judaic coloring, something which is not characteristic of second-century Gnosticism. There is no indication in the letters that the gnostic vaporings under attack are the full-blown systems which divided the second-century church. The teachings seem rather to be half-formed and ill-formed; and while some of the teachers have been excommunicated, many of them are still, apparently, working within the church.

d. *The doctrinal substance of the letters:* Judgment in this area is bound to be somewhat subjective. For example, the fact that the work of the Holy Spirit receives relatively little emphasis has been used as an argument against the authenticity of the Pastoral Letters. It is always dangerous to argue from what an author does not say: The Letter to the Colossians, today generally accepted as authentically Pauline, has the word "Spirit" just once and the adjective "spiritual" only twice. Moreover, these letters abound in teaching so completely Pauline in content and formulation that it has no real parallel except in the accepted letters of Paul. It should be remembered also that these letters were written to addressees and for purposes quite different from those of Paul's other letters. In general, a judgment like that of an able modern commentator would seem to be fair and reasonable: There is nothing in the Pastorals which Paul could not have written; there is much that only he could have written.

e. *The style and language of the letters:* The style resembles, as one would expect, the practical and hortatory portions of the other Pauline letters rather than that of the doctrinal portions. Besides, Paul's style varies considerably from letter to letter and even within a single letter, so that arguments based on style must be used with considerable caution.

The vocabulary presents the greatest difficulty. Over 36 per cent of the words that make up the vocabulary of the Pastoral Letters are not found in any of the other Pauline letters.

This large percentage of new words is in part explained by the newness of the subject matter of these letters, but only in part; for the little words (connectives, prepositions, etc.) that have no connection with the subject matter have changed too. How can one account for so radical a change?

First of all, Paul's vocabulary changes considerably within the range of his undoubtedly genuine letters too, though not as radically as in the case of the Pastoral Letters. Secondly, part of the change may be accounted for by the fact that Paul quotes or paraphrases "sure sayings" of the early church more freely here than anywhere else in his writings. Thirdly, it must be remembered that Paul probably spoke and wrote Greek as a second language, which he picked up largely by ear. His language would change more readily than that of a born Greek under changing conditions and surroundings. Thus his long stay in Rome would tend to make his Greek more like that spoken in Rome. And as a matter of fact the new words in the Pastoral Letters are found in much greater frequency in those early church fathers who are connected with Rome than in non-Roman writings. All in all, there is no conclusive evidence to overthrow the early and practically unanimous testimony of the church that the Pastoral Letters are Paul's.

CHAPTER VIII: "They devoted themselves to the apostles' teaching": The First Three Gospels and the Book of Acts

READINGS: MATTHEW, MARK, LUKE, and ACTS

The Character of the Written Gospels

Paul refers to himself in the Pastoral Letters as "preacher and apostle and *teacher*" (2 Tim. 1:11; cf. 1 Tim. 2:7); and it is the teaching aspect of his apostolate that these letters show us most clearly and fully. There is in them a strong and persistent emphasis on teaching, teaching formulated, defended, applied to life, teaching to be preserved and handed on to faithful men for the enduring health of the church (cf., e. g., 1 Tim. 1:11; 4:6; 6:3; 6:11-14; 2 Tim. 1:13; 3:10; 4:3; Titus 1:9; 2:10). But the teaching apostle is not essentially different from the herald (preaching) apostle; the trainer of the church remains what the founder of the church is, namely, "set apart for the Gospel of God." (Rom. 1:1)

The content of the teaching which is to motivate and mold the conduct of those who have in repentance and faith obeyed the initial Gospel call is not essentially different from the content of the missionary Gospel which proclaimed Jesus as Christ and Lord and summoned men to repentance and faith and to the baptism which incorporates them in the new people of God. Here as there, in the teaching as in the *kerygma,* "the truth is in Jesus" (Eph. 4:21). The worship life of the church is controlled by the basic fact of the Gospel: The church prays for all men because Christ Jesus died for all men (1 Tim. 2:1-5). Timothy's conduct in the church of the living God has its norm and standard in the truth which the church has, proclaims, and defends, the fact of the incarnation of the Son of God (1 Tim. 3:15, 16). The line between the true teacher and the heretic is determined by the fact that his words agree or do not agree "with the sound words of our Lord Jesus Christ" (1 Tim. 6:3). The honesty and fidelity of the Christian slave has its source in the fact that the transforming and training grace of God has appeared to *all* men, that our "great God and Savior Jesus Christ" has died in order "to purify for Himself a people . . . who are zealous for good deeds" (Titus 2:9-14). The act of teaching is anything but a merely intellectual one and is far removed from the secular idea of developing a potential which is in man and needs only to be called into active play. Teaching in the New Testament sense is the shaping of the whole man, including his will and especially his will; and this shaping is done, not by human persuasion using the tools of human wisdom but by divine revelation; the content of the teaching is simply the Gospel revelation, with all that serves and supports that revelation (the Old Testament, both Law and Promise); it is the Gospel as a formative and disciplinary power, "the word of God . . . *at work in you believers.*" (1 Thess. 2:13)

Our written Gospels, too, belong under this heading of apostolic "teaching." They are the written result, the precipitate in writing, of that "apostles' teaching" which Luke speaks of (Acts 2:42) as the first and basic formative element in the life of the first church. The Gospels are not primarily the apostolic *kerygma,* as we see it reflected in the sermons of Peter in the Book of Acts or see it summarized in Pauline passages like 1 Cor. 15:1-8, proclamations of the basic facts which summon men to the obedience of faith; they are the expansions of that *kerygma,* the apostolic teaching which builds up the church already called into being by the *kerygma.*

They are rightly called Gospels, Good News (and not "teaching"), nevertheless. For they, of course, include all that the *kerygma* includes: the sending of the Messiah by God in fulfillment of His promises, the Messiah's ministry to men, culminating in His death for the sins of men, His resurrection and His exaltation and the promise of His return. They have the same basic historical outline, as a comparison between Peter's sermon in the

house of Cornelius (Acts 10:34-43) and the Gospel according to
Mark shows at a glance. Their content is not a biography of
Jesus but the Way of the Messiah from the time that John the
Baptist prepared the way before Him to the time when God
raised Him from the dead; and they have the same basic intention, namely to lay bare the redemptive meaning of the Way
of the Messiah.

The goal of the apostolic *kerygma* is, then, that men may
in faith call Jesus "Lord" in all the fullness of meaning which
that word had for the apostles and for the first apostolic church.
The goal of the apostolic "teaching" is that this faith may be in
every sense the *obedience* of faith, that men may (as Jesus Himself put it) both call Him Lord and do what He tells them
(Luke 6:46). The apostolic teaching was from the first, therefore, the natural and necessary extension of the missionary Gospel,
an organic growth of the growing word of the Lord. As our
Gospels show, this teaching took the form of an ever fuller recital
of the words and deeds of Jesus, a filling in of the outlines of
the *kerygma* with the concrete details of what Jesus taught and did.
This teaching thus satisfied the natural desire of the believing and
hoping church to have a distinct and rounded-out picture of Him
who was the object of her faith and hope; but the satisfaction of
the historical interest was not the primary concern of this teaching.
If it had been, one would expect the accounts to be much fuller,
more nearly complete. As it is, the accounts are anything but
complete; John in his old age was able to supplement the first
three Gospels from his own recollections, and even he makes
plain that there is much that remains unwritten (John 20:30;
21:25). Likewise, if the historical interest were primary, we
should expect the accounts to be more detailed; as it is, they
are sparse and terse even in Mark, the most dramatic narrator
of them all, while Matthew cuts away everything that is not
religiously essential. And in all the evangelists much that is invaluable from a historical point of view (the exact sequence
of events, for example) is disregarded. The basic interest of the
teaching is religious; its aim is to confront men with the Christ
(Matt. 1:1; Mark 1:1), to preserve and strengthen men's faith in
Him (John 20:31) and to bring men into a disciple's total obedience to Him (Matt. 28:20).

The Gospels are genuinely historical; they record facts, and their account of Jesus' words and deeds follows a historical sequence which is common to the first three Gospels (ministry in Galilee, a period of wanderings, last days and death and resurrection at Jerusalem). But their interest and intent are not merely historical; they do not aim merely at reconstructing a piece of the past. For them history is the dress in which the Messiah of God is clothed in order that He may be revealed and may enter men's lives as the present and potent Christ. The Gospels reflect both halves of Jesus' last words to His disciples, both the command which looks backward, "Teaching them to observe all that I *have commanded* you," and the promise which marks Him as perpetually present, "Lo, I am with you always." (Matt. 28:20)

The Gospel According to Matthew

The religiously didactic character of the Gospels is very apparent in the Gospel According to Matthew. Within a generally chronological framework which is common to the first three Gospels, the arrangement of the deeds and words of the Christ is topical rather than chronological. The facts are massed and marshaled in impressive and easily remembered units of three, five, and seven. Thus we have in Matthew three major divisions in the genealogy of Jesus with which the Gospel opens (Matt. 1:1-17), three illustrations of hypocrisy and pure piety (Matt. 6:1-18), three parables of planting and growth (Matt. 13:1-32). Jesus' words are presented in five great discourses (chaps. 5—7, 10, 13, 18, 23—25), and within the Sermon on the Mount Matthew records five examples which illustrate the full intention of God's Law (Matt. 5:21-48). Jesus in this Gospel pronounces seven woes upon the scribes and Pharisees (Matt. 23:13-36), and the great parable chapter (Matt. 13) contains just seven parables. This topical arrangement is not absolutely peculiar to Matthew; Mark, for instance, twice gives a grouping of five disputes between Jesus and his Judaic adversaries, once in Galilee (Mark 2:1—3:6) and again in Jerusalem (Mark 11:27—12:44). But it is found in Matthew in a fuller and more highly developed form than in any of the other evangelists.

Another feature which illustrates the didactic character of the first Gospel (again not wholly peculiar to Matthew) is Matthew's use of what one may call the "extreme case" method; that is, Matthew illustrates the bent of Jesus' will by means of words and deeds which indicate the extreme limit to which Jesus went — as we illustrate a man's generosity, for instance, by saying, "He'd give you the shirt off his back." The first discourse of Jesus in Matthew begins with the beatitude upon the "poor"; Jesus promises the Kingdom and all its blessings to the beggar, to the poor in spirit (Matt. 5:3); this removes every limitation from the grace of God and makes it as wide and as deep as the need of man. In Matthew's account of Jesus' miracles the first three miracles are extreme-case miracles, which illustrate the lengths to which the compassion of Jesus will go (Matt. 8:1-15). Jesus heals the leper whom the Law cannot help, but must exclude from the people of God; He helps the Gentile who is outside the pale of God's people; and He restores to health the woman whom Judaism degraded to the rank of a second-rate creature of God. Now men can take the measure of the potent grace of God present and at work in the Christ. And men can measure the greatness of the divine forgiveness which Jesus brings by another extreme case, by the fact that Jesus calls a tax collector (whom the synagog branded as sinner and excluded) to be His disciple and His apostle and His table companion. (Matt. 9:9-13)

How rigorous and all-inclusive Jesus' call to repentance is can again be seen by the extreme case: Jesus calls just the righteous to repentance; more, He imposes the call to repentance upon the men who have become His disciples too (Matt. 18:1-4). When Jesus bids His disciples love their *enemies,* He has removed every limitation from their loving (Matt. 5:44). When He threatens Peter, the disciple who was ready to forgive seven times, with the wrath of the divine King if he will not forgive without limit, the fullness of the fraternal charity which Jesus inspires in His disciples and demands of His disciples is spelled out in unmistakable clarity. How completely Jesus binds the disciple to Himself can be seen in the fact that Jesus makes His own cross (the climax of His life of ministry) the impulse and the standard of the disciple's ministry. (Matt. 10:38; 16:24; 20:25-28)

Still another feature prominent in Matthew's evangelical teaching is the use of contrast. In the genealogy of Jesus, Matthew marks Jesus as son of Abraham and son of David, the crowning issue of Israel's history (Matt. 1:1-17); the immediately following section is in sharp contrast to this: Here it is made plain that God gives to Israel what her history cannot give Israel; the Messiah is not the product of Israel's history, but God's creative intervention in that history of guilt and doom; Jesus is conceived by the Holy Spirit (Matt. 1:18-23). Jesus in the Beatitudes promises to His disciples all the blessings of the kingdom of the heavens, all the glory of the world to come (5:3-9) — and puts them under the yoke of persecution "for righteousness' sake" (5:10-12). The Christ miraculously multiplies the loaves and fishes and sets a table for thousands in the wilderness (15: 32-39) — and yet refuses to show a sign from heaven when the leaders of Judaism demand one (16:1-4). The woman who spent her money lavishly in order to anoint the dying Christ is put in close and sharp contrast with the disciple who betrayed Him for money (26:6-13; 26:14-16). The Messiah who in sovereign grace gives Himself, His body and His blood, to His disciples and goes freely into death to inaugurate the New Covenant is set side by side with the Messiah whose "soul is very sorrowful, even to death" in Gethsemane (26:26-29; 26:36-46). The Son of man who claims a seat upon the very throne of God and proclaims that He will return upon the clouds of heaven (26:64), upon the cross cries out, "My God, My God, why hast Thou forsaken Me?" (27:46). These contrasts are a sort of chiaroscuro in narrative, similar to that process in the pictorial arts which creates its impression not by the clearly drawn line, but by the skillful blocking out of figures and features by means of contrasting areas of light and shade. Thus the Christ is portrayed by portraying the absoluteness of His grace for men and the absoluteness of His claim upon men, by recording both His claim to an absolute communion with God, which strikes His contemporaries as blasphemous, and His full and suffering humanity, which makes Him a stumbling block to His contemporaries. It is the historical Jesus of Nazareth who is being portrayed, but He is in His every word and work portrayed and proclaimed as the Christ the Son of God: He is *the* Son who alone of men gives

God the glory that is due Him, who alone does battle with Satan and overcomes him, who alone gives His life a ransom for many. He is not a sage, so that His significance for men can be told in His words alone; He is not a hero, whose deeds alone can signify what He means in history. He is the Christ, and His whole person, His words and works as a unity, must be recounted if men are to know Him, believe in Him, and have eternal life in His name.

The deep interest in the disciples of Jesus displayed by all the Gospels and the amount of attention devoted to them in all the Gospels are further testimony to their "teaching" character. In all the Gospels Jesus' first Messianic act (after His baptism and temptation) is the calling of disciples; in all of them the story of Jesus' ministry is told in terms of the widening cleavage between Jesus and Israel on the one hand and the deepening communion between Jesus and His disciples on the other. And in all the Gospels the supreme revelation of the Messiah, the appearance of the risen Lord, is vouchsafed to the disciples alone. But Matthew gives us the fullest account of the creation of the disciples, how Jesus called them, how He trained them, how they failed in the face of the cross, and how the risen Lord forgave and restored them. The five discourses of Jesus, which determine the structure of Matthew's Gospel, are all addressed to disciples; and the last word of Jesus in Matthew's record of Him is, "Make disciples" (Matt. 28:19). The thought which is in all the Gospels, that Jesus sought nothing and found nothing in the world except the men whom the Father gave Him, His disciples, comes out with especial force and clarity in Matthew. As God is known by His works, so the Christ becomes known to men by His disciples, by the men whom He called and molded in His own image.

Content of the Gospel According to Matthew

The Gospel is symmetrically constructed, built up around the five great discourses of Jesus, each marked at its conclusion by the recurrent formula, "When Jesus had finished these sayings" (7:28; 11:1; 13:53; 19:1; 26:1). The five discourses are preceded by an introductory section and followed by the culminating conclusion of the death and resurrection of Jesus. Each of the five discourses is introduced by a recital of deeds of Jesus which prepare for the following discourse and are in turn interpreted by the discourse. Thus there are seven major divisions.

I. *Introduction,* 1:1—4:16

Jesus the Messianic Fulfiller

A. The genealogy of Jesus (Jesus the climax of the history of God's people), 1:1-17.

B. The beginnings, seven fulfillments of prophecy: (1) The birth of the Christ — "Emmanuel," 1:18-25; (2) The birth at Bethlehem and the coming of the Magi — "From you shall come a ruler," 2:1-12; (3) The flight to Egypt — "Out of Egypt have I called My Son," 2:13-15; (4) Slaughter of the children at Bethlehem — "Rachel weeping for her children," 2:16-18; (5) The return to Nazareth — "He shall be called a Nazarene," 2:19-23; (6) The ministry of the Baptist, the baptism and the temptation of Jesus — "The voice of one crying in the wilderness: Prepare the way of the Lord," 3:1—4:11; (7) The beginning of Jesus' ministry in Galilee — "The people who sat in darkness have seen a great light," 4:12-16.

II. First Group of Messianic Deeds and Words: The Annunciation of the Kingdom and the Call to Repentance, 4:17—7:29

A. Deeds, 4:17—4:25. The theme of Jesus' proclamation, 4:17; the calling of the first four disciples, 4:18-22; general description of Jesus' Messianic ministry: teaching, preaching, healing, expulsion of demons, 4:23-25.

B. Words, 5:1—7:29. The Sermon on the Mount, the meaning of Jesus' call to repentance: The free grace of the Kingdom and the higher righteousness which that grace makes possible and demands.

III. Second Group of Messianic Deeds and Words, 8:1—11:1: The compassionate Messiah seeks the lost sheep of the house of Israel

A. Deeds, 8:1—9:35. Ten Messianic deeds of power which reveal the authority and the compassion of the Messiah.

The twofold reaction to the Messianic revelation, 9: 33, 34.

B. Words, 9:36—11:1. The compassionate Messiah extends His ministry to the whole twelve tribes of Israel through the twelve apostles, whom He authorizes and instructs to proclaim the Kingdom in word and deed. He prepares them to carry on their gracious work in the face of contradiction and opposition.

IV. Third Group of Messianic Deeds and Words, 11:2—13:53: The contradicted Messiah conceals the Kingdom from those who have rejected it (those who "have not," Matt. 13:12) and further reveals it to those who have accepted it (those who "have," Matt. 13:12)

A. Deeds, 11:2—12:50. The contradicted Christ: John's question from prison, 11:2-6; the fickle and petulant crowds who have rejected both the Baptist and the Son of man, 11:7-19; the impenitent Cities of the Lake, 11:20-24; the Son of God concealed from the wise and prudent, but revealed to babes, 11:25-30; Sabbath controversies, 12:1-14; the unspectacular ministry of the Servant of the Lord, 12:15-21; the Beelzebub controversy, 12:22-37; the demand for a sign and Jesus' judgment upon His contemporaries, 12:38-45; the true family of Jesus, 12:46-50.

B. Words, 13:1-53. Seven parables of the Kingdom as judgment upon unbelief and as deepened revelation to the faithful disciples.

V. Fourth Group of Messianic Deeds and Words, 13:54—19:1. Toward the new Messianic people of God, the church: The Messiah separates His disciples from the mass of old Israel and deepens His communion with His own

A. Deeds, 13:54—17:27: (1) Separation: Jesus withdraws when Nazareth is offended and the king grows suspicious, 13:54—14:13; He separates His disciples from the false tradition of Judaism, 15:1-20; He rejects the demand for a sign and warns His disciples against the leaven of the teaching of Pharisee and Sadducee, 16:1-12. (2) Communion: Jesus provides for those who seek Him (Feeding of the Five Thousand), comes to His own across the waters, gives access to Himself by faith, and continues to help all those who come to Him in their need, 14:14-36. He confounds no faith that trusts in Him (Canaanite woman), heals the afflicted, and provides for those who abide with Him, 15:21-39. He evokes the confession of His disciples and sets them on His way of the cross, 16:13-28; He permits the Three to see Him in the glory of His transfiguration, 17:1-13; He gives His disciples His unlimited promise to faith, 17:14-23, and asserts their freedom from Israel's temple, 17:24-27.

B. Words, 18:1—19:1. The Messiah deepens His communion with His disciples by making their fellowship a fellowship of faith and love, a fellowship in which divine forgiveness holds sway.

VI. Fifth Group of Messianic Deeds and Words, 19:2—26:1. The Messiah gives His disciples a sure and sober hope

A. Deeds, 19:2—22:46. The Messiah orders the relationship of the hoping disciple to the orders of this age: His relationship to marriage, children, property, 19:2 to 20:16. He makes plain why Israel has no hope: Israel contradicts and rejects the Messiah who comes in ministry, 20:17-28, mercy, 20:29-34, and meekness, 21:1-11. Israel's worship is corrupt and therefore doomed, 21:12-22; instead of heeding the voice of the Baptist, 21:23-27, and Jesus' call to repentance, 21:28—22:14, Israel's leaders seek to discredit and entrap Israel's Messiah, the Son of God, 22:15-46.

B. Words, 23:1—26:1. The doom of Israel and the hope of the disciple: Jesus' Messianic indictment of scribe and Pharisee and His lament over doomed Jerusalem, chap. 23; the destruction of the temple, the return of the Christ, and the close of the age; parables of comfort, warning, and encouragement; the Last Judgment, chaps. 24 and 25.

VII. Conclusion, chaps. 26—28. The Passion, death, and resurrection of the Messiah. The risen Lord in the perfection
of His power: the universal commission to the disciples

Author of the First Gospel

Who is the author of this massive and architectonic work?
The book itself does not name its author. The ancient church,
which from the first read and used the first Gospel more assiduously than any other, is unanimous in attributing it to Matthew.
No other claimant to authorship is ever put forward by anyone.
Little is known of Matthew. Matthew, Mark, and Luke all tell
us that he was a tax collector at Capernaum and therefore a member of the outcast class publicly branded by the Jewish community as "sinners." Mark and Luke call him Levi (Mark 2:14;
Luke 5:27), the son of Alphaeus; only the first Gospel calls him
Matthew. It may be that he was originally called Levi and that
Jesus gave him the name Matthew (which signifies "Gift of God"),
just as He named the sons of Zebedee Boanerges and gave Simon
his significant name Peter. Or he may have had two names to
begin with. At any rate, we may assume that "Matthew" was
the name by which he was best known in the Jewish Christian
community and thus became the name attached to the Gospel
attributed to him.

Matthew is not prominent in the New Testament record of
the Twelve Apostles. All three of the early evangelists tell the
story of his call and of the feast which he gave to celebrate this
turning point in his life, and all three record that he was among
the Twelve; but they tell the story of his calling (the only one
recorded after the calling of the first four disciples) not as a part
of the record of a prominent apostle, but as a testimony to the
supreme grace of the Christ, who called into His fellowship and
made His messenger one whom Judaism expelled and degraded
(Matt. 9:9-13; Mark 2:13-17; Luke 5:27-32). As a tax collector,
either under the Roman government or under Herod Antipas at
Capernaum, he would be a man of some education, skilled in
numbers, speaking both Aramaic and Greek, and a man of substance. Early tradition has it that he first preached the Gospel
to his countrymen in Palestine, originally wrote his Gospel in

their tongue, and later went abroad as missionary to other nations. The tradition concerning his later career is relatively late, tends to be fantastic and legendary in character, and often confuses Matthew with Matthias, so that it offers little or no basis for constructing a reliable history of Matthew the evangelist.

Theological Character of the First Gospel

The surest thing we know about Matthew is that Jesus called him as a tax collector. Like Paul, he therefore experienced the call of Jesus under circumstances which marked it most vividly as the absolute divine grace that it was. Matthew no doubt deserved the title which the synagog gave him — he was a "sinner." He had, in becoming a tax collector, turned his back upon the promise and the blessing given to Israel and had expressed his indifference toward the Law; he had turned to a life whose basic note was a self-seeking materialism. Jesus' call therefore meant for him a radical break with a sinful past; repentance was for him a complete 180-degree turn from sin and self to the grace of God which confronted him in Jesus. Matthew's own experience had given him an unusually keen awareness of how completely and hopelessly man's sin can separate him from God and had impressed upon him with unforgettable sharpness the fact that only the grace of the Christ can recall man from that separation into fellowship with God. This gave Matthew a keen perception of two significant features in the words and works of Jesus, features which are consequently prominent in his Gospel.

First, Matthew clearly saw and recorded with emphasis the fact that Jesus' call to repentance is an absolute call, demanding the whole man wholly. His Gospel is marked by a stern and unsparing opposition to any compromise with evil, whether that compromise be a Jewish one or a Christian one. He makes it clear that the call to communion with the Christ is a call to a never-ending struggle against the evil in man which is perpetually threatening that communion. It is no accident that the words of Jesus which impose on the disciple the duty of correcting and winning the sinning brother are peculiar to Matthew and that the necessity of perpetual forgiveness toward the errant brother is reinforced by one of the most powerful of Jesus' parables, again peculiar to Matthew. (Matt. 18:15-35)

Secondly, Matthew saw that the way to obedience can only
be the way of faith, faith which is purely the attitude and action
of the beggar who receives the grace of God. Jesus' call had
taught him: "One there is who is good" (Matt. 19:17). Only
One is good, namely God; and no man dare make his own
goodness count before Him. But God the Good is surely and
wholly good; no man may therefore doubt His goodness and
come to God with a divided heart or serve Him with half a devotion. That was the sin of scribe and Pharisee; and Matthew's
Gospel is therefore the severest indictment of scribe and Pharisee
in the New Testament. But Matthew indicts the scribe and
Pharisee not out of personal animus, but on religious grounds.
He knew the hollowness and falsity of a religion that could and
did degrade the sinner and thus hold him fast in his sin but could
not help him by forgiving him. Scribe and Phraisee had shut up
the Kingdom before him; Jesus had called him into the Kingdom.

If the call of Jesus set Matthew free from all the authorities
that were leading Israel to her doom (chap. 23), it did not separate him from the Old Testament or from the God of Abraham,
Isaac, and Jacob. Jesus made a true Israelite of him: His Gospel
is marked by a rich and constant use of the Old Testament, the
fullest of any of the Gospels. He sees in the Christ the consummation of Israel's history and the fulfilling of Old Testament
prophecy. Of the 29 Old Testament prophecies recorded in the
first Gospel, ten are peculiar to Matthew. And the influence of
the Old Testament is not confined to the direct citation of the
Old Testament. The Old Testament constitutes the ever-present
background and the all-pervasive atmosphere of the Gospel. For
example, the grouping of the words of the Christ in five great
discourses is no doubt intended to recall the five books of the
Law and the five divisions of the Psalter. The Gospel According
to Matthew is fittingly placed at the beginning of our New Testament, for it constitutes the New Testament's most powerful link
with the Old.

The Gospel According to Matthew is the most austere of the
Gospels, stern in its nay to evil, uncompromising in spelling out
the inexorable claim of God's grace upon the disciple, almost
fearfully conscious of how precarious man's hold upon that grace

is, summoning men to a sober and responsible adoration of the Christ. The austerity of the message is reflected in the style; the style is sober, restrained, almost colorless. A monumental quiet seems to brood over the work. The artistry of the Gospel is almost entirely confined to the architectonic symmetry of its structure. It is as if Matthew had said: "We cannot embellish the Christ with words; we cannot make His grace speak more eloquently by making it speak more beautifully. Let the facts be marshaled and built up into a clear and cleanly articulated whole; let the Christ Himself appear and call men as He once called me. Let the church see how this Jesus of Nazareth once confiscated men by His gracious call. Let the church hear the call of the Christ as I once heard it and let our human words be but the colorless and transparent vehicle of that call, and the church will remain the church of the Christ." The Gospel According to Luke has been called the most beautiful book in the world; the Gospel According to Matthew has been termed the most powerful book ever written. A comparison of the parable of the Prodigal Son, peculiar to Luke (Luke 15:11-32), and the parable of the Merciless Servant, peculiar to Matthew (Matt. 18:23-35), serves to confirm both judgments. The parable peculiar to Luke portrays God's saving act in a warm and moving way, as the act of a father who welcomes home the errant son, and concludes with an appeal to the righteous elder brother to give his glad assent to this free forgiveness of the father. The chief emphasis is on the gratuity of the grace which has appeared in Jesus Christ, a grace offensive to the Pharisee. The parable peculiar to Matthew records God's saving act as the sovereign grace of the king who restores his indebted servant to life and freedom, and the parable is told in order to impress upon the disciple what this freedom means for him: God has set him free for his fellow man, in order to forgive as freely and fully as he has been forgiven. The holy obligation which the grace of God imposes, the holy fear in which forgiven man must live by the divine word of forgiveness in his relation to his fellow man, that is the chief emphasis here. Without the peculiar emphasis of Matthew in the Gospel, the church is always in peril of becoming careless and callous, is in danger of ceasing to be church. It is no wonder that the Gospel which was first written for Jewish Christians and is the most Judaic of them all became also the prime Gospel of the Greeks.

Time and Place of Writing

The early church generally deemed the Gospel According to Matthew the earliest of the Gospels; somewhere between A. D. 50 and 60 is a probable date. The book itself offers no certain data for determining the time of writing.

If the tradition that the Gospel was originally written in Aramaic is correct, Palestine is, of course, the obvious and natural place of writing. Even a Greek Gospel would not be an impossibility, historically, on Palestinian soil. We can trace the use of the Greek Matthew first at Antioch on the Orontes, which early became a great Christian center and grew in importance after the fall of Jerusalem. But whether the Gospel was first translated there or not, cannot really be determined.

Canonicity: Homologoumenon

Authenticity: The authenticity of Matthew was unquestioned until modern times. See below, under Synoptic Problem.

THE GOSPEL ACCORDING TO MARK

The "Teaching" Character of Mark's Gospel

The second Gospel begins with the words, "The beginning of the Gospel of Jesus Christ, the Son of God." This is too comprehensive and solemn a phrase to be the title of the opening section only, as some have thought, the part which deals with John the Baptist and Jesus' baptism and His temptation, the preparation for Jesus' Messianic ministry. It is designed to be the title to the whole work, and it is a significant one. Mark's book aims to set before the readers the record of the beginning and origin of that Good News which they knew and believed, that powerful and saving word of God which the Son of God first proclaimed in word and deed (1:14, 15), a word which was still the voice of Christ when proclaimed to men by human apostles and evangelists. Mark is answering the question of converts who, once they had heard the basic *kerygma,* naturally and rightly asked, "How did this great Good News that has revolutionized our lives begin? What is its history? Tell us more of the strong Son of God who loved us and gave Himself for us. Recount for us His words and works, which will make clear His will for us who have become His own." Mark is doing what Luke did when he wrote "an orderly account" for Theophilus, in order that he might know the truth concerning *the things of which he had been informed* (Luke 1:3, 4). Mark's book is "teaching" in the sense defined above; it is the filling in of the outline of the *kerygma* for Christian readers. This is confirmed by many details in the book itself; for instance, the noun "Gospel" occurs seven times in this Gospel, while it occurs only four times in Matthew's much longer work and not at all in Luke and John. And it is in Mark's Gospel that Jesus identifies "Gospel" so closely with His own person that the two are practically one entity, as when He says, "Whoever loses his life for My sake *and the Gospel's* will save it." (Mark 8:35; cf. 10:29)

The earliest tradition of the church confirms this view of the Gospel as "teaching." Papias, bishop of Hierapolis, writing about A. D. 130 and citing as his authority the "Elder John" (perhaps John the Apostle, certainly a man close to the apostolic age), writes concerning the second Gospel: "Mark, having become Peter's interpreter, wrote down accurately, though not in order, as many as he remembered of the things said or done by the Lord. For he neither had heard the Lord nor followed Him, but at a later time, as I said, [he followed] Peter, *who delivered his instructions* according to the needs [of the occasion]. . . ." Other early notices locate this preaching of Peter's and Mark's recording of it in Italy, more specifically in Rome. An early prolog to the Gospel (one of the so-called Anti-Marcionite prologs) says that Mark wrote his record of Peter's preaching "in the regions of Italy," and Clement of Alexandria reports an early tradition that Mark wrote his Gospel in Rome at the request of those who had heard Peter preach there. Since Christianity had been established in Italy and Rome long before Peter ever worked there, both these notices are taken most naturally as referring to a *teaching* activity of Peter in Rome rather than to a strictly missionary activity.

Author of the Gospel

Mark (referred to in the New Testament also as John and as John Mark, Acts 13:5, 13; 12:12), was the son of a certain Mary, who owned a house in Jerusalem. At the time of Peter's imprisonment, A. D. 44, Jerusalem Christians assembled there for prayer, and it was thither that Peter turned when he was miraculously released from prison. Peter evidently knew the family, and since he calls Mark his "son" in 1 Peter 5:13, we may assume that Mark was converted by him. A. D. 46 Mark accompanied Paul and Barnabas on the First Missionary Journey as far as Perga in Pamphylia, whence he returned to Jerusalem (Acts 13:13). Barnabas wished to take his cousin Mark along on the Second Missionary Journey also, but Paul objected so violently that the two missionaries parted ways (Acts 15:37 ff.). Barnabas took Mark with him to Cyprus. Mark was with Paul again during the first Roman imprisonment, according to Philemon 24 (A. D. 59—61) and Paul bespeaks a warm welcome for him on the part of the Christians of Colossae (Col. 4:10 f.). In 1 Peter 5:13 Peter includes greetings from his "son" Mark to the Christians of Asia Minor; apparently he had worked there and was known there. Mark was with Peter in Rome at the time of writing, in the early sixties. A few years later, at the time of Paul's last imprisonment, he was again in Asia Minor. Paul urges Timothy to bring Mark with him when he comes to Rome (2 Tim. 4:11). This is the last New Testament notice of Mark. According to the church historian Eusebius, Mark was the founder of the church at Alexandria in Egypt and its first bishop. He is said to have died a martyr's death there.

Early tradition is unanimous in ascribing the second Gospel to Mark, the interpreter of Peter. There is one bit of evidence in the Gospel itself which also points, although only indirectly, to Mark. Only this Gospel records the incident of the young man who ran away naked at the arrest of Jesus (Mark 14:51, 52). Since no other convincing reason can be found for the inclusion of this detail, many scholars assume that the young man was Mark himself; the evangelist is thus appending his signature, as it were, to the Gospel. It may even be that the house of Mark's mother, Mary, was the house in whose upper room our Lord celebrated the Passover with His disciples on the night in which He was betrayed.

Place and Date of Writing

The style and character of the Gospel itself, which make it probable that the book was written for Gentile readers, confirm the tradition that Mark wrote his Gospel in Rome. The Gospel is therefore to be dated in the sixties of the first century, since Peter did not reach Rome until his later years. Some of the early witnesses declare that Mark wrote after the death of Peter. This would necessitate a date after A. D. 64. But since the tradition is not unanimous on this point, there can be no absolute certainty on it.

Content of the Gospel According to Mark

Formally, the Gospel According to Mark can be outlined in three major divisions (following the Introduction, which portrays the ministry of the Baptist and the baptism and temptation of Jesus, 1:1-13) according to the place and time of the three stages of Jesus' ministry:

I. 1:14—6:6a, Jesus' Galilean Ministry

II. 6:6b—10:45, The Period of Wandering, Including the Last Journey to Jerusalem

III. 10:46—16:20, The Last Days in Jerusalem

But an outline such as the following, which recognizes that the confession to Jesus as the Christ at Caesarea Philippi is the crisis and the turning point of the account and that the cross and resurrection are its climax (not only its end), will probably serve better as an indication of the teaching intent of the Gospel.

The Good News of Jesus the Christ, the Son of God

I. 1:1—1:45, The Coming of the Christ (the Anointed King of God) Ushers in the Promised Reign of God

A. The Preparation for His Coming, 1:1-13

1. John the Baptist prepares men for His coming by his baptism of repentance for the forgiveness of sins and by his announcement of the coming Mightier One, 1:2-8.

2. Jesus is prepared for His coming, 1:9-13.

a. by submitting to the baptism of John, an act which marks His solidarity with sinful man;

b. by being endowed with the abiding fullness of the Spirit of God;

c. by being hailed from heaven as the Son, the Messiah, and the Suffering Servant of God, cf. Ps. 2:7; Is. 42:1;

d. by resisting the temptation of Satan, the great opponent of the reign of God.

B. His Coming in Might and Mercy, 1:14-45

1. Jesus announces the present coming of the promised kingdom of God and calls men to repentance and faith, bidding men turn to the God who is turning in might and mercy to them, 1:14, 15.

2. Jesus enacts the good news of God's reign by His sovereign call to discipleship, His word of authority, His expulsion of demons, His healing of the sick; in a word, by drawing men into fellowship with Himself and by overcoming the powers that oppose the sole reign of God, 1:16-45.

II. 2:1—3:6, The Coming of the Christ Provokes the Contradiction of "Religious" Man (that is, man who wants to make his own legal righteousness count before God and therefore resists the free grace of God)

Five Galilean Disputes: the scribes and Pharisees oppose

A. The divine forgiveness pronounced by Jesus, 2:1-12

B. Jesus' free fellowship with repentant sinners, 2:13-17

C. The festive wedding joy which Jesus' coming produces, 2:18-22

D. Jesus' freedom over against the Sabbath prescriptions of the Law, 2:23—3:5. They plot with the Herodians to destroy Jesus, 3:6.

III. 3:7—8:30, The Response of the Contradicted Christ to the Rising Opposition of Religious Man

Three ideas, or motifs, dominate this section of the Gospel;

A. The contradicted Christ *maintains an unbroken will of*

mercy toward all who will accept the gracious reign of God present in His words and works.

1. He continues to free men from the destructive tyranny of demons, 3:11, 12; 5:1-20; He responds to the unuttered petition of a believing woman, 5:25-34; raises the dead, 5:21-24, 35-43; spreads a table for multitudes in the wilderness and invites thousands into His fellowship, 6:32-44; 8:22-26; restores hearing, speech, and sight to the deaf, dumb, and blind, 7:31-37; 8:22-26; heals multitudes of the sick, 3:10; 6:53-56; and gives a Gentile part in the abundant mercies of the God of Israel, 7:24-30.

2. He appoints and sends the Twelve, an appeal to all the twelve tribes of Israel, 3:13-19; 6:6-13, 30, 31.

B. The *cleavage between the Christ and His contradictors* becomes ever sharper and deeper.

1. Jesus withdraws from the multitudes, silences the confessions of demons, and concentrates on His chosen disciples, 3:7-19.

2. The line of demarcation is drawn between the Christ, on the one hand, and His "friends," 3:20, 21, His enemies the scribes, 3:22-30, and even His family, on the other, 3:31-35.

3. Jesus' teaching in parables, 4:1-34, is a judgment upon the unbelief of His fellow countrymen, 4:11, 12; they continue to hear the word which they have rejected, but they hear it for their condemnation.

4. Jesus' fellow townsmen are offended at Him, so that He marvels at their unbelief. No sign is given to overcome their unbelief, 6:1-6.

5. The death of John the Baptist (told out of natural sequence) is prophetic of Jesus' own fate, 6:14-29; cf. 9:12, 13.

6. The charge of the scribes that He is in league with Beelzebub, 3:22, the insistence of scribe and Pharisee upon the tradition of the elders even when it leads to a contradiction to the holy will of God, 7:1-13, the unbelieving demand of the Pharisees for a "sign from heaven,"

8:11-13 — all show what a gulf separates them from the Messiah of God and leads Jesus to remove His disciples absolutely from their influence; they are as much the opponents of the Kingdom as the Herodians who adhere to the king who killed the Baptist, 8:14-21.

7. Jesus separates His disciples from those who praise Him without believing in Him as decisively as He separates them from His outspoken opponents, 8:27-29.

C. The Christ *deepens the communion* between Himself and His chosen disciples, until they, and they alone, are capable of confessing Him as Christ.

1. He appoints the Twelve, 3:13-19, and gives them a share in His Messianic authority and His Messianic task, 6:6-13, 30, 31.

2. He declares His disciples to be His true family, 3:31-35.

3. His teaching in parables, which is a judgment on the people's unbelief, is at the same time for His disciples a deepened revelation of the nature of the kingdom of God, 4:1-12, 33, 34, which equips them for their future task as Jesus' apostles, 4:21-25.

4. He permits them to witness heightened revelations of His might and mercy, 4:35-41; 5:21-43, and comes to them across the waters, 6:45-52.

5. He evokes from them the confession which He had refused from the demons, 3:11, 12, the confession of faith which sets them apart both from His enemies and His unbelieving admirers, the confession: "You are the Christ," 8:27-29.

IV. 8:31—10:31, The Contradicted Christ Puts the Imprint of the Cross upon His Disciples

A. The Christ *predicts His Passion* and brands as selfish and satanic any will, even Peter's, which would oppose His way to the cross, 8:31-33.

B. He makes His way to the *cross the pattern of the disciple's way;* it will be a way which goes through self-denying ministry to glory, 8:34—9:1.

C. The *transfiguration* of the Christ prefigures the glory to which His cross will lead Him, 9:2-8. But the way to that glory is through the depths: The Son of man must suffer and be rejected, as was the Baptist before Him, 9:9-13. He descends from the mount of transfiguration to minister to a doubting and agonized mankind, 9:14-29.

D. He *teaches His disciples,* and the content of His teaching is the cross, His own cross, 9:30-32, and His disciples'; their *greatness lies in unspectacular ministry, ministry to the child,* 9:33-37. It is a greatness which will free them from a narrow-hearted and proud exclusiveness, 9:38-41, a greatness whose mark is heroic self-sacrifice in the avoidance of all that might lead believers into the sin which dooms them to eternal judgment. They shall be men "salted with fire," made an acceptable sacrifice to God by passing through the fires of self-denial, 9:42-50.

E. He teaches His disciples that the *way of the cross* is a way which they must go *within the orders which God has established for this world:* He orders their relationship to marriage, 10:1-12, to children, 10:13-16, and to property, 10:17-31. Marriage is to be the pure communion between the sexes which the Creator ordained. They are to honor children as the prime objects of God's royal care. They are to be aware of the fatal hold which money has on man, but they are to know also that the God who alone is good can of His goodness free them from that hold and will graciously reward their renunciation with eternal life.

V. 10:32—13:37, The Christ Goes to Jerusalem to the Cross

The cross pronounces doom upon the empty and self-centered piety of Jerusalem and gives the disciples, the new Israel, their hope of glory.

A. The *Christ binds His disciples to Himself,* 10:32-52. Jesus predicts His death for the third time. Israel's leaders in Jerusalem will reject Him and deliver Him to the Gentiles for execution, 10:32-34. He is forced to remind His disciples again that participation in His glory comes only by participation in His suffering, that the measure of all greatness is the self-expending greatness of the Son of man who serves to the uttermost in order to redeem the "many," 10:35-45; and He once more sums up His whole serving and saving ministry in one miracle: He opens the eyes of the blind man in order that the new, seeing man may "follow Him on the way," 10:46-52.

B. *The Christ confronts Jerusalem,* the capital and heart of Israel, 11:1—12:37.

1. By His *entry into Jerusalem* He proclaims Himself as the Messiah, but as a Messiah without pomp or power, the Messiah who comes to Jerusalem to die, 11:1-10.

2. By the *cleansing of the temple,* 11:15-18, and the *blasting of the fig tree,* 11:12-14, 20-26, He pronounces judgment on the self-centered and fruitless piety of Israel, and therewith calls Israel to repentance.

3. By *refusing to validate His authority* for the Jewish authorities who have not heeded the Baptist's call to repentance He *again imposes that call to repentance* upon them, 11:27-33. He reinforces this call to repentance with the parable of the Rebellious Tenants; this parable calls (in vain), 12:12, upon Israel's leaders to give God what is God's, to beware of the doom that awaits them if they disobey, and to realize that they cannot prevent the triumph of the Christ and the rise of a new people of God, 12:1-12.

4. By His *answer to the Pharisees and Herodians,* to the Sadducees, and to the scribe, 12:13-34, He again shows what separates Israel's leaders from Israel's Messiah. The Pharisees scruple about paying taxes to Caesar, but will not give God what is God's — Jesus goes to the cross in order that God's grace and righteousness may prevail, 12:13-17; the Sadducees know neither the Scriptures nor the power of God, 12:18-27 — Jesus can go to the cross because the Scriptures point Him to the cross, cf. 9:12, and point Him to the power of the living God who will raise Him on the third day, cf. 12:36; the scribe fumbles with the commandments of God and cannot, for all his searching, be sure of the primal will of God — Jesus goes

to the cross sure of the will of God; He goes with a whole love for God which binds Him in love to man, 12:28-34.

5. By His question concerning the Son of David Jesus makes His Messianic claim an absolute one; He looks above and beyond the throne of David to the throne of God as His rightful place and sees in His descent from David not His greatness, but His humiliation, 12:35-37.

C. Jesus separates His disciples from the scribes, the teachers and guides of Israel, 12:38-44.

1. He warns them against the pride and self-seeking hypocrisy of the scribes, 12:38-40.

2. He points to the widow's offerings as an exemplar of true, selfless piety, 12:41-44.

D. Jesus predicts doom for Jerusalem and ultimate deliverance for His own, 13:1-37.

1. He predicts the fall of the temple, 13:1, 2.

2. He makes all history a "sign" which is to alert His disciples to the coming of the end, 13:3-23: the history of the world, 13:3-8; the history of the church, 13:9-13; the fall of Jerusalem and the great tribulation, 13:14-23.

3. He foretells His return in power and glory to gather His elect from all the earth, 13:24-27.

4. By the parable of the Fig Tree He instills in His disciples the calm patience of genuine hope, 13:28-31; by the parable of the Returning Master of the House He makes of their hope a responsible vigilance, 13:32-37.

VI. 14:1—16:20, The Christ, the Son of God, Suffers, Dies, and Rises Again

A. He goes alone into death

1. His people reject Him, 14:1, 2, 43-46, 53-65; 15:1-15; all men (passers-by, 15:29, 30; chief priests and scribes, 15:31, 32; and those crucified with Him, 15:32) mock the condemned and dying King of Israel.

2. His disciples all fail Him. Judas betrays Him, 14:10, 11, 43-50; the Three cannot watch one hour with Him, 14:

32-42; all flee at His arrest, 14:26-31, 43-52; Peter denies Him, 14:66-72.

3. Gentile justice abandons Him to His enemies, 15:1-15; Gentile soldiers mock Him, 15:16-20.

4. He is forsaken by God, 15:34.

B. He suffers in full humanity

1. The agony in Gethsemane, 14:32-42.

2. The cry from the cross, 15:34.

C. He endures with divine majesty

1. He unmasks His betrayer, 14:17-21.

2. He gives His dying Self to His disciples, 14:22-25.

3. He sings a hymn (the Passover psalms in praise of God the Deliverer) in the very hour of His arrest, 14:26.

4. He foretells the failure of His disciples, 14:27-31.

5. He rebukes His captors at His arrest, 14:48, 49.

6. He is silent and composed before the Sanhedrin, 14:61, and before Pilate, 15:4, 5.

7. He makes no answer to those who mock Him, 15:16-20, 29-32.

8. He departs in full consciousness, with a loud cry, 15:37.

D. His death is the ransom for many and establishes the New Covenant

1. His death is the ransom for many, cf. 10:45. In utter isolation He drinks the cup of God's judgment upon the sin of mankind, 15:33-39; cf. 10:39 and 14:36.

2. His shed blood inaugurates the New Covenant, 14:23, 24.

E. His resurrection is enacted forgiveness, "the beginning of the Gospel"

1. The risen Christ restores to His fellowship the disciples, who had failed Him, and Peter, who denied Him, 16:7.

2. He sends His disciples out to all the world, to preach the Gospel to all creation for the salvation of all men — "all the world" includes the Israel that had rejected Him and killed Him, 16:15, 20.

Thus the Gospel began; all that the Christ is and signifies

for man is present and at work in the Good News that proclaims Him.

Characteristics of the Gospel According to Mark

The Gospel According to Mark is a Gospel of action. As compared with Matthew, Mark emphasizes the deeds of Jesus. The deeds of Jesus are by no means isolated from His words; the word is Jesus' instrument in His deeds too; He speaks, and it is done. And Mark, besides giving two longer discourses of Jesus (4:1-34; 13:1-37), repeatedly emphasizes the centrality of the word in the ministry of Jesus and the effect of its authority upon men, 1:14, 22, 38 f.; 2:2, 13; 4:1; 6:1-7; 9:7; 10:1; 11:18; cf. also 8:38. But it is chiefly by His works that Jesus is marked as the proclaimer and the bringer of the almighty grace of the kingdom of God, as the Anointed King in whom man can trust, the Son of God in whom man can believe.

The Gospel According to Mark is Peter's Gospel. Papias' statement that Mark "became Peter's interpreter" can be variously interpreted; but his assertion that Mark's Gospel incorporates the preaching of Peter is certainly confirmed by the character of the Gospel itself; it begins with Peter's call (1:16); it reaches its critical point when Peter in the name of the Twelve confesses the Christ (8:29); it closes with a message from the risen Lord to His disciples *and Peter* (16:7). Peter's house is the center of operations at Capernaum (1:29), the followers of Jesus are called "Simon and those who were with him" (1:36), and Mark's use of an indefinite "they" for the disciples is most naturally understood as reproducing Peter's use of "we" (e. g., 1:21; 6:53). The resemblance of the structure of the Gospel to that of Peter's sermon in the house of Cornelius (Acts 10:34-43) points in the same direction.

The many vivid and dramatic touches in the Gospel which mark the account as that of an eyewitness also reflect the preaching of Peter and are quite in keeping with what we know of his warm, vivacious, and volatile nature. The expressions, bearing, gestures, and feelings of Jesus are often noted, as is the effect of His words and deeds on the disciples and the multitudes. The narrative frequently drops into the vivid historical present, and Jesus' words are usually given in direct speech. The occasional reproduction of Jesus' words in Jesus' own tongue is probably also an echo of Peter's concrete and vivid narrative. (E. g., 5:41; 7:34)

The ancient tradition that Mark wrote his Gospel for Gentiles, specifically at the request of Roman Christians, is confirmed by the Gospel itself. Hebrew and Aramaic expressions are elucidated (3:17; 5:41; 7:11; 15:22), and Jewish customs are explained (7:2-4; 15:42). The evangelist himself quotes the Old Testament explicitly but once (1:2), although his narrative shows by allusion and echo that the narrator is conscious of the Old Testament background of the Gospel story (e. g., 9:2-8, cf. Ex. 24: 12 ff.; 12:1-12, cf. Is. 5:1 ff.). Mark reduces Greek money to terms of Roman currency (12:42) and explains an unfamiliar Greek term by means of a Latin one (15:16, *praetorium*); and Latinisms, that is, the direct taking over of Latin terms into the Greek, are more frequent in Mark's language than in that of the other evangelists.

Canonicity: Homologoumenon

Integrity of the Gospel

The question of integrity concerns only the last twelve verses of the Gospel, as the mode of printing in the Revised Standard Version and other modern versions indicates. Most scholars doubt that these verses were a part of the original text of Mark's Gospel, for two reasons. One is the attestation of these verses in the early manuscripts and church fathers; the other is the content and style of the verses in question.

As for the attestation, we may confine ourselves to the most important facts. The verses were apparently known to the second-century fathers Irenaeus and Justin and seem to have been included in the first Gospel harmony of the church, the *Diatessaron* of Tatian. They are included in some of the early Latin and Syriac translations and in a number of important manuscripts from the fourth century on. But, on the other hand, the verses are omitted from our two most reliable and important manuscripts as well as from some of the early translations. Eusebius, writing in the fourth century, tells us that the "exact" Greek manuscripts known to him closed with 16:8. The fact that another, shorter ending exists in some manuscripts is, of course, also evidence against the originality of 16:9-20; the shorter ending would hardly have found acceptance anywhere if the longer ending had been known.

The content and style of the last twelve verses also make it doubtful whether they were part of the Gospel originally. The narrative of 16:1-8 is not really continued in them. Mary Magdalene is introduced anew (16:9), although she has already been mentioned (16:1); the promised reunion in Galilee (16:7) is not referred to again. Instead there is a listing of appearances of the risen Lord which looks very much like a summary of the appearances recorded in Matthew, Luke, and John. The compressed and colorless style of these verses is in marked contrast to Mark's usually rather broad and vivid narrative, and a number of expressions occur which are not found elsewhere in Mark.

It may be that the Gospel originally ended at 16:8, as some scholars maintain. It is difficult to explain how an original ending, if one existed, could have disappeared so completely as it apparently did. If it was lost or destroyed early, Mark himself could have supplied the loss; if later, how did it happen that it was lost from *all* copies of the Gospel? Still, it is hard to believe that a Gospel with the title "The beginning of the Gospel," did not include a record of the meeting of the risen Lord with His disciples and of His missionary command to them. The ending which the early church supplied to make good the loss of the original ending was probably never intended to pass as the original ending. It was a substitute for the ending, made up from the other Gospels. And it does, with its record of the commissioning of the apostles by the risen Christ, carry out the intentions of the Gospel according to St. Mark.

THE TWO-PART GOSPEL OF LUKE: THE GOSPEL ACCORDING TO LUKE AND THE ACTS OF THE APOSTLES

"Teaching" for Gentiles

The third Gospel is the most outspokenly "teaching" Gospel of them all. This is already obvious from the dedicatory preface (Luke 1:1-4), in which the author promises Theophilus a full and orderly account of things which Theophilus to some extent already knows, in order that he may have reliable information concerning the things which he has been taught. Luke is not proclaiming the Gospel for the first time to Theophilus and his Gentile readers generally; rather, he intends to expand and fill in the already familiar basic outline of the Gospel message with a full account of what Jesus did and taught (cf. Acts 1:1). This is borne out by the fullness and completeness of his narrative; it is likewise confirmed by the fact that Luke extends his narrative in the Acts of the Apostles to include not only what Jesus "began to do and teach," but also the continued activity of the exalted Lord through His messengers by the power of the Spirit. The words of the preface, "accomplished *among us,*" indicate that Luke had this extension of the account in mind from the very beginning; he is, like Mark, going to tell the beginning of the Gospel of Jesus Christ; but he is going to carry on the account of it to include that triumphant progress of the Gospel from Jerusalem to Rome, the center of the world. He is recording that mighty growth of the word of the Lord which he and his readers have come to know as the power of God in their own experience. The Spirit of God guided the mind of Luke to see that a man has not come to know the Christ fully until he has come to know also the church which the exalted Christ by His word and through His messengers creates.

The Gospel According to Luke, with its companion volume, The Acts of the Apostles, is teaching designed for Gentiles. The name Theophilus is best taken as a real name, not merely as a symbolical designation of the Christian reader; the adjective "most excellent" (1:3) would mark him as a man of some standing in society — Paul and Tertullus use the same term in addressing the Roman procurators Felix and Festus (Acts 24:2; 26:25). Luke was following a literary custom of antiquity in dedicating his work to Theophilus. The man to whom the book was dedicated often bore the cost of the publication and the distribution of the book; and this may well have been the case with Theophilus. Since the work follows the contemporary conventions of Greek literature, it would follow that it was designed for Greek readers. And the content of the work confirms this inference.

Author

The ancient church, from the second half of the second century onward, uniformly ascribes the third Gospel and the Acts of the Apostles to Luke, "the beloved physician," Paul's companion on his journeys and his faithful friend in his imprisonment. He was probably a Gentile, for Paul distinguishes him from his Jewish co-workers (Col. 4:10, 11, 14). He joined Paul at Troas during the Second Missionary Journey, as the use of the first person plural in Acts 16:11 indicates, accompanied Paul as far as Philippi on that journey and apparently remained there for the next seven years. He rejoined Paul A. D. 56 when Paul passed through Philippi on his last journey to Jerusalem and was with him continually thereafter. According to 2 Tim. 4:11 he was with Paul in his last imprisonment also.

The evidence of the two books themselves confirms the ancient tradition. The Gospel and Acts have one author: Both are addressed to Theophilus, and they are markedly alike in language and style; they also show structural similarities. Now, the author of Acts in a number of places speaks in the first person plural (the so-called "we" passages, e. g., Acts 16:11-17; 20:5—21:18; 27:1—28:16), thus indicating that he was an eyewitness of the events recorded. Since these "we" passages are in the same style as the rest of the work and fit naturally into the whole narrative, they can hardly be assigned to another author. This marks the author as a companion of Paul. Of all the known companions of Paul, only Titus and Luke come seriously into consideration; the rest are excluded by the content of the narrative itself or made unlikely by their obscurity. If the ancient church were guessing at the author, it might well have picked Titus, who is more prominent than Luke in the letters of Paul. The tradition which assigns the third Gospel and Acts to Luke is therefore in all probability a genuine tradition and is to be trusted.

Scholars have naturally examined the language of Luke to see whether it betrays the physician. The first findings of research in this area greatly exaggerated the medical character of Luke's language. Later investigation has shown that much which had been labeled "medical" was not peculiarly medical at all but part of the common language of cultured men of the day. But if the language of Luke is not sufficiently medical in character to *prove* that he was a physician, it does confirm the ancient tradition in so far as there is nothing in it which makes it unlikely or impossible that the writer was a physician.

Time and Place of Writing

Neither the time nor the place of writing can be fixed with any degree of accuracy. The ancient sources are either silent or vague about the place of writing. As to the time of writing, Irenaeus and the Anti-Marcionite Prologue imply that Luke wrote after the death of Paul. A date in the late sixties is therefore the most probable. This would take due account of the ancient tradition, such as it is, and of the fact that Luke apparently made use of the Gospel According to Mark in composing his own, but did not have access to a collection of Paul's letters. Many scholars date the books considerably later, A. D. 75—80, but the reasons for this later dating are hardly compelling. This later dating is supposed to allow time for the writing of the "many" Gospel narratives to which Luke refers in his preface to the Gospel (Luke 1:1-4). But is there really any reason to assume that these many accounts could not have been written in the 30-odd years between the resurrection and A. D. 65—70? It is said that Jesus' words in Luke 19:43, 44 (His lament over Jerusalem) and in Luke 21:20, 24 concerning the fall of Jerusalem are so precise, compared with the comparable statements in Matthew and Mark, that Luke must have given them a form dictated by the fulfillment of the prediction in A. D. 70. One may doubt whether Luke felt free to deal so freely with the words of Jesus as this argument presupposes; more important, the words of Jesus are in both passages strongly colored by Old Testament language, a characteristic feature of Jesus' predictions in the other evangelists also; they are therefore not conspicuously more specific than is His language in the parallel accounts.

An even later dating period proposed by some scholars (A. D. 95—100) is based on arguments even less tenable: It is alleged that Luke in some passages in Acts (e. g., Acts 5:34-39) is dependent on, or shows acquaintance with, the *Antiquities* of Josephus, published about A. D. 94. The argument is singularly weak, for if Luke did use Josephus, he either read him very carelessly or consciously differed from him.

Content of the Gospel According to Luke

The basic outline of Luke is that of Mark's Gospel. Luke prefaces this Marcan outline with an extensive account of the infancy and youth of both John the Baptist and Jesus, expands the Marcan account by means of two major insertions (Luke 6:20—8:3, between Mark 3:19 and 3:20; and Luke 9:51 to 18:14, between Mark 9:50 and 10:1) and by considerable additional material in the narrative of the Passion and Resurrection. He rather inexplicably omits the material covered by Mark 6:45 to 8:26. The peculiar quality of Luke's highly original work cannot therefore be very well indicated by an outline, which is consequently kept brief here. An appreciation of the individual accent of the third Gospel is best gained (a) by studying the material peculiar to it; and (b) by a study of Luke-Acts as a unified whole.

Preface, 1:1-4

I. Beginnings, 1:5—4:13. Infancy of John the Baptist and of Jesus; the twelve-year-old Jesus in the temple; the ministry of John the Baptist; the baptism of Jesus; genealogy of Jesus, tracing His descent from Adam; the temptation of Jesus

II. Jesus' Ministry in Galilee, 4:14—9:50

III. The Journey from Galilee to Jerusalem, 9:51—19:27. (The so-called Lucan Travel Account, 9:51—18:14, contains material largely peculiar to Luke)

IV. Jesus' Last Days in Jerusalem, 19:28—21:38

V. Jesus' Passion, Death, Resurrection, and Ascension, 22:1 to 24:53

Characteristics of the Gospel According to Luke

Formally, the work of Luke is obviously the most literary and the most thoroughly Greek of the three. The preface, with its formal structure, its conformity to Greek literary custom, its reference to the work of other writers, its claim to painstaking and systematic research as the basis of an ordered and articulated account, plainly bespeaks an acceptance of the work as a piece of Greek literature. The extensive proportions of the two-book work, its long perspective and broad scope, are in keeping with its announced literary intentions. The language and style have a purity and an elegance which set the work apart from the other Gospels. Hebrew and Aramaic words are in general avoided; Latinisms are relatively rare. But the work is in no sense a compromise with Greek thought and spirit, even in style. Especially when the narrative moves on Palestinian soil, as in the Gospel and the first 12 chapters of Acts, the style reflects the Semitically colored language of the Septuagint (the Greek translation of the Old Testament). And the Gospel, for all its fullness, remains a Gospel; it does not become a Greek biography. Likewise, the Acts of the Apostles is sacred history of a unique sort, the history not of heroic men, but of the embattled and triumphant word of the Lord.

The material peculiar to Luke emphasizes the absoluteness and the fullness of the forgiving grace which came into the world in the person of Jesus. Jesus' first Messianic words are "gracious words" (Luke 4:22); they reveal Him as the compassionate Servant of the Lord who brings good news to the poor, sight to the blind, liberty to the oppressed; His coming is the beginning of the great Year of Jubilee, the divinely appointed amnesty for all mankind (Luke 4:16-21). The story of Peter's call makes clear that the summons to discipleship is an act of divine forgiveness (Luke 5:1-11). The story of the sinful woman who anointed Jesus' feet, with its parable of the Two Debtors, shows how Jesus looked upon forgiveness as the source and wellspring of ministering love (Luke 7:36-50). In the parable of the Barren Fig Tree (Luke 13:6-9) Jesus pictures Himself as the intercessor for a people under the judgment of God. In the moving parables of the Prodigal Son and the Pharisee and the Publican the free and gracious forgiveness of God is put in sharp antithesis to the legalistic harshness and pride of Pharisaic piety (Luke 15:11-32; 18:9-14). The motif is continued in the story of Zacchaeus (Luke 19:1-10); one could inscribe over the whole Gospel the Messianic words in which that story culminates: "The Son of man came to seek and to save the lost" (Luke 19:10). It is found in the shadow of the cross — Jesus intercedes for the disciple who will deny Him (Luke 22:31-34) — and upon the cross itself; Jesus opens the gates of paradise to the criminal beside Him (Luke 23:42, 43). And the risen Christ sends out His disciples to preach repentance and forgiveness of sins in His name. (Luke 24:47)

The Christ of the third Gospel is the Seeker of the lost, the Savior of the lowly. His birth is announced to the shepherds, whom good Jews suspected and despised (Luke 2:8-20), and He is branded by the righteous in Israel as one who "receives sinners and eats with them" (Luke 15:2). Of a piece with this picture of Jesus as the compassionate and condescending Savior is the special attention paid to women in this Gospel, for woman was not highly regarded in Judaism or in the ancient world generally. The infancy story is Mary's story, not Joseph's as in Matthew; and Luke dwells more than the other evangelists on Jesus' relationship to women: Mary and Martha (Luke 10:38-42), the widow of Nain (Luke 7:11-17), the sinful woman (Luke 7:36-50), the women on the *via dolorosa* (Luke 23:27-31) — these are peculiar to Luke's account. And two parables dealing with women are peculiar to Luke also: the parable of the Lost Coin Luke 15:8-10) and that of the Importunate Widow (Luke 18:1-8).

The third Gospel emphasizes the universality of Jesus' grace and Saviorhood. The Gospel according to Luke is, to be sure, richly imbued with Old Testament language and thought, and the portions peculiar to Luke are pronouncedly Palestinian in coloring — no other Gospel gives us such sympathetic portraits of the pure Judaic piety which waited for the fulfillment of God's promises as the first chapters of Luke. Yet all that characterizes Jesus' earthly ministry as limited to Israel recedes into the background. Jesus' interpretation of the Law, which occupies so broad a space in Matthew (Matt. 5:17-48) has no counterpart in Luke. Luke does not tell of Jesus' dispute with the scribes and Pharisees concerning the tradition of the elders (Matt. 15:1-20), nor does he tell the story of the Syrophenician Woman with its emphasis on Israel's prior claim to the Gospel (Matt. 15:21-28). His is the universal, missionary outlook; he fits the life of Jesus into world history; the names of Augustus and Tiberius appear only in Luke (Luke 2:1 ff.; 3:1 ff.). His genealogy of Jesus does not stop with Abraham, but goes back to Adam, the father of all mankind (Luke 3:23-38), and thus points up the universal significance of the Christ. Little touches here and there keep this motif of universality before the reader; for example, Luke alone records the fact that soldiers, who would be Gentiles, came to be baptized by John (3:14); no other evangelist shows such an interest in Samaritans as Luke (Luke 9:52 ff.; 17:11 ff.; 10:29 ff.); his Gospel looks forward to the day when Samaria would receive with joy the word of God (Acts 8:8, 14), when Peter would be divinely led to preach the Gospel to a Roman centurion (Acts 10:1-48), to the time when the word of the Lord would grow and prevail mightily until it reached the end of the earth (Acts 1:8).

Perhaps it is because of Luke's emphasis on the completely gratuitous character of the grace of God in Christ, that Fatherly grace which makes man merciful and sets him free for a love that sees in never-ending ministry its obvious task (Luke 17: 7-10), that there is in Luke's Gospel a corresponding emphasis on the radical antithesis between Mammon and the kingdom of God. The evangelist who so completely took the measure of God's transfiguring grace had a keen eye also for those elements of Jesus' teaching which warned against the disfiguring power of wealth. The Magnificat of Mary sings of the God who has filled the hungry with good things and has sent the rich away empty (Luke 1:53). Only Luke records the Baptist's admonition, "He who has two coats, let him share with him who has none" (Luke 3:11). Only Luke records the Woe upon the rich as the counterpart to the Beatitude upon the poor (Luke 6:24). Only Luke tells of Jesus' rebuke to the man who wanted His help in getting his legal rights as heir: "Man, who made me a judge or divider over you?" (Luke 12:14, 15). Only Luke has the parables which speak of the false security of the rich (Luke 12:16-21) and of the wrong and right use of riches (Luke 16:19-31; 16:1-9).

The evangelist who was to write the Gospel of the Holy Spirit (as Acts has aptly been called) naturally emphasizes the activity of the Holy Spirit in the life of the Baptist (Luke 1:15, 17) and in the life and ministry of Jesus (Luke 1:35; 3:22; 4:1, 14, 18; 10:21). The "acceptable year of the Lord" is in Luke's Gospel greeted by a burst of inspired song. Elizabeth, "filled with the Spirit," hails the mother of the Lord (Luke 1:41, 42); Zechariah "was filled with the Holy Spirit and prophesied" over the child of his old age, the forerunner of the Lord (Luke 1: 67-79). The Holy Spirit was upon Simeon (Luke 2:25) and, "inspired by the Spirit" (Luke 2:27), he hailed the Child in his arms as God's salvation in person (Luke 2:29-32). The Messiah's gift will be the baptism with the Spirit (Luke 3:16); His disciples have the promise of the Spirit for their witness to the world (Luke 12:11, 12; 24:49). The Holy Spirit is the heavenly Father's best gift to His own. (Luke 11:13)

Scholars are inclined to see the influence of Paul in these religious emphases of Luke's Gospel; the emphasis on the absoluteness of God's grace in Christ, on the universality of Christ's redeeming work, and on the Spirit as the mark and the power of the new age are certainly central to Paul's proclamation too. The Lucan antithesis between Mammon and the kingdom of God has its counterpart in Paul's antithesis of flesh and Spirit. And since Paul performed his apostolic ministry to the music of prayer and thanksgiving and perpetually admonished his churches to prayer, it may be that Luke's emphasis on prayer owes something to Paul too. He does go beyond the other evangelists in depicting Jesus at prayer (Luke 3:21; 5:16; 6:12; 9:18; 9:28, 29; 22:41 ff.; 23:34, 46) and in recording Jesus' teaching on prayer. Jesus, in Luke's Gospel, illustrates the difference between a false, self-righteous piety and the genuine piety of repentance by recounting the *prayers* of the Pharisee and the tax collector (Luke 18:9-14); and two parables of encouragement to prayer are peculiar to Luke (Luke 11:5-8; 18:1-8).

If Matthew's Gospel is at once the most austere and the most compelling of the Gospels, if Mark's is the most vivid and dramatic recital of the deeds of the Christ, Luke's is the warmest and most winning story of them all. It is Luke who has filled the church with the moving music of the New Testament canticles; it is Luke's Nativity story that has most decisively shaped the church's Christmas celebration. And the church's teaching

has been immeasurably enriched by the warmth and pathos of
such Lucan narratives as those of the widow of Nain, Jesus
weeping over Jerusalem, the look of Jesus that called Peter to
repentance, Jesus' words to the weeping daughters of Jerusalem,
and the story of the walk to Emmaus.

Canonicity: Homologoumenon

THE SECOND HALF OF LUKE'S GOSPEL:
THE ACTS OF THE APOSTLES

Title of the Work

"Acts of the Apostles" can hardly be the title given to the
second part of his work by Luke himself. As an indication of
the content it is inaccurate. Of the apostles only Peter and Paul
are really leading figures. John appears a few times in the early
chapters and then disappears forever; James the son of Zebedee
appears only as a martyr, with one short sentence devoted to his
execution. On the other hand, men who are not apostles play
a considerable role in the narrative: Stephen, Philip, Barnabas,
Silas, Agabus. Furthermore, if the title were to be understood
in the sense suggested by similar works current in antiquity, such
as *The Acts of Alexander* by Callisthenes or *The Acts of Hannibal*
by Sosylus, it could actually be misleading. It would suggest
a narrative of human heroism and human achievement. Of course,
the very term "apostle," as defined by Jesus and as used by the
apostles themselves, should have excluded that idea, for the apostle
is by definition nothing of himself and everything by virtue of the
commission given him by his Lord. But would Luke have selected
a title which even suggested the idea of human greatness? His
book tells the story of men only because, and in so far as, men
are instrumental in the growth and triumph of the word of the
Lord. The Book of Acts is to be thought of as the rectilinear
continuation of Luke's Gospel, with the exalted Christ as its solely
dominant figure. (Acts 1:1)

Content of the Acts of the Apostles

Luke has himself outlined the structure of his work by in-
serting summarizing statements at six points in it (Acts 6:7; 9:31;
12:24; 16:5; 19:20; 28:31). Each of the units thus indicated

marks a step in the progress of the word of the Lord on its way from Jerusalem to Rome. It is probably not accidental that the first five of these summarizing statements alternate in stressing the word (6:7; 12:24; 19:20) and the church (9:31; 16:5), while the last one (28:31) gives the content (kingdom of God; Lordship of Jesus) which makes the word a creative power that has built and shall build the church. Where the word is spoken, even though it be by "defeated" men in prison, there God the King, revealed in Jesus the Lord, is gathering the new people of God, the church.

The Word of the Lord Grew

I. 6:1—6:7, The Word of the Lord in Jerusalem

The Spirit-filled apostolic word creates and sustains in Jerusalem a church which overcomes internal tensions and triumphs and grows despite opposition from without.

Summarizing statement: "And the word of the Lord increased; and the number of the disciples multiplied greatly in Jerusalem, and a great many of the priests were obedient to the faith," 6:7.

II. 6:8—9:31, The Word of the Lord Triumphs Over Persecution

The word goes to Samaria, and the persecutor Saul becomes the Lord's chosen instrument.

Summarizing statement: "So the church throughout all Judea and Galilee and Samaria had peace and was built up; and walking in the fear of the Lord and in the comfort of the Holy Spirit it was multiplied," 9:31.

III. 9:32—12:24, The Word of the Lord Becomes a Light to the Gentiles, cf. Acts 26:23.

Peter, mighty in deed and word, preaches the Gospel to the Roman centurion. The word goes to Antioch in Syria and creates a predominantly Gentile church there (Barnabas and Saul). Peter is rescued "from the hand of Herod and from all that the Jewish people were expecting"; he is preserved to promote the growth of the word by championing

Gentile freedom from the Law, Acts 15:7-11, while the persecuting king is destroyed.

Summarizing statement: "But the word of God grew and multiplied," 12:24.

IV. 12:25—16:5, The Word of the Lord Unites Jew and Gentile in One, Free Church

Paul's First Missionary Journey; the Judaistic controversy and its resolution at the Jerusalem Council.

Summarizing statement: "So the churches were strengthened in the faith, and they increased in numbers daily," 16:5.

V. 16:6—19:20, The Word of the Lord Goes in Conflict and Triumph to Macedonia, Achaia, and Asia

The Second and Third Missionary Journeys of Paul.

Summarizing statement: "So the word of the Lord grew and prevailed mightily," 19:20.

VI. 19:21—28:31, The Power of the Word of the Lord Is Made Perfect in Weakness

Paul the prisoner witnesses before "rulers and authorities," Luke 12:11, and brings his Gospel to Rome.

Summarizing statement: "Preaching the kingdom of God and teaching about the Lord Jesus Christ quite openly and unhindered," 28:31.

Purpose of Acts

It may be, as some scholars have supposed, that Acts has an apologetic purpose: to make plain to the Roman world that Christianity is no treasonable, subversive movement but is innocent of any politically dangerous intent; its preachers may be "turning the world upside down" (Acts 17:6), but not in any sense that threatens the stability of the empire. It has often been pointed out that Luke repeatedly notes the fact that Roman officials find Christianity politically innocuous (e. g., Acts 18: 14, 15; 23:29; 25:18, 19; 26:32). But that purpose is at most a secondary one. The prime intent of the work is religious. It portrays the impact of the risen and exalted Christ upon the wide world. The Christ confronts men in the inspired word of the messengers whom He Himself has chosen. He confronts all sorts and conditions of men, Jews, Samaritans, Greeks, Romans, the high and the lowly, the king and the cripple, suave metropolitan philosophers and superstitious, excitable louts of the hinterland; and He confronts them all with the gracious claim of His saving Lordship. Whether the response be the joyous and absolute submission of faith or the embittered resistance of unbelief or the polite mockery of skepticism, He looms divinely large as the Lord before whom the ways of men divide, as the Christ who is gathering the new people of God from among all the nations of the earth.

The book does not pretend to be a history of the first church or even a history of early missions; it would be woefully incomplete as either of the two. It is the continuation of the story of the Christ, and can therefore be as selective in recording the facts of history as the Gospel itself. Of all the ways which the Gospel went, Luke selects just one, the high road to Rome. And even that segment of the total history of missions is not fully portrayed but is leanly and monumentally sketched. There are, for instance, large gaps in the record of the career of Paul; both his two years' ministry at Corinth and his three years' ministry at Ephesus are merely illustrated by means of typical incidents rather than chronicled. Indeed, the whole work illustrates rather than chronicles the course of the word which proclaims and presents the Christ. Luke selects incidents and actions that illumine and bring out in clear outline the impact of that word upon men, the tensions and conflicts which ensue when the word of the Lord is heard, and the triumphant progress of that word despite tensions and conflicts.

If we understand the book thus on its own terms, the ending no longer appears strange or weak. Many have found the ending puzzling and inadequate: Why is the outcome of Paul's trial not told? Either his release or his martyrdom would seem to constitute a more fitting conclusion to the work than the one Luke has seen fit to give it. Some scholars have suggested that Luke perhaps intended to add a third volume to his work, one which would round out and conclude the story by recounting Paul's release, his voyage to Spain, and his martyr's death. But there is no real indication that Luke intended such a continuation of his book; neither is the suggestion very plausible that Luke did not record the outcome of Paul's trial because that outcome was martyrdom and he did not wish to conclude his account of the victorious Gospel on a sad and negative note. To judge from Luke's account of the martyrdom of Stephen (Acts 7:54-60) and from Paul's own attitude toward martyrdom as recorded by Luke (Acts 20:24; 21:13), neither Luke nor Paul looked on martyrdom as something negative and depressing.

The fact is that the present ending makes sense, both as the conclusion of Acts and as the conclusion of the two-part work. It is not merely the end but the conclusion of Acts; the goal pointed to in Acts 1:8 has been reached: The Gospel is being proclaimed in Rome, the capital of the world; it has stepped through the door which opens into all the world. That is *the* fact, the fact that counts; before it any man's fate, even Paul's fate, pales into insignificance. And the present ending is a meaningful conclusion to the whole work also. When Jesus "began to do and to teach" in His own city Nazareth, He offered His people God's free forgiveness on the basis of a word from Isaiah (Luke 4: 18-21). He had met with objection and resistance from His own people even then (Luke 4:22, 23, 28-30). And He had hinted even then that the word which they were rejecting would go to the Gentiles (Luke 4:24-27). Jesus' prediction is now being fulfilled; the Jews of Rome are following the course set by the Jews of Galilee and Jerusalem and the cities of Asia and Macedonia and Achaia. They are rejecting the proffered Good News of God. The prophet Isaiah is heard once more, this time uttering words of fearful judgment upon a people who will not hear (Acts 28:25-27). But God's purposes are being worked out nevertheless: "This salvation of God has been sent to the Gentiles; they will listen." (Acts 28:28)

Sources of the Book of Acts

What sources has the author of Acts used for his history? This question has been assiduously investigated by scholars, especially by those who are convinced that Luke is not the author of the work. But since conjecture plays so large a role in this kind of investigation, it is not surprising that no satisfactory or generally accepted answer has as yet been given to the question. If Luke is the author, as the ancient tradition asserts, he of course himself witnessed a large portion of the events recorded in the latter half of the work. And as a companion of Paul he had access to firsthand information from Paul and his co-workers (e. g., Silas and Timothy). And since he was with Paul in Jerusalem and during Paul's two-year imprisonment in Caesarea, he had abundant opportunity for obtaining information on the early church in Palestine from the apostles and men like Philip, Agabus, the "early disciple" Mnason, James the brother of our Lord, and the Jerusalem elders. He may, of course, have also utilized written sources, both Aramaic and Greek, but as to their nature and extent we can only guess. It is generally agreed that he did not utilize the letters of Paul — a fact which makes the remarkable agreement between Acts and the historical notices in the Pauline letters all the more remarkable.

Authenticity of Acts and Its Historical Accuracy

The historical accuracy of Acts has been seriously questioned by critical scholarship in modern times, for the following reasons: (a) The ancient tradition concerning Lucan authorship is heavily discounted. Only the "we" sections, at most, are attributed to some eyewitness and companion of Paul, probably, but not necessarily, Luke. This material, it is said, has been utilized by a writer of much later date. (b) The aim of the work, it is said, is obviously not primarily to convey historical information; since its purpose is edification (or apologetics), one cannot expect of it historical accuracy. For example, it is argued that the parallelism between the accounts of Peter (Acts 1—12) and Paul (Acts 13 to 28) is too complete and too pat to be convincing as history. (c) The account of Acts concerning Paul cannot, it is alleged, be squared with what the letters of Paul tell us of his life. (d) Most important of all, it is argued that no one who had really known Paul could have portrayed him as he is portrayed in Acts; for example, it is thought to be inconceivable that the man who wrote the Letter to the Galatians would make it a point to preach first to the Jews wherever he went or would so completely and unabashedly associate himself with Judaism as he does in Acts

21:23-26 or would call himself a Pharisee (Acts 23:6). The author of Acts has, so the argument runs, distorted the picture in order to give the impression that the development within the first church was more peaceful and harmonious than it in reality was. It is likewise maintained that Paul in Acts 17:22-31 makes concessions to pagan thought which cannot be paralleled in his letters.

To these arguments the answer is: (a) It is a good principle in historical study that a tradition stands until valid reasons have been given for rejecting it. Can any really valid reason be advanced for skepticism regarding the tradition of the Lucan authorship of Acts in the early church? (b) Acts is obviously written for the edification of the church; its preface already indicates that. But the argument that a book designed for edification is for that very reason not trustworthy as a record of facts rests on a false conception of what constitutes "edification." The New Testament itself is emphatic on the point that the apostles built and edified the church, not with myths and dreams and fancies but with the facts of God's wonderful works; the Gospels by their very title (Good News) assert that they want to be taken seriously as history; and Paul stakes the whole case for his apostolate, the apostolic message, and the church on the factuality of the Resurrection (1 Cor. 15:1-19). As for Luke, it should be remembered that Luke 1:1-4, with its claim to historical accuracy based on careful research and recourse to primary sources, is the preface to the whole two-volume work, which the secondary preface of Acts 1:1 is designed to recall. A feature like the parallelism between the lives of Peter and Paul does not, therefore, call into question the accuracy of the report concerning them. The parallelism was no doubt designed by the author and designed for edifying purposes; but that does not prove that he falsified the facts in order to produce it. A man may point out that Handel and Bach, both musicians, were born in the same year, were both treated by the same eye doctor, and both went blind without falsifying history. Moreover, the accuracy of Luke's account in many details has been strikingly confirmed by historical and archeological investigation. Luke, for instance, gets the titles of Roman officials right — and they varied not only from place to place, but also from time to time in the same place. And what is even more difficult for a noncontemporary, he accurately reproduces the atmosphere of the various places which are the scenes of events recorded by him — the fanatical Jewish nationalistic fervor at the time of a great festival in Jerusalem, the civic self-consciousness of the Philippian "colonists," the intellectual curiosity and rationality of Athens. The details of the narrative of Paul's voyage to Rome and his shipwreck on Malta in chap. 27 have been checked by experts and not found wanting. (c) The most remarkable feature about the relationship between Acts and the letters of Paul is the amount and kind of correspondence between the two. The notices of Paul and Luke frequently dovetail, and in such a manner as to exclude a calculated agreement on the part of Luke. It is only natural and, indeed, inevitable that there should remain unresolved tensions and unanswered questions in this area. The two men write from different points of view, and neither Paul nor Luke is writing a complete biography of Paul, so that we are often left ignorant of facts which might supply the connecting and unifying links between the Lucan and the Pauline notices. (d) If Acts has drawn a false picture of Paul, one that cannot be harmonized with the self-portrait of the letters, that would constitute a most serious indictment of its historical trustworthiness. But one may fairly ask whether those who have found Acts wanting in this respect have made the *whole* self-portrait of Paul's letters the standard for comparison. Have they not forgotten the Paul who spoke of the Gospel as the power of God for salvation "to the Jew first" (Rom. 1:16) when they question Luke's veracity in portraying the Paul who preached first in the synagog? If Paul avoided the synagog, how are we to account for the fact that he in his apostolic ministry received the 39 lashes at the hands of the Jews no less than five times (2 Cor. 11:24)? Paul writes, "To the Jews I became as a Jew" (1 Cor. 9:20); was that a theory, or did he put it into practice? And if Paul once calls himself a Pharisee, the situation in which he calls himself one must be borne in mind; he was not thereby saying, and his Pharisaic judges did not understand him to say, that he was returning to Judaism; he was saying with typically Pauline incisiveness that he shared with the Pharisees what he did not share with the Sadducees, the Messianic hope and the hope of the resurrection (Acts 23:6). And as for Paul's alleged concessions to paganism, does his speech on the Areopagus in Acts 17, rightly understood, really go beyond what he says in the first chapter of his Letter to the Romans (Rom. 1:19 ff.)? And is there not a remarkable agreement between his speech on the Areopagus and the description which he himself gives of his missionary preaching in 1 Thess. 1:9, 10?

The historical accuracy of Acts cannot be checked and verified at all points; where it can be checked, the results have been generally favorable to Luke. In many points no verification is possible; the miracles attributed to Peter and to Paul, for instance, lie quite outside the realm of historical verification. And what historical investigation can determine that which is for Luke the controlling fact of history, the fact of the presence and power of the Spirit? These realities can neither be proved nor disproved, and assent to the message which the facts spell out does not depend on the possibility of historical verification. That message is faith's inspired interpretation of the facts, and it appeals to faith; deep calls to deep and speaks a speech for which shallow rationality has no ear.

THE SYNOPTIC PROBLEM

The first three Gospels are called the Synoptic Gospels. The word "synoptic" means "affording, presenting, or taking the same or a common view," and these Gospels are called "synoptic" because they afford a view of the life, death, and resurrection of Jesus which is basically common to all three of them. One can set down the materials of these three evangelists in parallel columns and study them together, whereas the Gospel according to John would not lend itself to such a form of study.

The Synoptic Problem is posed by the fact that the Synoptic Gospels, for all their basic similarity, present a complex set of agreements and differences in detail. The question naturally arises: What is the historical relationship between these three? How is their striking similarity and dissimilarity to be explained? The problem has been under discussion for a century and a half, and a vast literature has grown up around the subject; but it can hardly be said that a really satisfactory solution has as yet been found. It is neither possible nor necessary to go into detail on this complex problem here; a brief indication of the types of solution which command the widest acceptance, together with a critique which indicates the strength and the inadequacies of each, will suffice by way of introduction.

The Two-Source Hypothesis (or, Two-Document Theory)

The chief features of the Two-Source Hypothesis are: (a) Mark is the earliest of the Gospels, and the authors of the first and the third Gospels both used his work as a source in constructing their Gospels. This is based on the observation that Matthew and Luke largely incorporate the subject matter of Mark, the wording of Mark, and Mark's sequence of events. Both follow Mark's basic outline and never depart from it together; where one departs from it, the other preserves it. (b) Matthew and Luke drew on another source for the material which they have in common; this source was a document containing chiefly sayings of Jesus and is for convenience labeled Q (from the German word "Quelle," meaning "source"). (c) The author of this document Q may have been the apostle Matthew. Papias, writing about A. D. 130, reports that "Matthew compiled the *oracles* in the Hebrew language and individuals translated them as they were able." A Greek translation of this document served as source for the first Gospel, and since that Gospel incorporated Matthew's "Oracles" more fully than any other Gospel, it came to be known as Matthew's Gospel. Its actual author or compiler is unknown.

The Four-Source Hypothesis

The Four-Source Hypothesis is an elaboration of the Two-Source Hypothesis and a recognition of the fact that the Two-Source Hypothesis is too simple to account for all the facts. According to this hypothesis the author of the first Gospel utilized another source in addition to Mark and Q, which is labeled M (material peculiar to Matthew). He also made use of material preserved by oral tradition, probably at Antioch. The third Gospel also utilized another document in addition to Mark and Q, which is labeled L (material peculiar to Luke), and an oral tradition which furnished the materials for the first two chapters of the Gospel.

It should in fairness be said that these theories are much more persuasive when presented in detail, with all the acumen and ingenuity which characterize many of the experts in this field, than in the skeleton form given above. But both theories, no matter how fully and ingeniously argued, suffer from basic weaknesses which must be briefly noted here.

Both theories work with the assumption that the Gospel According to Mark was the first to be written. The arguments for the priority of Mark are certainly strong; but they are based wholly on internal evidence, that is, on the nature of the documents themselves. There is no external evidence to support it; that is, no ancient source says that Mark was written first or that the other evangelists made use of Mark. Internal evidence, like circumstantial evidence in law, is a slippery business; and conclusions based on it alone are bound to be somewhat uncertain. One sees something of this uncertainty in the fact that some scholars believe that Matthew and Luke used an earlier form of Mark, not the Mark that we have today, or an early document having the basic outline of Mark, but not identical with our Mark. Still others see in Matthew the earliest Gospel and can support their case with a mass of data that cannot simply be dismissed out of hand, especially since the ancient tradition tends to make Matthew the first Gospel in point of time. Unless new evidence is discovered, there will probably always remain a reasonable doubt concerning the priority of Mark. Q is, of course, purely hypothetical, a sort of "X" used to identify an unknown quantity. One may rightly question whether such a document, consisting exclusively or predominantly of *sayings* of Jesus, ever existed. The apostles and the early apostolic church never thought of Jesus or proclaimed Jesus merely as a teacher; consequently His words were never thought of as a body of teaching which could be divorced from His acts or from His person as the crucified, risen and exalted Christ. Jesus was remembered and proclaimed as the Christ, mighty in word and deed, whose works and words were organically bound up together. In all the sermons in Acts Jesus is *quoted* just once (Acts 20:35) and it is at first glance a surprising fact that in the whole New Testament outside the Gospels Jesus is so seldom quoted directly, although His word and person dominate and permeate the whole. One can collect the sayings of a rabbi and have in them the distillate of his life's work; the words of the Christ are part of the seamless robe of His Christhood and have their true meaning only as part of the texture of that robe. The way in which Matthew has built the discourses into the structure of His Gospel testifies to this, as does the intimate connection between work and word in the Gospel of John (e. g., John 6, the Feeding of the Five Thousand and the discourse on the Bread of Life).

One may also legitimately question the way in which the problem of the authorship of the first Gospel is treated in these theories. The ancient church unanimously attributed the first Gospel to Matthew, the tax collector and apostle. It is hard to find a reason for this attribution in anything but in the fact that Matthew did write the Gospel. The theory that the Gospel was called Matthew's because it incorporated so much material from his supposed collection of the "oracles of the Lord" can hardly stand up; for the ancient church knew that Mark's Gospel incorporated the preaching of Peter and emphasized that fact, but the ancient church did not for that reason call it the Gospel According to Peter. Even if the priority of Mark were established beyond all doubt, and the literary relationship between Matthew and Mark could be explained only by assuming that Matthew used Mark as one of his sources, that would not yet disprove the Matthean authorship of the first Gospel. The apostles were practical, praying, hard-working men, not literary men concerned about their reputation as authors. What would have prevented Matthew from utilizing a document by a nonapostle, a document which, moreover, incorporated the preaching of Peter the apostle?

The more elaborate the theories become, the larger the hypothetical element in them becomes. The Two-Source Hypothesis operates with one unknown quantity, Q; the Four-Source Hypothesis (which is really a six-source hypothesis) operates with five unknowns. Where is the evidence by which these conjectures are to be controlled?

Form Criticism

It was perhaps the sterility of synoptic studies of the type treated above that turned some scholars from the investigation of literary relationships in terms of documents to an investigation of the oral Gospel which preceded written documents and in the last analysis underlies all of them. This type of investigation is known as Form Criticism (German, *Formgeschichte*). Its aim is to penetrate beyond the written Gospels and the documents underlying the written Gospels to the Gospel as it was proclaimed by missionaries, preached by evangelists, and taught by catechists in the church.

Basic to this type of investigation is the perception of the fact that our present Gospels are made up of a series of relatively short, self-contained units of narrative and discourse. These units, it is thought, follow rather definite patterns similar to those in which the traditions of other primitive communities are cast. The task of the form critic is, first, to classify these units according to their characteristic forms. Once he has classified them (e. g., as Pronouncement Stories, Miracle Stories, Myths, Legends, Wisdom Sayings, Parables, etc.), he seeks to recover the original form of the story by stripping the present written account of what he considers to be additions and modifications introduced in the course of oral transmission or by the compilers of the written Gospels. When he has recovered the original form of the unit, he seeks to establish its *Sitz im Leben,* that is, its life situation; in other words, he attempts to answer the question: For what purpose or to meet what need did the first church preserve, shape, modify, or even invent the story or saying? The critic's ultimate aim is to reconstruct the history of the unit from the time of its oral telling, through the time when modifications were imposed upon it in the process of constant retelling, to the time when it was fixed in writing in our present Gospels.

The merits of this relatively new (since 1920) approach are readily seen: It has again called attention to something which, for all its obviousness, has often been lost sight of when the Gospels were studied merely as literary documents, namely to the *preaching* character of the Gospels, their historical connection with the living voice of the proclaiming church. And it has called attention to another pretty obvious feature of the Gospel materials, namely to their practical, church-centered character. Our Gospels are again seen to be books which gather up and perpetuate the "teaching" by which men of the church lived and died.

But when one has recognized these legitimate concerns of the method and has appreciated these legitimate emphases, one has said about all that can positively be said for the method. In practice the emphasis of Form Criticism is all on the Christian community as the creator and bearer of the Gospel tradition; the fact of the apostolate, the fact that Jesus Himself prepared men to be witnesses to Him with divinely given authority and equipped them for their task by His gift of the illumining and empowering Spirit, this fact is largely, if not entirely, ignored. The teaching tradition of the church is treated as if it were completely parallel to the folklore and the myth making of all primitive communities, and classifications derived from non-Palestinian folklore are applied to the Gospel materials without regard for the uncertainty of these classifications and without questioning their applicability to the Gospel materials. Form critics attribute to the "community" a creative power which is really incredible; while the Gospels themselves and the Book of Acts with one voice proclaim that Jesus the Christ created the church, the form critics seem to conclude that the church somehow created the Christ. The net result of their study is the conclusion that the Gospels, which incorporate the tradition of the Christian community, tell us a great deal about the faith of the early Christian community, but very little about Jesus of Nazareth. Not all practitioners of the method are equally radical and negative, of course; but the main current of Form Criticism does set in that direction.

It is scholarly heresy to say so, but one wonders whether the church of God is well served by any of these attempts to penetrate into the substrata of the Gospels which it has pleased God to give to His church. All of the theories must, in view of the paucity of the evidence, remain highly speculative. None of them in the last analysis contributes much to the understanding of the Gospels as we have them. The three Synoptic Gospels loom in large and mysterious grandeur, like three great mountains, before the eyes of the church. The Lord of the church has given us in our generation abundant materials for the study of their geography; He has given us practically none for the study of their geology. Perhaps our main business is geography, not geology; perhaps it is our business to understand the three Gospels, each on its own terms, in their individual and yet consentient witness to Jesus Christ the Son of God, without exercising ourselves overmuch about the unanswerable question of their origins and their historical interrelationships. There will be unanswered questions and unrelieved tensions enough even so; but the big questions, the question of life-and-death import, the question of the Christ, will be answered; and men can learn to live well and die peacefully without having answers to the others.

CHAPTER IX: The First and Second Letters of Peter: "Strengthen your brethren" — The Letter of Jude

READINGS: 1 and 2 PETER; JUDE

It is because the word of the Lord comes from God to man as a pure gift and as creative grace that it lives and grows from man to man. On the night in which He was betrayed Jesus foretold the failure of His disciples. Satan, He said, would sift them like wheat, in the hope and to the intent that they might prove chaff, to be burnt in the unquenchable fire. On that occasion Jesus gave Peter, who was to fail most signally, a special proof of His love: "Simon, Simon," He said, "I have prayed for you that your faith may not fail" (Luke 22:31, 32). That forgiving love of Jesus laid the divine claim of grace upon Peter even then, on the principle that he who is forgiven much shall love much (Luke 7:47). Jesus went on to say, "And when you have turned again, strengthen your brethren" (Luke 22:32). Because he had failed and had been forgiven, because he knew both the fragility of man's resolves and the strength of divine grace, Peter was fitted for his task as the strengthener of his brethren. We find him working as strengthener in his letters, as the strengthener of persecuted brethren (First Letter of Peter) and as the strengthener and warner of brethren whose hold upon the Christian hope is growing weak (Second Letter of Peter).

THE FIRST LETTER OF PETER
Occasion of the First Letter of Peter

The First Letter of Peter is addressed to the Christians of five provinces of Asia Minor. Peter calls them "exiles of the dispersion" (1 Peter 1:1), a term which suggests "the dispersion of the Jews" and might naturally be thought to imply Jewish Christian readers, especially since Peter was primarily the apostle to the circumcised (Gal. 2:7-9). But the letter itself shows that the readers have a Gentile background (e. g., 1 Peter 1:14; 2:9, 10; 4:3, 4); they are therefore "exiles of the dispersion" in a figurative sense, strangers and sojourners on this earth (1 Peter 1:17; 2:11), dispersed in an unbelieving world. There is nothing to indicate that Peter and his readers knew each other personally.

The Christians addressed are undergoing some form of persecution (1 Peter 3:16, 17) and are perhaps being threatened by an even severer form of persecution (1 Peter 4:12-19). They are being slandered, ridiculed, and suspected of disloyalty to the state (1 Peter 4:14, 16; 4:4; cf. 2:13-17); but there is nothing to indicate a full-scale official persecution. We hear nothing of a demand for emperor worship, for instance; nor is there any hint of confiscation of property, imprisonment, or martyr's death. Yet it is a time of severe trial; they are going through a "fiery ordeal" (1 Peter 4:12), perhaps the first great ordeal they have been called upon to endure, since they are finding it "strange" (1 Peter 4:12). And Peter writes to them out of the riches of the grace which he has himself experienced, out of the fullness of the glorious hope which Christ has implanted in him, to encourage them in steadfast endurance in the strength of that grace and for the sake of that hope. He writes to admonish them to a life which befits the great salvation that is in store for them, a life whose moral comeliness is to be in itself a proclamation of that salvation to the world about them. He writes in order to make these afflicted men see once more the full, eternal dimensions of the true grace of God, in order that they may stand fast in it. (1 Peter. 5:12)

Place and Time of Writing: Silvanus' Part in the Letter

Peter sends greetings to his readers from her "who is at Babylon, who is likewise chosen" (1 Peter 5:13). This no doubt refers to a church (the Greek word for church is feminine); and the church referred to is in all probability the church at Rome. Christianity seems to have taken over this name for Rome from late Judaism. Babylon had been branded by Old Testament prophecy as the embodiment of world power at enmity with God and His people. Peter is, in using this name for Rome, reminding his readers that the hostile world which now has power to impose the fiery ordeal upon the scattered and homeless people of God is doomed to destruction under the judgment of God. The letter was thus written at Rome.

The place of writing helps fix the time of writing. There is no reason to doubt that Peter did reach Rome and did die a martyr's death there. But Peter did not reach Rome until the latter years of his life, after Israel had been called to repentance and had been called in vain. Since the persecution to which the letter refers does not seem to be an official one like that under Nero and since Peter can still call for absolute loyalty to the state (1 Peter 2:13-17), a date before the Neronian persecution of A. D. 64 is probable.

As for the circumstances which prompted Peter to write to Gentile churches, some of which had their origin in Paul's missionary labors, one can only guess. A recent commentator on the First Letter of Peter has made a suggestion which is probable and attractive, to the effect that Peter may have written at Paul's suggestion. Paul, about to leave for Spain in A. D. 61 or 62, having heard of the situation of the churches of northern Asia Minor, laid it upon Peter's heart to write to them a circular letter, just as Paul himself had written somewhat earlier to a group of churches in Asia Minor (Letter to the Ephesians). This receives some confirmation from the fact that Silvanus, Paul's long-time companion, had a part in the writing of the letter. Peter's words, "By [or "through"] Silvanus, a faithful brother as I regard him, I have written briefly to you" (1 Peter 5:12), probably indicate that he was more than merely a secretary to Peter. Perhaps he acted as translator; Peter as a Galilean would know

Greek but was doubtless more at home in Aramaic. Or perhaps Silvanus worked more freely, carrying out Peter's general instructions as to content and submitting his work to Peter's supervision, a practice not uncommon in ancient letter writing. Silas as the trusted companion of Paul and a man endowed with the gift of prophecy (Acts 15:32) may have been called into the consultation between Peter and Paul when the letter was planned and was thus acquainted with its purpose and content from the outset.

Content of the First Letter of Peter

"This is the true grace of God; stand fast in it," 1 Peter 5:12.

Salutation, 1:1, 2 with a strong and comforting emphasis on the elective love of God.

I. The Exultation of Hope, 1:1-12. Opening doxology: By God's great mercy Christians have been born anew to a living hope by the resurrection of Jesus Christ from the dead, to a sure and eternal inheritance in Christ, who has brought the salvation which the prophets promised and desired. No suffering can dim this joyous hope or quench their love for Christ or shake their faith in Him.

II. The Ministry of Hope, 1:13—4:6. "Set your hope fully upon the grace that is coming to you at the revelation of Jesus Christ," 1:13.

God's gift of a living hope claims the Christians wholly.

A. It claims them as children, 1:14—2:3

God's gift of a new birth makes them children of God who obey Him, 1:14, whose conduct reflects the holiness of the Father who gave them life by His call, 1:15, 16. They honor their Father in lives of holy fear, for they know the fearful cost of the redemption which a righteous God has provided; it cost the life of the Lamb of God, 1:17-21. Since they owe their new life to the living word of God, their lives express God's will of love which that word reveals: in obedience to that word they love their brethren, 1:22-25, make that word the constant nurture of their lives, and grow in stature as the sons of God, 2:1-3.

B. It claims them as the new people of God, 2:4-10

By being joined to Christ, the living Stone to whom the Scripture points as the rock of salvation for all who believe and the Stone over which unbelief stumbles and falls — by being joined to Him they become living stones in a new and better temple, priests who offer acceptable sacrifices of praise to the God who has called them out of darkness, to be His own special people, a holy nation of kings and priests to serve and glorify Him.

C. It claims them as aliens and exiles in this world, 2:11—4:6

This new position as God's peculiar people sets them apart as aliens and exiles in this world. They are therefore called upon so to live amid an alien and hostile mankind that all slander is silenced and men are led by their good deeds to glorify God, 2:11, 12. This applies to their every social relationship, as subjects to civil authorities, 2:13-17, as servants, especially if servitude involves undeserved suffering after the example of Christ, 2:18-25, as spouses, 3:1-7, as members of a Christian community united in love and humility, 3:8. As inheritors of a blessing, their function in this world is to bless, not to return evil for evil, 3:9-12. Though their task as the blessers of mankind involves them in undeserved suffering, no harm can come to them if they take Christ for their Lord, their Example, and their Savior, and with Him pass through suffering to glory, 3:13—4:6.

III. The Sobriety of Hope, 4:7—5:11. "The end of all things is at hand," 4:7.

The approaching end of all things calls for a sober vigilance in prayer, a life of love and mutual ministry, to the glory of God through Jesus Christ, 4:7-11. It alerts Christians to see in their suffering both a sharing in the suffering of Christ, and therefore a guarantee of their participation in His glory, and also the sign and dawn of the approaching judgment, 4:12-19. It calls for a sober and responsible congregational life: The elders are to exercise their shepherd's office with a pure zeal, conscious of their responsibility to the Chief Shepherd who is about to be manifested. The church is to submit obediently to its elders. All are to be clothed in humility, 5:1-5. It calls upon all to submit to the governance of God and to trust in His care, to be vigilant and firm in resisting the devil, in the assurance that suffering is the normal lot of the people of God and that the God of grace will sustain them, 5:6-11.

Conclusion, 5:12-14: Silvanus' part in the letter. Greetings from the church of Rome and from Mark. The kiss of peace. Benediction.

Peculiar Value of the Letter

The First Letter of Peter is often, and rightly, called the Letter of Hope. Hope in the full Christian sense of a serene and confident dependence on God, hope based on the unshakable certainty of the resurrection of the dead which is begun and guaranteed in the resurrection of Jesus Christ, hope as a mighty energizing power for the whole life of men in the church is certainly a dominant note of the letter. But such convenient catchword summaries are necessarily oversimplifications and can serve to conceal from the student the variety and riches of the letter. These qualities of variety and richness have been noted by many students of the letter. Erasmus called it "an epistle sparse in words, crammed with content." The comprehensiveness of the letter is taken into account by those scholars who have suggested that the section 1:3—4:11 represents a baptismal homily, or address, which laid before the newly converted all that their new life in the church conferred upon them as God's gift and all that it asked of them as the response of faith and hope to that gift. Others have taken the whole letter as a record of an early Christian service of worship, beginning with an address to the newly baptized converts (1:3—4:11) and concluding with an address to the whole church (4:12—5:11). One of the greatest of modern New Testament scholars makes the penetrating comment that the compressed fullness of the letter marks it as the production of a *worker* who knows how to utilize his time; he sees in the "luminous" power of Peter's sentences the hallmark of that composed and settled intellectual strength which results from a life of constant prayer. Luther included the First Letter of Peter in his list of the prime and capital books of the

New Testament. Anyone looking for a key book which will unlock for him the meaning of the whole New Testament would do well to give his days and nights to this letter.

Canonicity: Homologoumenon

Authenticity of the First Letter of Peter

The authenticity of the First Letter of Peter is questioned by some scholars on the grounds that (a) the Greek of the letter is too delicately idiomatic and literary to be the work of a Galilean fisherman like Peter; (b) that the letter borrows from the Letter of James and from Paul to an extent that makes authorship by one of apostolic stature unlikely; (c) that the persecution which the letter has in view is of a kind not possible within the lifetime of Peter, since persecution for the "name" itself (that is, for merely being a Christian) did not take place before the time of Emperor Domitian (A. D. 81—96) or even that of Trajan (A. D. 98—117).

a. We should remember that we really have no way of knowing how much Greek Peter could or did know. Peter's home country, Galilee, was more open to Greek influence than any other part of Palestine. The part which Silvanus, the Roman citizen and the companion of Paul on his mission to the Gentiles, had in the composition of the letter must be reckoned with also.

b. The so-called dependence of Peter's first letter on other New Testament writings can easily be overstated. Not every similarity between New Testament writings is proof that one of the authors drew upon the work of the other. The apostles and other leaders of the first church did not merely read one another's letters in studious seclusion; these men heard and knew one another; they confessed together, worked together, and above all, they had one Lord and possessed one Spirit. Moreover, they lived for and with the church, enriching the life of the church and being enriched by it (cf. Rom. 1:11, 12), so that whatever one apostle gave the church became the property of all. The question of the interrelationship of the apostolic writings cannot be determined by the study of the coincidences of language in the writings alone; the whole historical picture must be considered. Thus considered, the coincidences between Peter and John (who is closely associated with Peter in the Book of Acts) is in many ways as striking as that between Peter and Paul or Peter and James: both Peter and John link the Christ closely with the hope and the predictions of the Old Testament prophets (1 Peter 1: 10-12; John 12:41); both portray Jesus as both Lamb and Shepherd (1 Peter 1:19; 5:4; John 1:29; 10:11); both see the office and duty of apostles and elders as one of tending the sheep of Christ (1 Peter 5:2; John 21:16); both see in the death of Christ the basic norm for Christian conduct (1 Peter 2:21-25; 3:17, 18; 1 John 3:16; 4:9-11); and both describe themselves as "witness" and "elder" (1 Peter 5:1; 1 John 1:1; John 1:14; 19:35; 2 John 1; 3 John 1). One can hardly, therefore, draw long conclusions from a limited number of literary coincidences between the Letter of Peter on the one hand and the Letter of James and the letters of Paul on the other, even if some of these coincidences are very close.

c. As was noted above, the kind of persecution indicated by the letter does not demand a dating later than the lifetime of Peter. Nothing points so definitely to a persecution of the type which occurred under Domitian and Trajan as to demand a dating under one of these Emperors. It should be remembered that from the point of view of the apostle and the church *every* persecution was a persecution for the sake of the "name" of Christ, whatever reason might be put forward by the persecuting power itself.

Positively, there are two features of the letter which speak strongly for authenticity. One is the claim of the writer to be an eyewitness of the sufferings of Christ (1 Peter 5:1), a claim supported by many little touches throughout the letter. The other is the amount and kind of agreement between the letter of Peter and the sermons of Peter as recorded by Luke in the Book of Acts. Neither of these would, of course, *prove* that Peter wrote the letter; but they do indicate that there is no reason to doubt the early, widespread, and clean-cut tradition that Peter wrote the letter.

THE SECOND LETTER OF PETER

Historical Uncertainties

The historical contours of the First Letter of Peter are tolerably distinct; we can answer with considerable assurance most of the questions that historical inquiry raises concerning it. The Second Letter of Peter, however, is wrapped in mystery, and the reconstruction of its historical background is beset at almost every point with perplexing uncertainties. While the place of the first letter in the canon has always been an assured one, the second letter is decidedly an antilegomenon, with the weakest historical attestation of any book in the New Testament. There are some faint indications that the letter was known and used in the second century, but there is no unmistakable evidence that it was known and used in the church before the time of Origen (A. D. 185 to 254), who uses the letter and considers it apostolic, but is aware of the fact that its place in the canon is in dispute. The authenticity of the First Letter of Peter, though questioned by modern critical scholarship, is actually quite solidly established by the external and internal evidence, whereas the authenticity of the second letter was questioned even in the early church and is denied by the great majority of scholars today. The circle of readers for whom the first letter was intended is clearly defined by the letter itself; the address of the second letter is very general: "To those who have obtained a faith of equal standing with ours" (2 Peter 1:1), and leaves the location of the readers uncertain. The words, "This is now the *second letter* that I have written to you, beloved" (2 Peter 3:1) make it likely, but not certain, that its destination is the same as that of the first letter. Concerning the time and place of writing of the second letter, we can only say that it must be dated toward the close of Peter's life and that it was therefore probably written from Rome. We can see what sort of tendencies and difficulties occasioned the second letter, but we cannot fix them as to place and time with any precision.

Content of the Second Letter of Peter

If all else is uncertain, there is no uncertainty about the intent and the message of the letter. Like the First Letter of Peter, it is written in the service of Christian hope. The letter has, to be sure, often been called the Epistle of Knowledge, and "knowledge" is a prominent motif in the letter; but knowledge is not being emphasized and imparted for its own sake, but for the purpose of strengthening the Christian hope and defending it against the

attack of error and to preserve it from the corrosion of doubt
(2 Peter 1:3 with 1:8 and 11; 3:17, 18). If the First Letter of
Peter is designed to keep hope alive and strong in men under the
stress of persecution, the Second Letter of Peter is designed to
maintain hope pure and strong in men whose hope is threatened
by false teaching and is in danger of being weakened by doubt.

The Christian Hope Strengthened and Defended
Salutation, 1:1, 2

I. The Greatness of the Christian Hope, 1:3-11

A. 1:3, 4. The greatness of its gift: the great and precious
promises of God call men into communion with God and
open up to them the eternal kingdom of our Lord and
Savior Jesus Christ.

B. 1:5-11. The greatness of its claim: the possession of this
hope calls for a life of strenuous sanctification.

II. The Certainty of the Christian Hope, 1:12—2:22

A. 1:12-21. The Christian hope is guided and sustained by
the inspired Old Testament prophetic word, now made
more sure by the apostolic witness to the majesty of the
Christ, the fulfillment of that prophecy.

B. 2:1-22. Therefore that hope need not be shaken by the
godless false teachers who shall come, for the church is
forewarned and knows in advance that their condemnation
is sure.

III. The Delayed Fulfillment of the Christian Hope, 3:1-18

A. 3:1-7. The scoffers who say, "Where is the promise of
His coming?" simply ignore the fact that the God who
once judged the world by water can and will judge the
world by fire.

B. 3:8-10. The church is to see in the Lord's delay a missionary command: the delay is the forbearance of the
God who wills the salvation of all men and would have
all men come to repentance.

C. 3:11-18. The church is to see in the Lord's delay a summons to a life of tense and holy expectancy: "According

to His promise we wait for new heavens and a new earth in which righteousness dwells. Therefore, beloved, since you wait for these, be zealous to be found by Him without spot or blemish, and at peace," 3:13, 14.

Authenticity of the Letter: Its Relationship to the Letter of Jude

As noted above, the majority of scholars today regard the Second Letter of Peter as unauthentic; they consider the letter to be a second-century work, written by one who wishes to invoke the authority of Peter to aid him in dealing with the dangers and difficulties confronting the church in his day. The letter, they say, is not a malicious forgery; the use of Peter's name is not designed to deceive anyone. It is merely the author's way of saying, "This is what the apostle Peter would say to our situation if he were still with us today."

This position is supported by a massive array of arguments, and the case is generally conceded to be proved beyond reasonable doubt. And yet there is room for reasonable doubt. There have been similar cases in the history of New Testament scholarship; there was, for instance, a time when practically nobody who was anybody in the world of scholarship cared to defend the authenticity and first-century origin of the Gospel of John, while today further study and new discoveries have put the matter in a different light. The evidence needs to be sifted. The impressive list of arguments against authenticity contains items of varying strength and validity. Some of the arguments are strong, and honest scholarship should not evade the fact that we are confronted by genuine reasons for uncertainty in this matter. There is no denying the fact that the letter is very weakly attested in the ancient church; and it is difficult to see why it should have been less well known and less widely acknowledged than the First Letter of Peter if it is a genuine work of the apostle. Similarly, the argument based on differences between the first and the second letter in vocabulary and style is strong. One may conjecture that the weakness of historical attestation is due to the fact that the second letter was designed for Jewish Christian readers; the gulf between Judaic Christianity and Gentile Christianity widened with the years, and books peculiar to Judaic

Christianity might for that reason remain relatively unknown to the Gentile churches for a considerable period. But this is conjecture, not verifiable fact. Likewise, one may conjecture that the differences in language and style are due not only to the different situation presupposed by the two letters, but also to the fact (as Jerome already suggested) that Peter employed a different helper for the second letter, that the associate "through" whom Peter wrote his second letter was a man different from Silvanus, the secretary "through" whom he wrote the first letter. But again this is conjecture; and we are left with unsolved problems.

Other arguments used to support the thesis that the Second Letter of Peter must be a second-century non-Petrine work are less strong. Arguments on what the letter does not say are of dubious validity; it is argued that the second letter is less profoundly Christ-centered than the first letter, that the second letter is more somber about the approaching end of all things than the first letter. The argument from silence is always dubious; Paul, for instance, is silent on the Lord's Supper in all his letters except the First Letter to the Corinthians, but this neither calls into question the authenticity of the other letters nor does it prove anything concerning the importance which Paul attaches to the Lord's Supper. Similarly, the fact that the second letter quotes and recalls the Old Testament less often than the first letter, does not have much weight, especially when we consider that the second letter contains one of the most powerful statements in the whole New Testament on the authority and the inspiration of Old Testament prophecy (2 Peter 1:19-21). Neither is the alleged fact that the author speaks of Paul's letters as a *collection* known to the church (2 Peter 3:16) sufficient to prove a late date and exclude Peter as the author. The phrase "in all his letters" does not necessarily imply that everyone everywhere in the church knew the collected letters of Paul. And to argue that Peter could not have ranked Paul's letters with "the other Scriptures" (that is, the Old Testament) involves the whole question of apostolic authority. If Paul himself considered the word which he spoke to be no less than the word of God (1 Thess. 2:13), there is no reason why Peter, who gave Paul the right hand of fellowship (Gal. 2:9), should not have placed the same value on it.

The relationship between the Second Letter of Peter and the Letter of Jude is usually considered one of the strong arguments against the authenticity of the Second Letter of Peter. The Letter of Jude and the second chapter of the Second Letter of Peter are so similar in language and thought that there is obviously a historical connection between the two; they can hardly have originated altogether independently of each other. Most scholars today argue that the Second Letter of Peter is the later of the two documents and has incorporated the Letter of Jude. The arguments used to prove the dependence of Peter's second letter on Jude cannot be discussed in detail here. But it should be noted that this theory of borrowing on the part of a second-century writer leaves a good many unanswered questions. For example, if Jude is the earlier document and the Second Letter of Peter the later, why is it that Jude's account of the false teachers is the darker and more sinister of the two? In Jude the false teachers are compared not only to Balaam, but also to Cain and Korah — why should a second-century writer, engaged in so desperate a struggle against such a dangerous heresy that he must invoke the name of Peter in order to combat it, tone down the indictment of Jude? Note also that Jude twice (Jude 4 and 17) refers to an older apostolic writing which predicts the errorists who at Jude's time are present in the church. The Second Letter of Peter answers to that document; it predicts future errorists (2:1, 3) whose coming and working Jude notes as present in his time. It would seem to follow that Jude knew and prized as apostolic a document which must have been very similar to the second chapter of our Second Letter of Peter. If the Second Letter of Peter is not apostolic but later than Jude, the original apostolic document referred to by Jude (Jude 4 and 17) must have been lost early and without leaving a trace.

The greatest difficulty about the theory that the Second Letter of Peter is a forgery is to discover a motive for the forgery. Men who write in the name of others, especially great authorities, have a reason for doing so. In the case of the Second Letter of Peter such a reason is hard to discover. The author is not using an apostle's authority to support a heresy, as is so often the case with early forgeries. He is not indulging in a romantic glorification of an apostle as the *Acts of Paul,* for instance, does. The allusions to Peter's life and experience remain within the limits of what we know of Peter from the Gospels. And there are no anachronisms, that is, the writer imports nothing from his own time and experience into the picture of the apostle.

Another difficulty which is usually overlooked by those who assign the Second Letter of Peter to the second century is the fact that it was just in this period that heretical sects were producing pseudoapostolic works in support of their heresies. The early church had every reason to be cautious and critical about works which claimed to be Peter's; and the church *was* cautious, as the history of the Second Letter of Peter in the canon shows. The fact that this letter did nevertheless impose its authority upon the church under just these circumstances must be given due weight.

The church cannot erase the line between antilegomena and homologoumena. The church cannot rewrite or unwrite history. And the weakness of the historical witness to the Second Letter of Peter and the difficulties posed by its peculiar history and its peculiar character cannot and should not be simply ignored. But a coolly rational balancing of probabilities will never see the whole of the problem and will not find the whole answer. The most important fact about the Second Letter of Peter is in the last analysis the fact that it has in generation after generation "strengthened the brethren" of Peter in a genuinely apostolic way. The church has been strengthened for battle and heartened in its hope by the living words of this letter, words which are as clear and sure as the history of the letter is dark and uncertain. Whatever the historical difficulties attending it, the Second Letter of Peter has had, and has, an undeniable part in that peculiar history which gives meaning to all history, the history of the growing and victoriously prevailing word of the Lord.

THE LETTER OF JUDE

Author of the Letter

The author calls himself simply "Jude, a servant of Jesus Christ and brother of James" (Jude 1); he does not call himself an apostle, and the way in which he speaks of the apostles makes

it clear that he is not one of them (Jude 17). He cannot therefore be identified with the apostle Judas, the son of James (Luke
6:16). "Brother of James" serves to identify him, and there is
really only one James so generally known in early Christendom
as to serve as identification, and that is James the brother of
Jesus, the "pillar" and head of the Jerusalem church (Gal. 1:19;
2:9; cf. 1 Cor. 15:7; James 1:1). Jude is, then, one of the
brothers of Jesus; we find his name listed in Mark 6:3 and Matthew 13:55. Luke refers to these brothers as a group, and he
associates them with the Twelve during the early days in Jerusalem (Acts 1:14). We learn from Paul (1 Cor. 9:5) that these
brothers of Jesus were active in missionary work. Jude, like the
other brothers of Jesus, had not believed in Jesus during the
time of His ministry on earth (John 7:5). Perhaps it was the
example and the witness of his brother James after the resurrection (1 Cor. 15:7) that won him for the faith. Nothing more
is known of him. It is at first glance surprising that he does not
call himself "brother of Jesus" in order to identify himself. But
James, it should be noted, is similarly reticent; he too calls himself
not brother, but "servant" of Jesus (James 1:1). The men of
the first church remembered the word which the Lord had spoken
concerning His disciples: "Whoever does the will of My Father
in heaven is My brother" (Matt. 12:50); they knew that faith
and only faith established the tie which bound a man to Jesus
and made him an obedient son of God.

Occasion and Purpose of the Letter

Jude leaves us in no doubt as to what occasioned his writing.
It was the appearance and the activity of men who answered Paul's
question, "Are we to continue in sin that grace may abound?"
(Rom. 6:1) in a way that was the very opposite of Paul's. These
were men who saw in the freedom which Christ had won for man
not a freedom from sin, but the freedom to sin. Jude calls them
"ungodly persons who pervert the grace of our God into licentiousness and deny our only Master and Lord, Jesus Christ" (4).
There was, moreover, nothing furtive or apologetic in their assertion and proclamation of this liberty; they did so quite openly
and, indeed, arrogantly (4, 8, 13, 16, 18, 19). They had not
broken with the church, but carried on the propaganda for their

views within it — they have "gained admission secretly" (4), are present at the common meals of the church (12), and create divisions within the church (19). The images which Jude uses to describe them indicate that they set themselves up as teachers of the church — they are clouds, from which men might expect water; trees, from which men might expect fruit; stars, from which the sailor expects guidance. (12, 13)

Jude centers his attack on the impiety of these men; he does not honor whatever theological "system" they may have had by describing and refuting it — he is following the guidance of the word of his brother and Lord, Jesus ("You will know them by their fruits," Matt. 7:16), in pointing to the evil fruits of this bad tree. But that they did have a system by which they defended and asserted their vicious liberty is evident not only from the fact that they appear as teachers, but also from other indications in Jude's letter. Jude speaks of their "dreamings" (8); this would indicate a speculative kind of theology, perhaps akin to the emphasis on "knowledge" with which the brilliant and irresponsible misleaders of the Corinthian Church had justified their claim to liberty; their arrogance and their mercenary character (11, 16) would also characterize them as men of similar bent. When Jude calls them "worldly people, devoid of the Spirit" (19), he is ironically using terms which gnostics later used; they, of course, described the simple Christian who had only faith as "worldly" (unspiritual) and themselves, the men of knowledge, as "spiritual."

The very vehemence with which Jude exposes these teachers is indication enough that they were persuasive and impressive men, and therefore a fearful threat to the church. They were all the more fearful a threat because they would not break with the church; Jude therefore insists that the church break with them. He rouses holy fear in his readers; they are called upon to do battle for that which the Lord and His apostles have given them (3) and to avoid all contact and compromise with the false teachers, lest they fall under the judgment of God which once struck a disobedient Israel, doomed the disobedient angels, destroyed Sodom and Gomorrah, and will surely destroy these destroyers of the church of God (5—7, cf. 13—15). Even their attempts to save those brethren who have not yet succumbed completely to the propaganda of the doomed teachers are to be marked by this holy fear: "Save some, by snatching them out of the fire; on some have mercy with fear." (23)

But fear is not Jude's only weapon; he instills also the high confidence of faith. The arrogant, contentious, and mercenary blasphemers are surely doomed (4); judgment awaits them, and they will perish in their pride (11, 14, 15). His readers are forewarned by the apostolic word (17, 18); and, above all, they have their security in the love of God as men "beloved in God the Father and kept for Jesus Christ" (1). And so the letter closes with a doxology filled with the exuberant confidence of hope: "Now to Him who is able to keep you from falling and to present you without blemish before the presence of His glory with rejoicing, to the only God, our Savior through Jesus Christ our Lord, be glory, majesty, dominion, and authority, before all time and now and forever. Amen."

Content of the Letter of Jude

1, 2. *Salutation,* with strong emphasis on the protective love of God.

3, 4. *Purpose of the letter:* An appeal to contend for the faith which is being endangered by the intrusion of men who pervert the grace of God in Christ by making of it a permission to sin.

5-13. *Solemn warning against these false teachers,* who despite the fearful record of God's judgment upon unbelief and disobedience (Israel in the wilderness, the fallen angels, Sodom and Gomorrah) pursue a godless and licentious way which invites the judgment which befell Cain, Balaam, and Korah. They are all the more dangerous because they appear as Christian teachers.

14-23. *The safeguard of the church:* The church is doubly forewarned and forearmed — Enoch has foretold the judgment of God on such boastful and mercenary apostles of licentiousness, and the apostles of the Lord Jesus Christ have warned the church of the coming of these scoffers who follow their ungodly passions. The church's duty is clear: to preserve the church itself in a pure faith and a sure hope and to save (with a courage made sober by holy fear) those entangled in the meshes of falsehood.

24, 25. *Closing doxology,* with a powerful assurance of God's protective and sustaining love.

Time and Place of Writing

We know so little of the life and activity of Jude that any attempt to fix the place of writing or to localize the church or churches addressed is bound to be pure guesswork. As to the date of writing, the way in which Jude refers to the apostles (17) would seem to indicate that they belong to a time that is for him and his readers past; a date around A. D. 70 is not improbable.

Canonicity

The Epistle of Jude is an antilegomenon, but its attestation in the early church is quite strong. According to some ancient authorities, doubts concerning the epistle were occasioned by its use of noncanonical writings such as the Book of Enoch (14, 15) and the *Assumptio Mosis* (9). It may be that such apocalyptic writings were being used by the false teachers and that Jude in quoting these writings is meeting them on their own ground. It is noteworthy that he uses these writings only insofar as they serve to enforce the call to repentance, that is, as warnings against any proud self-assertion of man.

Value of the Letter

When Jesus warned His disciples against false prophets, He gave them only one simple test by which they were to distinguish the false prophets from the true: "You will know them by their fruits" (Matt. 7:16). The test seems almost absurdly simple when one considers the history of error in the church, error in its various, ever new, and plausible disguises. But the little, powerful Letter of Jude is living proof that Jesus' confidence in His followers was not misplaced. Endowed with the Spirit of Jesus, Jude rightly saw and roundly declared that what these men produced was not a fruit of the Spirit; for the Spirit teaches men to call Jesus Lord and to live under His Lordship (1 Cor. 12:3), and neither the brilliance nor the persuasiveness nor the arrogant boldness of these men could conceal from the keen eye of faith the fact that they did in fact deny Him whom they professed as their only Master and Lord, Jesus Christ. Thus the word of the Lord prevailed; and the presence of Jude in the canon is an assurance that it will continue to prevail.

CHAPTER X: "In these last days He has spoken by a Son": The Letter to the Hebrews

READING: HEBREWS

The Letter to the Hebrews is surely a part of the story of how the word of the Lord grew and prevailed. Here if anywhere in the New Testament we are made conscious of the fact that God's speaking is a mighty onward movement, an impetus of revelation which is designed to carry man with it from glory to glory. And here it is impressed upon us that if a man resists that impetus, he does so at his own deadly peril; we are warned that stagnation and retrogression invite the destroying judgment of God. But the letter is itself also the proof that God does not abandon the weak and sickly stragglers of His flock; He sends forth His word and heals them.

Destination of the Letter

The title "To the Hebrews" is not part of the original letter itself, but was probably added in the second century when the New Testament letters were gathered into a collection. Moreover, there is no salutation which would identify the readers. The destination of the letter must therefore be inferred from the letter itself. The letter to the Hebrews is not so personal as a letter of Paul's. It is more on the order of a sermon (cf. Heb. 13:22, "my word of exhortation"), and it is more literary, with its high stylistic finish and its strictly unified theme. Still, it is not merely an essay in letter form, but a genuine letter. It grows out of a personal relationship between the author and his readers. The author has lived among the people whom he is now addressing; and though he is at the time of writing separated from them, he hopes to be restored to them soon (Heb. 13:18, 19, 23). The content of the letter indicates that these readers were Jewish Christians, so that the title given by the men of the second century is not unfitting.

Many modern scholars are inclined to see in the readers not Jewish Christians in danger of relapsing into Judaism, but Gentile Christians (or Christians in general) in danger of lapsing into irreligion. And they have often argued their case with considerable ingenuity. But it is difficult to see why the letter should in that case be from beginning to end one great and emphatic exposition of the superiority of the New Testament revelation over that of the Old Testament. Why should an appeal to *Gentile* Christians in danger of apostasy take just this form? Jewish Christians seem to be more likely as recipients of the letter.

Where these Jewish Christians lived cannot be definitely made out. Italy is the most likely place, and within Italy, Rome. The letter contains greetings to the church from "those who come from Italy" (Heb. 13:24), evidently from members of the Jewish Christian church who are now with the author and are sending greetings to their home church. This is confirmed by the fact the Letter to the Hebrews is first quoted and alluded to by Roman writers, namely Clement of Rome and Hermas. These readers have their own assembly (Heb. 10:25) but are also connected with a larger group, as the words "greet *all* your leaders and *all* the saints" (Heb. 13:24) indicate. It has therefore been very plausibly suggested that the recipients of the Letter to the Hebrews were one of the house churches to which Paul refers in his Letter to the Romans (Rom. 16:5, 14, 15).

Occasion and Purpose of the Letter

These Christians had in the past given evidence of their faith and love (Heb. 6:10). They had stoutly endured persecution themselves and had courageously aided others under persecution (Heb. 10:32-34). Their believing courage had not failed them in times of crisis; but it was failing them in the long-drawn, unending struggle with sin (Heb. 12:4). They were growing dispirited and slack (Heb. 12:12); the continuous pressure of public contempt, particularly the contempt of their fellow Jews (Heb. 13:13), had revived in them the old temptation to be offended at the weakness of the Christ they believed in, at His shameful death, and at the fact that the Christ did not fulfill their Judaic expectation and "remain forever" on earth (cf. John 12:34) but was removed from sight in the heavens. They had ceased to progress in their faith (Heb. 5:11-14) and were neglecting the public assembly of the church which could strengthen them in their faith (Heb. 10:25). Some had perhaps already apostatized (Heb. 6: 4-8); all were in danger of falling away (Heb. 3:12) and reverting to Judaism (Heb. 13:9-14). Judaism, with its fixed and venerable institutions, its visible and splendid center in the Jerusalem temple and its cultus, its security and exemption from persecution as a *religio licita* under Roman law must have had for them an almost overwhelming fascination.

The letter is therefore basically just what its author calls it, a "word of exhortation" (Heb. 13:22), an appeal to "hold fast the confession . . . without wavering" (Heb. 10:23; cf. 10:38; 3:14). The author points his readers to Jesus and urges them to look to Jesus, "the pioneer and perfecter of our faith, who for the joy that was set before Him endured the cross, despising the shame, and is seated at the right hand of the throne of God" (Heb. 12:2). They are to consider Him with the eyes of faith and find in Him the strength to overcome their weariness and faintheartedness (Heb. 12:3). The whole long and detailed exposition of the highpriesthood of Christ is anything but a merely informative theological treatise. It is wholly pastoral and practical in its aim and intent. The author is a leader like the leaders whom he describes in his letter (Heb. 13:17); he is keeping watch not over the theology of his people, but over their souls, as one who will have to give an account of his leadership.

Content of the Letter

The pastoral intent of the writer dictates the structure of his letter; instruction alternates regularly with admonition, warning, and appeal. The indicatives which expound the surpassing significance of Christ as God's last word to man are always followed by the imperatives which summon men to heed that word.

    I. 1:1—4:13. Introductory Section: God has spoken His ultimate word in His Son, who surpasses all previous mediators of divine revelation; therefore give heed to His word.

A. 1. Instruction, 1:1-14. Jesus is high above the angels, who mediated the message of the Law, cf. 2:2.

2. Admonition, 2:1-4. "Therefore we must pay the closer attention to what we have heard, lest we drift away from it."

B. 1. Instruction, 2:5-18. The humiliation of Jesus does not call into question His unique greatness; His humiliation is necessary to His priesthood.

2. Admonition, 3:1. "Therefore . . . consider Jesus, the Apostle and High Priest of our confession."

C. 1. Instruction, 3:2-6. Jesus is superior to Moses, the mediator of the Law.

2. Warning, 3:7—4:13. Therefore give heed, lest you, like the ancient people of God in the wilderness, forfeit the promised rest by unbelief and lose your portion in the promises given to the people of God.

II. 4:14—12:29. Main theme: The superiority of Jesus, the New Testament High Priest, and the need of unwavering faith in Him.

A. 1. Instruction, 4:14—5:10. Jesus is marked as a true High Priest by the fact that He is

a. one with man and therefore capable of sympathy with man's frailty and

b. is appointed by God.

2. Warning and Encouragement, 5:11—6:20. Go on to maturity in knowledge of your great High Priest, lest you stagnate, fall away, and come under the judgment of God, 5:11—6:8. Your goodly past has in it the promise that you will overcome your present torpor and go on to realize the full assurance of hope, 6:9-12, a hope based on the certainty given by the promise and oath of God and by the work of Jesus as the High Priest after the order of Melchizedek, 6:13-20.

B. 1. Instruction, 7:1—10:19

a. Jesus is a High Priest of a higher order, not that of Aaron, but of Melchizedek, both priest and king forever; His priesthood antiquates and supersedes the old Levitical priesthood, chap. 7.

b. He performs His priestly ministry in a better sanctuary, the heavens, and by it mediates the promised new and better covenant, chap. 8.

c. He offers the final and perfect sacrifice for sin, 9:1 to 10:18.

2. Exhortation, 10:19—12:29

a. Draw near to God in word and work by "the new and living way" which the great High Priest has consecrated, 10:19-25.

b. Beware of apostasy, that deliberate rejection of the proffered redemption which will deliver you up to the judgment of God, 10:26-31.

c. Recall the believing steadfastness of your former days, remember that you stand in the succession of the ancient men of faith, and look to Jesus, the pioneer and perfecter of your faith, 10:32—12:3.

d. Remember that your present suffering is proof of God's fatherly love for you; He is the Lord who chastises every child whom He receives, 12:4-11.

e. Repent and grow strong again before the time of repentance be past; do not refuse the God who has spoken His supremely gracious word for the last time, before His last judgment comes, 12:12-29.

III. Concluding Admonitions, 13:1-19

A. 13:1-6. Continue in brotherly love, in charity toward the stranger and the prisoner, in sexual purity, in contentment based on a confident trust in God.

B. 13:7-19. Remember your past teachers and imitate their faith in the abiding and unchanging Christ, their resistance to false teaching, their resolute break with Judaism, their pure worship, their sacrifice of praise and well-doing. To the same end, obey your present leaders and pray for us.

Close, 13:20-25. Intercessory prayer, appeal to receive the admonition of the letter, news, greetings, benediction.

The Author of the Letter

The letter does not name its author, and there is no consistent tradition in the early church concerning the authorship of the Letter to the Hebrews. In the East the letter was regarded either as directly written by Paul or as in some sense owing its origin to Paul. Origen of Alexandria reflects this tradition; he says of the letter: "Its thoughts are the thoughts of the apostle, but the language and composition that of one who recalled from memory and, as it were, made notes of what was said by the master. . . . Men of old times handed it down as Paul's. But who wrote the epistle God only knows certainly." The Western church did not attribute the letter to Paul; Tertullian of Carthage assigned it to Barnabas, while in Rome and elsewhere the letter was anonymous.

The fact that the author counts himself and his readers among those who received the word of salvation at second hand from those who had heard the Lord is conclusive evidence that the author is not Paul (Heb. 2:3), for Paul appeals repeatedly to the fact that he has seen the Lord and has received the Gospel directly from Him (1 Cor. 9:1; 1 Cor. 15:8; Gal. 1:11, 12). The general character of the theology of the letter and the author's acquaintance with Paul's companion Timothy (Heb. 13:23) point to someone who moved in the circle of Paul's friends and co-workers. The characteristics of the letter itself further limit the possibilities: they indicate that the author was in all probability a Greek-speaking Jewish Christian, thoroughly at home in the Old Testament in its Greek translation, and intimately acquainted with the whole worship and cultus of the Jews, a man capable, moreover, of the most finished and literary Greek in the New Testament. Barnabas, the Levite from Cyprus (Acts 4:36) and companion of Paul, would be a not unlikely candidate for authorship. Whether Tertullian attributed the letter to him on the basis of a genuine tradition or was making a plausible conjecture, cannot be determined. Apollos, whom Luther suggested as the possible author, is even more likely. He was associated with Paul, though not in any sense a "disciple" of Paul, and Luke in the Book of Acts describes him as a Jew, a native of that great center of learning and rhetoric, Alexandria, an eloquent man, well versed in the

Scriptures, and fervent in spirit (Acts 18:24, 25), all characteristics that we find reflected in the Letter to the Hebrews.

Luther's conjecture remains the most reasonable of all the
ancient and modern conjectures, which have attributed the letter
to a great variety of authors — Luke, Clement of Rome, Silvanus,
Aquila and Priscilla, Priscilla alone, etc. But Origen's word still
holds: "Who wrote the epistle, God only knows certainly." More
important than the man's name is the kind of man he was; he was
an earnest teacher of the church, deeply conscious of his responsibility for the church, whom the Holy Spirit moved to employ
all his resources of language and learning in order to restore to
health and strength the weak and faltering church.

Date of the Letter

Since the Letter to the Hebrews is quoted by Clement of Rome
in his Letter to the Corinthians of A. D. 96, the letter must be
earlier than that date. There is no evidence which enables us to
determine exactly how much earlier the letter was written. Timothy is still alive at the time of writing (Heb. 13:23), but since
he was a young man when Paul first took him as his companion
in A. D. 49 (Acts 16:1-3), he may have lived to the end of the
first century or beyond. The readers have been converted by
personal disciples of the Lord (Heb. 2:3), and a considerable
time has elapsed since their conversion: they have had time for
development and growth (Heb. 5:12). Some of their first leaders
are now dead (Heb. 13:7). They have endured one persecution
(probably the Neronian persecution A. D. 64) and are apparently
facing another (Heb. 10:36). All this points to the latter half
of the first century. Since the author dwells on the fact that the
old system of priesthood and sacrifice was destined to be superseded by a greater and more perfect priesthood and sacrifice,
it would seem strange that he does not mention the fall of Jerusalem (which put an end forever to the old cultus) if that event
had taken place. The argument from silence is strong in this case,
and a dating before A. D. 70, probably shortly before, seems very
probable. But it should be said that many scholars today are not
inclined to attach much weight to this argument; they argue that
the author is thinking not of the Jerusalem temple and its cultus,

but of the cultus as he knows it from the Old Testament, and date the letter somewhere in the 80s.

Canonicity: Antilegomenon

Characteristics of the Letter

The purpose of the Letter to the Hebrews is practical, like that of every book of the New Testament; its aim is to strengthen faith and hope, to inculcate stout patience and a joyous and resolute holding fast to the Christian confession. The message which provides the basis for the exhortation and the impetus and power for the fulfillment of the exhortation has three primary characteristics. It is founded on the Old Testament; it is centered in Christ; and it is marked by an intense consciousness of the fact that all days since the coming of the Christ are last days.

The message is, first, founded on the Old Testament. It is to a large extent an interpretation and exposition of Old Testament Scriptures. It has been likened to a Christian sermon or a series of sermons on selected Psalms (Pss. 2, 8, 95, 110). The letter therefore contains high testimony to the inspiration and authority of the Old Testament Scriptures. In the first verse the whole Old Testament is designated as the very voice of God speaking to men, and throughout the letter words which men of God spoke of old are presented as spoken by God Himself (e. g., Heb. 1:5, 6, 13; 5:5) or by Christ (e. g., Heb. 2:11-13; 10:5) or by the Holy Spirit (Heb. 3:7; 10:15).

The author's characteristic use of the Old Testament is that which has been termed the typological use; that is, he sees in the history and the institutions of the Old Covenant events, persons, and actions which are typical, foreshadowings and prefigurings of that which was to become full reality in the New Covenant. In one sense the whole epistle is a set of variations on a theme from Paul: "These [the Old Testament sacral institutions] are only a shadow of what is to come; but the substance belongs to Christ" (Col. 2:17). Thus Melchizedek, both priest and king, is divinely designed to point beyond himself to the great High Priest Jesus Christ (Heb. 7:1—10:18). The fate of God's people in the wilderness, their failure to attain to the promised Sabbath rest, points beyond itself to the eternal Sabbath rest which awaits the New Testament people of God (Heb. 3:7—4:13). This view and use of the Old Testament never degenerates into mere allegory; that is, the Old Testament figures are never merely symbols of eternal truths, as in the allegorizing interpretation of the Jewish philosopher Philo; rather, the Old Testament history is always taken seriously as history. As such, as history, it points beyond itself to the last days. This use of Scripture is therefore an eloquent expression of the faith that God is Lord of all history, shaping all history for His purposes and leading all history toward His great redemptive goal. The Old Testament is therefore of abiding value and enduring significance for the people of God in the last days, for it enables them to see the whole sweep and direction of the mighty redeeming arm of God.

The message is, secondly, centered in Christ. Christ, the Son of God, dominates the whole, and Christ colors every part of the whole. He stands at the beginning of history as the Son through whom God created the world; He stands at the end of all history as the divinely appointed "heir of all things" (Heb. 1:2). He dominates all history and rules the whole world, "upholding the universe by His word of power" (Heb. 1:3). He is God's ultimate and definitive word to man (Heb. 1:2), and His highpriestly ministry is God's ultimate deed for man — a whole, assured, eternal deliverance from sin. That highpriestly, atoning ministry spans the whole of Jesus' existence: His entry into mankind, His sacrificial suffering and death, His entering into the heavenly Holy of Holies, His presentation of His sacrifice at the throne of God, and His return in glory to the waiting people of God are all highpriestly acts. (E. g., Heb. 2:17, 18; 9:11-14; 4:14; 9:28)

His highpriestly ministry marks Him as full partaker in the Godhead and as completely one with man. Indeed, no letter of the New Testament is so full of the humanity of Jesus as the Letter to the Hebrews. Since He is both Son of God and a Priest fully one with man, His priesthood and His sacrifice have a real and eternal significance and top and supersede every other priestly ministration. The impress of the incarnate Christ is upon His people; His history of suffering and triumph is their history; His obedience and fidelity to the Father make possible their faithful obedience to God. His entering into the Holy Place gives them access to the throne of God.

The message is, thirdly, marked by the consciousness that the days since God spoke in His Son are "these last days" (Heb. 1:2). Christ has appeared "at the end of the age to put away sin by the sacrifice of Himself" (Heb. 9:26). It is the beginning of the end; the new world of God has become a reality in the midst of the old, and men "have tasted . . . the powers of the age to come" (Heb. 6:5) even now. What former ages had possessed in an imperfect form, a form which itself pointed to a fuller realization, is now a present blessing — a better covenant (Heb. 7:22), better sacrifices (Heb. 9:23), a better possession (Heb. 10:34), and a better hope (Heb. 7:19). Men still hope, and the full realization of all that Christ has wrought is still to come. But the Day is drawing near (Heb. 10:25) when all that is now a sure hope shall be fully realized. This "last days" character of Jesus' work, its eschatological character, gives it a final, once-for-all character and makes the decision of faith one of terrible urgency; eternal issues are being decided now, in faith or unbelief. Man is confronted by an eternal and inescapable either-or. Seen in this eschatological light, the sternness of the warnings in 6:4-8 and 10:26-31, warnings which at first glance seem to preclude the possibility of a second repentance, is not strange. (These warnings seemed to Luther to be "hard knots" and made him dubious about the letter.) God has spoken His last word, and the time is short; men must not be left under the delusion that they can coolly and deliberately sin and then repent in order to sin again. Such sinning is the last step on the way toward apostasy; it is the expression of an "evil, unbelieving heart" (Heb. 3:12) which cannot find the way to repentance because it has deliberately cut itself off from God, the Giver of repentance.

CHAPTER XI: "I chose you and appointed you that you should go and bear fruit and that your fruit should abide": The Gospel, Letters, and Revelation of John

READINGS: JOHN; 1, 2, 3 JOHN; REVELATION

Author: Literary Activity of John

"The word of the Lord grew." It continued to grow to the very end of the apostolic period, to the time of the death of John, the apostle who long outlived the rest. And it remained the Lord's word to the very end. The words which John heard Jesus speak to His disciples during His last meal with them might be written over all his works: "I chose you and appointed you" (John 15:16). In all his writings John is at pains to underscore the fact that he is freely giving what he has received freely, that in all his life and ministry it is the Christ who has taken and retains the initiative, and that this initiative is pure grace: "From His fullness have we all received, grace upon grace," he writes in his Gospel (John 1:16); the incarnate Word has given him the new birth which makes him a child of God (John 1:12, 13); it was the Son of God who made known to him the Father (John 1:18); it was the risen Christ who breathed on John and gave him the gift of the Holy Spirit, the Spirit who made his word a divinely valid word, effectual for forgiveness and for judgment (John 20: 22, 23). "This is the message *we have heard from Him,*" John writes in his first letter (1 John 1:5). And the second and third letters too make plain that the word which John defends and promotes is not his own, but his Lord's; it is "truth" received "which abides in us" (2 John 2), not the doctrine of John, but "the doctrine of Christ" (2 John 9). All that John, or any man, may do is to become a "fellow worker" *in* that truth (3 John 8). The Revelation of John is the most outspoken of all on this point. When John beheld the exalted Christ, he "fell at His feet as though dead" (Rev. 1:17). It was purely the grace of the Christ that restored him from death to life: "But He laid His right hand upon me saying, 'Fear not' " (Rev. 1:17); and it was the gracious Lord of the churches who raised him up from impotence and empowered him for ministry: "Now write what you see" (Rev. 1:19). The word of John is the growing and prevailing word of the Lord.

"I chose you and appointed you that you should go and bear fruit and that your fruit should abide" (John 15:16). The elective grace of the Christ gave John a long and fruitful apostolic ministry, both in Palestine and in Asia Minor. The Book of Acts gives us glimpses of his Palestinian ministry: we find him associated with Peter in the healing of the lame man at Jerusalem (Acts 3:1-26), in his subsequent trial and defense before the Sanhedrin (Acts 4:1-22), and in his ministry to the young church in Samaria (Acts 8:14-25). Paul can speak of John as one of the three men "who were reputed to be pillars" of the Judaic church (Gal. 2:9). He was associated with Peter in Palestine; like Peter, he left Palestine when the skies over Israel grew dark with judgment and it became increasingly clear that his apostolic mission to Israel had been fulfilled and the debt of love to Israel had been paid. Early Christian tradition, a tradition which there is no real reason to doubt (a tradition which archeological discoveries in Ephesus have, moreover, served to confirm) says that John went to Asia Minor and settled at Ephesus. John's rich literary activity falls in this period. His Lord's promise that the fruit of his labors should abide thus found a twofold fulfillment, both in the thousands whom his spoken word brought to Christ and in the millions who have drunk of the living waters of his written word and have come to know the validity of the inspired promise: "These are written that you may believe that Jesus is the Christ, the Son of God, and that believing you may have life in His name." (John 20:31)

The writings of John are, as it were, a recapitulation of the whole New Testament. For their own day they meet the same needs of the church and defend it against the same dangers as the earlier New Testament writings. The church's need for "teaching" (in the full Biblical sense of "teaching") is met: the Gospel of John, like those of Matthew, Mark, and Luke, holds before the church a true and mighty picture of the Christ who is the Author of her salvation and the Lord of all her life, in order that men may hold to Him and serve Him. As Paul, Peter, and Jude had labored to defend the church against the false teaching which endangered her faith and her life, so John in his first and second letters, and in the letters to the churches in Revelation, strives to open the eyes of the church to the satanic weeds that grow among God's wheat; his Gospel, too, perhaps has a polemical cutting edge. As Paul had to defend his apostolic authority against the arrogant presumption of men, so does John in his third letter. As Paul wrote in the interest of the advance of missions in his Letter to the Romans, so does John in his third letter. As Peter and Paul wrote to persecuted churches in order to make them brave and submissive and to keep their hope pure and strong, so does John in that wondrous and mysterious last book of the Bible, the Revelation.

John in his writings meets the same needs as the earlier writings; and he meets them in the same way, by the same means. The three basic notes of the New Testament proclamation are sounded with thunderous fullness and insistence by the apostle whom Jesus had surnamed a "Son of Thunder" (Mark 3:17). He proclaims Jesus as Lord; his whole Gospel is a rich and manifold explication of what His Lordship signifies, a full and varied witness to the glory of Him who is God's incarnate Word, very God; the Life and Light of men; the only Son; the Lamb of God; the Anointed of God; the Bread of Life from heaven; the eternal Son who can say, "Before Abraham was, I am"; the Resurrection and the Life; the Light of the world; the Way, the Truth, and the Life. The cry which the appearance of the risen Christ wrung from Thomas the doubter is the free, witnessing cry of John: "My Lord and my God!" And the Gospel spells out with unequaled insistence that He alone is Lord, that there is no other name under heaven whereby man may be saved but His alone, that there can be no way to the Father but by Him; he confronts men with the ultimate and inescapable alternative of life or death: "He who believes in Him is not condemned; he who does not believe is condemned already, because he has not believed in the name of the only Son of God" (John 3:18). In the letters of John, too, Jesus appears as the Son of God, the only Son, the Word of life, God-given eternal Life in person, manifested to men in the hard historical reality of His incarnation, "in the flesh"; to deny Him is to lose God, and to confess Him is to have the Father. Before Him the ways of men divide: they are either the Christ's or the antichrist's. And the Revelation of John, while holding fast the Jesus of history, the Lamb that was slain, blazons forth the glory of the risen and exalted Christ, "the Lord of lords and King of kings," the gracious and dread Lord of the church, the Lord of all history and the goal of all history, the whole content of the church's hope. ("Come, Lord Jesus!")

John is at one with the whole New Testament also in proclaiming the reality and the power of the Holy Spirit. His Gospel gives us Jesus' promise of the Spirit in an unrivaled fullness and clarity. And his book is itself a monument to the fulfillment of the promise of his Lord which said: "When the Spirit of truth comes, He will guide you into all the truth. . . . He will glorify Me" (John 16:13, 14). His Gospel is the witness of one in whom the Spirit has through all his years done His gracious revelatory work; it is the witness of one before whose eyes the Christ loomed in ever greater grace and majesty. John's first letter is filled with the certitude of the presence and the sure perpetual witness of the Spirit of truth (1 John 3:24; 4:2, 13; 5:7, 8). In his Revelation he outspokenly attributes the gift and the task which has been assigned him to the Spirit's working: "I was in the Spirit on the Lord's day" (Rev. 1:10; cf. 4:2; 17:3; 21:10); the exalted Christ, who appears to John and speaks through him, bids the seven churches "hear what the Spirit says to the churches" (2:7, 11, 17, 29; 3:6, 13, 22); and the Spirit helps the embattled church in her weakness and gives her prayer new strength: "The Spirit and the Bride say, 'Come'" (Rev. 22:17). The apostle in his prophetic task, the church in her struggle with weakness, error, and sin, and the church that hopes and prays in the world's last evil days — all these know the power and the blessing of the Spirit.

The word of the Lord as spoken and written by John is also, finally, an eschatological word, the word of a man who knows that he is living in the world's last days. The words of Jesus in John's Gospel mark out with peculiar clarity the fact that the end of all things presses hard upon the present and gives the present its decisive eschatological character: "The hour *is coming, and now is,* when the dead will hear the voice of the Son of God, and those who hear will live" (John 5:25). Eternal life, as Jesus proclaims and promises it, is not merely a far-off possibility; it has, in Jesus, moved into the present: "Truly, truly, I say to you, he who hears My word and believes Him who sent Me, has eternal life; he does not come into judgment, but has passed from death to life" (John 5:24). The resurrection of the dead is no longer a remote event; it is, in Jesus, a present reality: "I am the Resurrection and the Life" (John 11:25). And this reality moves surely toward its final consummation; Jesus' promise to the believer is: "I will raise him up at the last day" (John 6:40). In his first letter John confronts the "many antichrists" who have come, and thunders them down, with serene assurance; for their presence in the world marks this hour as the "last hour" (1 John 2:18); the time is therefore near at hand when the children of God whom the world does not recognize will be manifested as the children of God: "When He appears, we shall be like Him, for we shall see Him as He is" (1 John 3:2). And all of John's Revelation cries out: "The time is near" (Rev. 1:3); the God who speaks through John to the afflicted and dying church is the God "who is and who was and *who is to come*" (Rev. 1:4), and His strong angel who bestrides the sea and land cries out: "There shall be no more delay!" (Rev. 10:6)

John's writings constitute a résumé of the New Testament proclamation, but they are anything but a mere résumé. They are a new and fresh revelation of the "unsearchable riches of Christ" (Eph. 3:8). This growth of the apostolic word is, to many hearts and minds, the richest growth and the finest flowering of them all.

THE GOSPEL ACCORDING TO JOHN

Occasion and Purpose of the Gospel

The central and controlling purpose of the Gospel is stated by the evangelist himself: "Now Jesus did many other signs in the presence of the disciples, which are not written in this book; but these are written *that you may believe that Jesus is the Christ, the Son of God, and that believing you may have life in His name*" (John 20:30, 31). The book is not a missionary appeal; it addresses men who are already Christians and seeks to deepen and strengthen their faith in Jesus as the Christ. It does so by interpretatively recounting the words and deeds of Jesus, His "signs," or significant actions. It is, therefore, like the first three Gospels, "teaching," teaching as we defined it in the opening paragraphs of chapter VIII, teaching in the sense of Acts 2:42. Like the other Gospels, it no doubt had behind it a long history of oral teaching; it is, as ancient tradition also indicates, the final precipitate of John's many years of oral apostolic witness to Christ in the churches of Asia Minor. Some scholars see indications that the book had its origin in the worship life of the church of Asia Minor in such features of the Gospel as its peculiarly simple and exalted style, its dramatic structure, its highly selective way of dealing with the career of Jesus, and its rich use of the solemn "I am" sayings of Jesus. They may well be right.

John's teaching did not take place in a vacuum. The church which he taught was in the world, a church in conflict and a church under temptation. And we can tell, from the Gospel's particular emphases, what some of these conflicts and temptations were. The Gospel of the Crucified was a stumbling block to the Jew and folly to the Greek in John's day as it had been in Paul's (1 Cor. 1:23). The fierce hatred of the Jews of Asia had pursued Paul (Acts 20:19; 21:27); we find the same embittered Jewish offense at the cross active against Christians a generation later than John in Smyrna at the time of the martyrdom of Polycarp (*Mart. Pol.* 13:1). And in the letters to the churches at Smyrna and Philadelphia in Revelation (most probably written within a few years of the time of the Gospel of John), we find references to Jews opposed to the church, "those who say that they are Jews and are not, but are a synagog of Satan" (Rev. 2:9; 3:9; cf. John

8:44). Conflict with the Jews had not ended with the death of Jesus nor with the death of Paul. Rather, according to the witness of the Fourth Gospel, it persisted in intensified form; the Gospel of John presents the conflict between Jesus and the Jews in even stronger colors than does the Gospel of Matthew. He speaks of the Jews for the most part simply as "Jews." He knows the distinctive coloring of the various Jewish parties, but the distinction between Pharisees and Sadducees no longer is of import to him or his readers. John speaks of his people simply as of the people who rejected Jesus as their Messiah, and "Jew" is practically equivalent to "unbelieving Jew" (John 2:18, 20; 5:10, 16, 18; 6:41, 52; 7:13; 9:22, etc.). The "Jews" are the opponents of Jesus, blind and stubborn in their refusal to recognize Him, persecuting Him with an ever-mounting hatred. They deny that He is the Son of God (John 5:18; 8:40-59); they seek His life (John 5:18; 8:40, 59; 10:31, 39; 11:8, 50), and in all things show themselves not as true children of Abraham, but as children of the devil (John 8:39-44). Jesus predicts that this hatred will persist; they will deem it a service rendered to God if they kill Jesus' disciples (John 16:2). The Spirit whom Jesus will send will enable His disciples to continue the struggle which He had in His lifetime carried on against them. (John 16:2-4, 7-11)

This feature of John's Gospel may be due in part to the fact that he devotes so much space to Jesus' ministry in Jerusalem, where opposition to Jesus was concentrated most strongly. But only in part; it is due chiefly to the fact that the lines have been drawn by Israel's national rejection of her Messiah, that judgment has been executed on Jerusalem and a gulf has been fixed between the ancient people of God and the new Israel, the church. But this does not mean that the Fourth Gospel has an anti-Semitic bias. John is at one with the other evangelists and with Paul (Rom. 9:1-5) in his positive appreciation of what the Jew had by the grace of God received and in his hope that the Jew may still receive of that grace. John's harsh indictment of the Jew is therefore to be construed as a call to repentance addressed to the Jew. It is in the Fourth Gospel that Jesus declares, to the Samaritan woman, that "salvation is *from the Jews*" (John 4:22); the Scripture given to the Jews is for the Jesus of John the supreme

authority as it is for the Jesus of Matthew (e. g., John 10:35).
The flock for which the Good Shepherd dies is a flock gathered
out of Israel (John 10:16); the hour of the Gentiles, the hour
for the Greeks who would see Jesus, is yet to come (John 10:16;
12:20, 32). Israel's own high priest must declare that Jesus is
the One who dies for the whole people (John 11:50, 51). The
title of the Crucified is "King of the Jews" (John 19:19). Jesus
is "King of Israel" (John 1:49), and the Gospel still pleads with
the Jew to become an "Israelite indeed," an Israelite "in whom
is no guile," by acknowledging Israel's King as Nathanael acknowledged Him (John 1:47). Indeed, this motif is so strong that one
modern scholar has advanced and defended the theory that the
Fourth Gospel is primarily a missionary appeal addressed to the
Jew — an overstatement, of course, but an indication of the
tendency of the Gospel.

Another, less direct form of Judaic opposition to Jesus and
His church is combated by the Fourth Gospel also. There were
those in Israel who became disciples of John the Baptist but
did not accept his witness to Jesus as the Christ. These continued
to exist as a separate group or sect, and apparently their reverent
esteem for the Baptist was such that they assigned to him the
titles and functions of the Messiah. The incident recorded in
Acts 19:1-7 (Paul's encounter with "disciples" who knew only
the Baptism of John) would seem to indicate that this movement
had spread as far as Ephesus, where the Fourth Gospel was
written. This would account for the fact that the Fourth Gospel
enunciates with special emphasis the fact that the Baptist has his
significance and his honor in his subordination to Jesus as the
Christ: "He was not the light, but came to bear witness to the
Light" (John 1:8); in John's account of him, the Baptist will
accept no title of honor at all, but calls himself merely the Voice
in the wilderness — his whole significance lies in his function as
the herald of the Christ (John 1:19-23). He must decrease, as
the Messiah must increase; and he finds his perfect joy in the
Christ's increasing (John 3:28-30). He points his disciples to the
Lamb of God who takes away the sin of the world (John 1:29-36).
But the evangelist is not minded to belittle the true stature of the
Baptist; he sees in him "a man sent from God" (John 1:6), a valid

and mighty witness to the only Son from the Father (John 1:
14, 15). John alone records the witness of the people to John
("Everything that John said about this Man was true," John
10:41), and he alone records the words with which Jesus Himself places His seal upon the Baptist's mission: "You sent to
John, and he has borne witness to the truth. . . . He was a burn-
ing and shining lamp" (John 5:33, 35).

The Gospel was a stumbling block to the Jew; it was foolish-
ness to the Greek. And the Gospel of John is also directed
against a Greek perversion of the Gospel which was in effect
a denial of the Gospel. According to the second-century father
Irenaeus, the Gospel of John was written to combat the heresy
of Cerinthus. This is hardly the whole purpose of the Gospel;
but John's emphatic declaration that the eternal Son, the Word,
"became *flesh*" (John 1:14) does seem to be aimed at one of
the tenets peculiar to the sect of Cerinthus. For Cerinthus denied
that the "heavenly Christ" had been identified with man, the
creature of flesh, in any real and lasting way; he maintained that,
not the Christ but only the man Jesus (in whom the Christ had
dwelt guest-fashion from the time of His baptism onward up to
the eve of His Passion) had suffered and died. This could
also be the historical background to the fact that in the Fourth
Gospel, and in it alone, Jesus is hailed at the very beginning of
His ministry as the dying Christ, as "the Lamb of God" (John
1:29), and is at the end of His ministry worshiped by Thomas
as the Crucified: Thomas says, "My *Lord* and my *God*" to the
Christ who bears on His body the marks of the crucifixion (John
20:27, 28). Perhaps John's insistence, in the opening verses of
his Gospel, that "all things were made through Him [the Word],
and without Him was not anything made that was made" (John
1:3) is also pointed at Cerinthus, who maintained that the world
was created not by the highest God who sent the heavenly Christ
into the world, but by a Power which had separated itself from
God. The fact that the First Letter of John is patently directed
against a heresy like that of Cerinthus lends great plausibility to
the suggestion that the Gospel, too, has a polemical point that
is aimed at Cerinthus.

Content of the Gospel According to John

John begins his Gospel with a compressed, thematic statement which contains in essence the message of the whole book (John 1:1-18). Everything that follows is really only an ever fuller and ever profounder development of this statement, and unfolding of all that is implicit in it. The recital of the words and deeds of Jesus which follows does not pretend to be a complete record of Jesus' activity (John 20:30); the words and deeds are freely selected from a much larger mass of material (some of it, no doubt, familiar to John's readers from the other Gospels), freely arranged, and told in stylized form, with one aim only: to proclaim what Jesus is and signifies; to present Jesus to men as John and his fellow witnesses had been led by the Spirit to behold Him, as the very Word of God, the only Son in whom God has uttered His whole will for man, the grace and truth of God in person, grace and truth enacted in the history of a human life which men have witnessed.

The movement of the Gospel is therefore not so much movement in a straight line as movement in spiral form, a spiral which rises higher and higher and grows wider and wider but remains always over the same area, the area marked out by the first eighteen verses of the Gospel. For example, the theme of the cross is already stated in the first unit, 1:10, 11: "The world knew Him not . . . His own people received Him not." It recurs in the witness of the Baptist in 1:29, "Behold the Lamb of God, who takes away the sin of the world!" This spiral comes around to it again in 3:14, "As Moses lifted up the serpent in the wilderness, so must the Son of man be lifted up," and again and again — in 6:51, "The bread which I shall give for the life of the world is My flesh"; in 8:28, "When you have lifted up the Son of man, then you will know that I am He"; in 10:11, "I am the Good Shepherd. The Good Shepherd lays down His life for the sheep"; in 12:24, "Truly, truly, I say to you, unless a grain of wheat falls into the earth and dies, it remains alone; but if it dies, it bears much fruit"; and in 12:31, 32, "Now is the judgment of this world, now shall the ruler of this world be cast out; and I, when I am lifted up from the earth, will draw all men to Myself," to mention only a few passages. The spiral movement touches the cross again in Chap. 13, for the cross is the luminous background of Jesus' action when He washes His disciples' feet (13:1-20). The spiral movement of the cross runs through the last discourses of Jesus (e. g., 15:13, 18-21; 16:20). The spiral movement does not cease at the actual crucifixion; it goes on over the narrative of Jesus' appearance to Thomas — Thomas beholds the Crucified (John 20:25-29) — and continues over the narrative of Jesus' last conversation with Peter, for Jesus' words, "Feed My sheep" (21: 15-19) unmistakably recall the Good Shepherd who lays down His life for the sheep.

Theme: 1:1-18. Jesus the Word of God in the Flesh, the Word which Men Would Not Heed

The Explication of the Theme, 1:19—21:25: How the Word of God Was Spoken to Men

I. The Word Is Spoken to All Israel, 1:19—4:54 ("He came to His own home," 1:11)

A. The Witness of John the Baptist, 1:19-34. Jesus is the Lamb of God, the Giver of the Spirit, the Son of God. John's witness points the first disciples to Jesus.

B. The Confession of the First Disciples, 1:35-51. He is the Messiah of prophecy.

C. The First Sign at Cana, 2:1-12. Jesus reveals His glory.

D. The Cleansing of the Temple, 2:13-22. Jesus states His Messianic claim and points to His cross.

E. The Conversation with Nicodemus, 2:23—3:21. Jesus is the Giver of life, by His cross and death.

F. The Baptist's Last Witness to Jesus, 3:22-36. "He must increase."

G. The Conversation with the Samaritan Woman, 4:1-42. Jesus is the Giver of living water, the Savior of the world.

H. The Second Sign: The Healing of the Official's Son, 4:43-54. Jesus gives the gift of healing and the gift of faith in His word.

(Note that this first sketch of Jesus' activity covers all Israel: Judea, Samaria, and Galilee.)

II. The Word Is Rejected by Israel, 5:1—12:50 ("His own people received Him not," 1:11)

Jesus reveals Himself amid a hostile and obdurate people.

A. Healing at the pool of Bethesda in Jerusalem on the Sabbath, 5:1-47. Jesus' oneness with God; the Jews' estrangement from God.

B. Feeding of the Five Thousand in Galilee, 6:1-71. Jesus is the Bread of Life; all forsake Him except the Twelve — and one of them is a devil.

C. Jesus and Jerusalem, 7:1—10:42.

1. Controversy at the Feast of Tabernacles, 7:1—8:59. Jesus is the Water of Life and the Light of the World. The rulers of Israel determine to arrest Him. Of the crowd, some believe, while others seek to stone Him.

2. Healing of the Man Born Blind, 9:1-41. Jesus' gracious coming issues in a judgment on unbelieving men: "For judgment I came into this world, that those who do not see may see, and that those who see may become blind," 9:39.

3. Jesus the Door to the Sheepfold and the Good Shepherd, 10:1-21. Jesus claims sole authority as Teacher of the people of God, brands all teachers who oppose Him as false, and proclaims His will to die for His own.

4. Are You the Christ? 10:22-42. Jesus points to the works which attest His oneness with God and points those who find His claim blasphemous to the God who has revealed Himself in the Old Testament.

5. The Raising of Lazarus, 11:1-54. Jesus is the Resurrection and the Life; Jerusalem's leaders determine that He must die for His people.

D. The Result of Jesus' Ministry, 11:55—12:50. Jesus is anointed at Bethany, 12:1-8, hailed by the crowds at His Messianic entry into Jerusalem, 12:9-19, sought out by Greeks, 12:20-26; even in official circles there are many who believe in Him, though secretly, 12:42,43. But to Israel as a whole the word has been spoken in vain, 12:37-40: the chief priests and Pharisees, the most influential group in Israel, are hardened against Him, 11:57; cf. 12:19, 42. Jesus knows that His Passion impends, 12:23-26, 27-34. The Light of the world has but a little while to shine, 12:35, 36; the word of God, spoken to save, will at the last day judge those who have rejected it, 12:44-50.

III. The Word Is Received by the Disciples, chaps. 13—17. ("To all who received Him, who believed in His name, He gave power to become children of God," 1:12).

Jesus loves His disciples to the end. He enacts His ministering love for them in the footwashing, and by identifying His betrayer shows them the way His ministering love must go, the way of the cross; thus He imposes on them His commandment of love, 13:1-38. He prepares the disciples for the time when they shall be separated from His bodily presence, by showing them what they will gain by His departure: He promises them that the Father will send them the Spirit, who shall be their Counselor in their conflict with the world, lead them into all truth, and complete the presence of the Christ among them, 14—16. He prays for His disciples and for those who shall come to faith through their word, 17.

IV. The Word of God Speaks God's Grace and Truth, chaps. 18—20. ("And from His fullness have we all received, grace upon grace," 1:16).

In the crucifixion and the resurrection of Jesus His disciples behold His glory, the glory of the Good Shepherd who dies for His sheep, the glory of the King whose kingdom is not of this world, the glory of the ministering Lord who on the cross commits His mother to the disciple whom He loves, the glory of the Word made flesh in full reality, who cried, "I thirst," the glory of the Savior of the world who said, "It is finished," the glory of the risen Lord of life who breathed on them with creative breath and gave them the Holy Spirit for their apostolic task, the glory of the Lord and God who overwhelmed the stubborn doubt of Thomas and called them blessed who without seeing believe.

Conclusion: Jesus and Peter and John, chap. 21.

Once more Jesus admits His own to the fellowship of the
common meal. They see Him once more in the glory of His
Lordship: He restores Peter to his apostolic task and appoints
for him the death by which he is to glorify God. He determines the fate of the disciple whom He loved, He alone.
It is he, the apostle wholly determined by his Lord, who
witnesses to the Word of God in written words, and his
witness is true. Through it, men may behold the glory of
the Christ, believe in Him, and live.

Integrity of the Gospel

There is general agreement among scholars that the section
John 7:53—8:11, the story of the woman taken in adultery, is
a later insertion into the text of the Gospel. Many of the ancient
manuscripts omit this section, and it is unknown to the commentators of the Greek church down to the eleventh century.
Further doubt is thrown upon this section as constituting a part
of the Fourth Gospel by the fact that other manuscripts insert the
story at Luke 21:38, and still others at John 7:36 or John 21:24.
Besides, the section differs from the Gospel in language and style.
The story is probably true, a genuine part of the story of Jesus;
but it is not a part of the Gospel which John wrote.

Many scholars are of the opinion that the twenty-first chapter,
too, is not an original part of the Gospel but the work of a second
hand. But here the situation is quite different from that of the
story of the woman taken in adultery: every ancient manuscript
and translation contains the chapter; it is linguistically and stylisti-
cally in harmony with the first twenty chapters. While it is a sort
of appendix to the Gospel proper, which obviously closes at 20:31,
it is an appendix written by the author himself.

THE FIRST LETTER OF JOHN

Occasion of the Letter

The Gospel of John was to some degree polemical. It was
probably not directly occasioned by false teaching, but some
characteristic accents and features of the Gospel are most readily
understood as John's answer to a false teaching which perverted

the true Gospel. The First Letter of John is wholly and vigorously polemical. It is aimed at false teachers, and although the letter never enters into a detailed refutation of their error, much less a full presentation of their teaching, the general character of the heresy can be ascertained with tolerable accuracy from hints given in the letter.

The false teachers had arisen within the church: "They went out from us," John writes, "but they were not of us; for if they had been of us, they would have continued with us; but they went out, that it might be plain that they all are not of us" (1 John 2:19). At the time when John wrote, they had separated themselves from the church — or had been expelled by the church: "You are of God, and have overcome them," John tells the church (1 John 4:4). They had apparently constituted themselves as a separate community, and they continued to make vigorous propaganda for their cause (cf. 2 John 7 and 10) and still constituted a threat to the church (1 John 2:27; 3:7).

They were a real threat, for they were very "religious" men. They were "spiritual" men and claimed the prophetic authority of the Holy Spirit for their teaching (1 John 4:1). They propagated a high and solemn sort of piety, a piety which claimed immediate communion with God and operated with slogans like "I know Him," "I abide in Him," "I am in the Light" (1 John 2:4, 6, 9), and "I love God" (1 John 4:20). They probably felt themselves and professed themselves to be a new elite in Christendom, the "advanced" type of Christian. John is probably referring to them in his second letter when he speaks of those who "go ahead" and do not abide in the doctrine of Christ (2 John 9). It was no wonder that they deceived many and that many who remained in the church were perhaps not fully convinced that the church had been in the right when it separated itself from them. Or there might well have been some who were still secretly attracted to this brilliant new theology.

They deceived many, these new teachers. But they could not deceive the heart of John, for that heart was in fellowship with the Father and with His Son Jesus (1 John 1:3). The eyes that had seen the Word of life in the flesh (1 John 1:1) saw these men for what they were. They are, in John's clear vision of them,

not prophets of God, but false prophets (1 John 4:1); their words
are inspired not by the Spirit of truth, but by the spirit of error
(1 John 4:6); they are not the Christ's, but the very embodiment
of the antichrist of the last days (1 John 2:18), impelled and
informed by the spirit of the antichrist (1 John 2:22; 4:3) who
inspires the lie.

What was this lie? They denied not the deity, but the full
humanity of the Christ. They denied that Jesus, the man in
history, was the Christ, the Son of God (1 John 2:22; cf. 4:3;
4:15; 5:5); they denied that Jesus was the Christ who had come
"in the flesh" (1 John 4:2; cf. 2 John 7). We get a hint of how
far this denial went in the words of John which state positively
the significance of the Christ who came in the flesh: "This is He
who came by water and blood, Jesus Christ, not with the water
only, but with the water and the blood" (1 John 5:6). These
words are in themselves somewhat obscure; but they become
clearer against the background of the heresy which they combat.
That heresy was most probably the heresy of Cerinthus and his
followers, of which Irenaeus has left us a description (*Adv. Haer.*
I. 26, 1). Cerinthus, according to Irenaeus, taught that Jesus
was a man among men, a superior man but still merely man,
the son of Joseph and Mary; at His baptism the "heavenly Christ"
descended upon Him in the form of a dove and enabled Him to
reveal the hitherto unknown God and to perform miracles; at His
Passion, however, the "heavenly Christ" again left Jesus, and only
Jesus the man suffered and died. In other words, the Christ
came "by water" (the baptism of Jesus), but did not come "by
blood" (the Passion and death of Jesus). The cross of Jesus,
the shed blood of the Son of God, which the apostolic witness
celebrated as the crown and culmination of the ministry of Christ,
was thus ignored or relegated to the background. The blood of
Jesus, the Son of God, was no longer the blood which "cleanses
us from all sin." (1 John 1:7)

Where the cross is not taken seriously, sin is no longer taken
seriously either. Men whose proud piety centers in their assumed
knowledge of God and ignores the cross in which God has revealed Himself as both the Judge of sinful man and the Forgiver
of sinners, can think of sin as something which need not concern

them; they can deceive themselves and say that they have no sin; they can say, "We have not sinned," and thus make a liar of God, who has in the cross declared that all men have sinned (1 John 1:8, 10) and has in the cross given His Son as the "expiation . . . for the sins of the whole world" (1 John 2:2). Such a piety can be comfortable in this world; the offense of the cross is gone, and the lives of Christians are no longer a walking indictment of the sins of the world. The world which does not recognize the children of God, but rather hates them (1 John 3:1, 13), can come to terms with these men and with the Christ whom they proclaim: "They are of the world; therefore what they say is of the world, and the world listens to them" (1 John 4:5).

Over against these men John asserts, with all the concentrated power that this inspired Son of Thunder can command, the full reality of the incarnation, the fact that life and communion with God are to be found in Jesus, the Christ who came and died for man's sin in the flesh, or they will not be found at all; that any claim to know and love God which does not produce a life of righteousness and love is a blank lie; that the child of God cannot ever, without denying himself and his God, be at home in the world which is in the power of the Evil One. The letter is controversial and polemical, but it is not merely or one-sidedly polemical. John meets the danger which threatens the church by a powerfully positive restatement of what the Christian life really is, a passionate appeal to recognize in action the full measure of the gift and the full extent of the claim of that grace of God which has given man fellowship with the Father and with the Son.

Content of the First Letter of John

The thought movement which is characteristic of John's Gospel is apparent in this letter also. The utterances of John move not step for step in a straight line, but spiral-fashion, circling around three great themes with a continual enrichment of the thought at each turn. Consequently, there is a considerable overlapping, both in the main divisions and in the subdivisions, and no formal outline is a really adequate guide to the letter. It is, in the last analysis, best grasped and appropriated meditatively by giving oneself to its movement with energetic sympathy and without too

much concern for grasping it structurally. But as a first guide to
the letter the kind of outline developed by Robert Law and
Theodor v. Haering is useful. The letter is viewed as a series of
tests of the Christian life, tests which enable us to examine and
assay the genuineness of the Christian's life under the revelation
given by God in His Son.

Test Yourselves

Introduction: The Revelation, 1:1-4. God has spoken His
ultimate Word, the Word of eternal life in the concrete, visible,
palpable historical reality of His incarnate Son. With that Word
He has admitted man to fellowship with Himself, and has placed
men into fellowship with one another.

The Tests of the Christian Life Under That Revelation

I. The First Standard: "God is light and in Him is no darkness
at all," 1:5. Fellowship with God means "walking in the
light"; test yourselves to know if you are walking in darkness
or in the light, 1:5—2:28.

A. The Test of Righteousness, 1:8—2:6

1. Walking in the light means facing the fact of your sin,
confessing your sin, and receiving forgiveness of sins by
the atoning death of Christ; only thus is your fellowship
with God a genuine fellowship, 1:8—2:2.

2. Walking in the light means keeping the commandments
of God, keeping His word, and walking as Christ walked,
2:3-6.

B. The Test of Love, 2:7-17

1. Walking in the light means keeping the old, and yet new,
commandment of love; you cannot hate your brother and
walk in the light, 2:7-14.

2. Walking in the light means loving the Father, not the
dying and doomed world which is in revolt against Him,
2:15-17.

C. The Test of True Belief, 2:18-28

Walking in the light means holding to the Christ as revealed to you from the beginning by the Spirit as the incar-

nate Christ; it means rejecting the lie of the antichrist who denies the incarnate Christ and thus denies the Father too.

II. The Second Standard: "We are God's children now," 3:2. Fellowship with God means being God's children; test yourselves to know whether you are born of God, 2:29—4:6.

A. The Test of Righteousness, 2:29—3:10

The Son of God, through whom you are children of God, appeared to take away sins, 3:6, to destroy the works of the devil, 3:8; being born of God therefore means a radical antagonism to the devil (who "has sinned from the beginning," 3:8), and a total aversion from sin, 3:9. Those who sin are children of the devil, not children of God, 3:10.

B. The Test of Love, 3:11-24

The Son of God laid down His life for us, 3:16; thereby He laid upon the sons of God His commandment that they should love one another, 3:11. To believe in the name of God's Son and to love one another as sons of God, these two things cannot be separated from each other. To hate, as Cain hated, is to be a murderer and a child of the devil and to abide in death; to love as Christ loved, in deed and in truth, is to be a child of God, with a child's confidence before God, the assurance of being heard by Him.

C. The Test of True Belief, 4:1-6

God's final revelation has been the Word made flesh, 4:2; cf. 1:1-4; this revelation has drawn the line of division between the children of God and the world: Christ and antichrist, true prophecy and false prophecy, the Spirit of truth and the spirit of error, the Spirit of God and the spirit of antichrist, confront one another in absolute antithesis. The test of true belief is therefore clear and simple: whether or not a man believes the final Word of God as God has spoken it, that is, as the Word spoken "in the flesh," 4:2, determines whether a man is a child of God or not.

III. The Third Standard: "God Is Love," 4:7—5:12

Test yourselves to know whether you are of God. The three tests recur in this section, but not in the same order.

Rather, the thought that they are all three closely related with one another and therefore inseparable is stressed; therefore the three tests in this section interlock and overlap.

A. The Test of Love, 4:7-12; 4:16-21; 5:1, 2

B. The Test of True Belief, 4:13-15; 5:5-12

C. The Test of Righteousness, 5:2-5

Conclusion: The Great Certainties to Which We Hold, 5:13-20

1. The certainty of eternal life, 5:13.

2. The certainty that our prayer is heard, 5:14-17.

3. The certainty that our life as God's children means separation from sin, 5:18.

4. The certainty that the Christian life means radical antagonism to the world, which is dominated by the Evil One, 5:19.

5. The certainty that in the Son of God we have the true revelation of the true God and eternal life, 5:20.

Closing admonition: "Keep yourselves from idols." Faith in any Christ but the Christ who came in the flesh, faith in any God but the Father whom the Christ has revealed, is idolatry, 5:21.

Canonicity: Homologoumenon

Date of the First Letter of John

About all that can be said certainly is that the letter dates from John's long ministry in Asia Minor, which leaves a wide margin, from about A. D. 70 to about A. D. 100. The date of Cerinthus helps to narrow down the date of the letter somewhat more. Cerinthus was a contemporary of Polycarp, who died about A. D. 150. His activity as false teacher would thus probably fall into John's later years, somewhere between A. D. 90 and 100.

Value of the Letter

The First Letter of John is a letter written to Christians, to men whose faith is being endangered by heresy and is being tried by temptation. Although the usual letter forms (salutation, close, etc.) are missing, it is nevertheless a genuine letter, written for a specific situation by a father in Christ to his "children," and it is pervaded by an intense personal and pastoral concern for these "children." In its white-hot passion for the truth, for a Christian Gospel and a Christian life that is genuine, whole, and uncompromised, it remains a tonic and bracing word for the church always. It summons a church grown easy and comfortable to bethink itself penitently of the basic facts and the basic laws of its existence. Nowhere is black so black and white so white as in this letter; the antithesis of truth-lie, Christ-antichrist, God-devil leaves the church no possibility of doubt as to where she must stand. And the letter likewise leaves no doubt that the church *can* stand where she must stand; the greatness of God's enabling gift is lettered out in pithy statements which are as profound as they are brief and pointed. Perhaps no New Testament book of like compass has furnished so many brief sayings, sayings that Christian men can lay up in their hearts, to live by and to die on, as this First Letter of John. (E. g., 1:5, 8; 2:2, 9-11, 15-17, 23; 3:1, 2; 4:1-3, 7-12, 19; 5:3-5, 11, 12)

THE SECOND LETTER OF JOHN

Destination of the Second Letter

The Second Letter of John is addressed by one who calls himself simply "the elder" to "the elect lady and her children" (2 John 1). This is probably a figurative way of addressing a church (the word for church is feminine in Greek), rather than a literal address to some Christian woman and her children. The very broad statement of the salutation, "whom I love in the truth, and not only I, but also all who know the truth" (2 John 1) is more suitable to a church than to an individual. The expression in verse 4, "I rejoiced greatly to find some of your children following the truth," is most naturally understood of a church, some of whose members had resisted the inroads of the heresy which was then ravaging the church of Asia Minor. The greeting of verse 13, "The children of your elect sister greet you," also seems to be more naturally taken as a greeting from a sister church in whose midst the Elder is writing. And finally, the content of the letter (the renewal of the commandment of love and a stern warning against false teachers) seems eminently suitable as a message to a church. Besides, if the "elect lady" is an individual, why is she not named, as Gaius is named in the Third Letter of John?

Occasion, Purpose, and Content of the Second Letter of John

The letter was occasioned by the activity of false teachers, most probably the same group that John dealt with in his first letter. There is the same emphasis on the commandment of love (5, 6), the same emphasis on the reality of the incarnation of the Son of God (His "coming . . . in the flesh," 7), the same designation of the false teaching as deceit and the work of the antichrist (7), the same insistence on the fact that no one can know the Father except through the incarnate Son (9). The letter contains one of the sternest warnings in the New Testament against participating in, or furthering, the activities of those who pervert the Gospel (10, 11). It is this furthering of the work of the false teachers that is referred to, of course, in the words, "Do not receive him into the house or give him any greeting" (10); evangelists were dependent on the hospitality of Christians as they moved from place to place, as the Third Letter of John shows; they had no missionary fund to draw on.

Date of the Second Letter

The second letter is probably to be dated about the same time as the First Letter of John. The designation, the "elder," would seem to indicate that John had outlived his generation and had become the grand old man of the church in Asia Minor.

Canonicity: Antilegomenon

THE THIRD LETTER OF JOHN

Occasion and Purpose of the Third Letter

The Third Letter of John gives us another glimpse into the apostolic activity of John in his latter years. If the first and second letters dealt with heresy, the third letter deals with a missionary problem. The recipient of the letter, "the beloved Gaius," had distinguished himself by his loyal support of some traveling evangelists (5-8). These evangelists had meanwhile reported to their home church, probably at Ephesus, and had there testified to the love which Gaius had shown them (6). He had done so in the face of grave difficulties; a certain Diotrephes had sought, and was at the time of writing still seeking, to put himself in control of the church to which Gaius belonged and had refused to welcome the missionary brethren. He went even farther than that and sought to stop those who wished to receive the missionaries and "put them out of the church" (9, 10). In so doing he was consciously opposing the Elder himself. (9)

Content of the Third Letter of John

John in his letter warmly commends Gaius, who has by his support of the missionaries shown himself as a "fellow worker in the truth" (8); at the same time he commends to Gaius the bearer of the letter, Demetrius, who is probably the leader of a group of evangelists (12). Since a letter to the church dominated by Diotrephes has not had the desired effect, John promises to come himself and to deal with Diotrephes and to put an end to his malicious "prating." (9, 10)

When the Lord called Paul to be His apostle, He said, "I will show him *how much he must suffer* for the sake of My name" (Acts 9:16). What the Lord said of Paul held for all the apostles; they remained servants and sufferers to the end. John never became his serene highness, the lord of the church of Asia; he remained the apostle of the Crucified, with no power but that of the word with which he was entrusted, the contradictable word of the Gospel. He lived and worked "in honor and dishonor, in ill repute and good repute" (2 Cor. 6:8). The New Testament has preserved the record of the apostle's dishonor too; these things are written for the apostolic church and for our learning.

Canonicity: Antilegomenon

Date of the Third Letter

The third letter probably dates from the same period as the first and second letters. Some scholars think that the letter to the church referred to in 3 John 9 may be our Second Letter of John. This cannot be either proved or disproved.

THE REVELATION TO JOHN

Occasion and Purpose

Revelation is, in form, a letter addressed to seven churches in the Roman province of Asia (Rev. 1:4), complete with salutation and closing benediction (Rev. 1:4; 22:21). The situation which called forth the writing is made clear by the writing itself: the churches are being troubled by false teachers (Rev. 2:6, 14, 15), slandered and harassed by Jews, the "synagog of Satan" (Rev. 2:9; 3:9), and are undergoing a persecution (Rev. 1:9) which has already cost the lives of some faithful witnesses (Rev. 2:13; 6:9, 10) but has not yet reached its height (Rev. 6:11). To these churches John, himself in banishment on the island of Patmos "on account of the word of God and the testimony of Jesus" (Rev. 1:9), writes the account of the visions vouchsafed to him there, the record of "the revelation of Jesus Christ, which God gave Him to show to His servants" (Rev. 1:1). He writes in order to strengthen them in their trials, both internal and external, to hold before them the greatness and the certitude of their hope in Christ, and to assure them of their victory, with Christ, over all the powers of evil now let loose upon the world and, to all appearances, destined to triumph on earth. The book is thoroughly practical, like all the books of the New Testament, designed to be read in the worship services of the churches, as the first of the seven beatitudes which the book pronounces shows: "Blessed is he who reads aloud the words of the prophecy, and blessed are those who hear, and who keep what is written therein; for the time is near." (Rev. 1:3)

Time and Place of Writing

Irenaeus' statement (*Adv. Haer.* V, 30, 3) that Revelation was written toward the close of the reign of the emperor Domitian (A. D. 81—96) gives us the most probable date for the book, A. D. 95 or 96. Domitian was the first Roman emperor to make an issue of emperor worship; and since the emperor cult was propagated with great zeal in the province of Asia, the collision between the emperor who laid claim to men's worship as "Lord and God" and those who would call no one Lord but Jesus and would worship Him alone proved to be inevitable in Asia. That

John should have been banished from Ephesus to Patmos, off the coast of Asia, "on account of the word of God and the testimony of Jesus" (Rev. 1:9), that Antipas should have died a martyr's death at Pergamum in Asia (Rev. 2:13), that the souls of men who had been slain for the witness they had borne should cry aloud for vindication (Rev. 6:9, 10) — all this fits in naturally with the historical situation in Asia in the latter years of Domitian's reign. The payment of divine honors to the emperor was made the test of loyalty; the Christian had to refuse, and that refusal made him liable to the penalty of death. The visions given to John made it unmistakably plain to the churches why the Christian had to refuse and die; and these visions wrote out in letters of gold and fire the promise that such dying was not defeat but triumph, a triumph which man shared with the Lamb that was slain, with Him who is King of kings and Lord of lords, whose people go His way through death to victory and royal reign.

The Literary Form of the Book

Revelation, with its visions of riders, trumpets, and bowls, of dragon and beasts, its use of number symbolism, and its mysterious and suggestive style generally, strikes the modern reader as strange and bizarre, and he is inclined to agree with Luther when he says, "My spirit cannot adapt itself to this book." Much in the book that puzzles us today was familiar to John's first readers; much that we can gain access to only by laborious study and by a gradual process of sympathetic immersion into this alien world spoke directly to them. They had been familiarized with the imagery of John's vision by a form of Judaic religious literature known as "apocalyptic." Apocalyptic elaborated certain elements or aspects of Old Testament prophecy, found in such passages and books as Isaiah 24—27, Zechariah 9—14, Ezekiel, Joel, and Daniel. It sought to interpret all history on the basis of purported visionary experiences of the author. It was especially interested in eschatology, that is, in the end of history and the ushering in of the world to come. It utilized pictures, allegories, and symbols (which soon became traditional); numbers, colors, and stars were in these images endowed with a profound significance. Books of this type were The Book of Enoch, The Book of Jubilees, Fourth Esdras, The Assumption of Moses.

Formally, Revelation belongs to this class; apocalyptic, as it were, furnished the familiar vocabulary of its speech. But Revelation is set apart from the general run of apocalyptic literature by profound differences. Apocalyptic itself drew heavily on the Old Testament; John draws even more heavily. No other New Testament book can compare with it in the number of allusions to the Old Testament; Revelation is saturated with the Old Testament. In fact, it is the Old Testament itself and not apocalyptic that constitutes the immediate background and the richest source for Revelation. Revelation is at bottom much more deeply akin to the Old Testament than it is to the apocalyptic which it resembles so strongly on the formal side. Other differences are equally striking. Apocalyptic works are generally pseudonymous; that is, they claim some great figure from Israel's past, such as Enoch, as author; and the past course of history as known to the actual author is made a prediction in the mouth of the purported author. John, however, writes in his own name. Apocalyptic has speculative interests and seeks to calculate the times and seasons of the world's last days and the world's end. John has no such speculative interest; he does not aim to satisfy men's curiosity but to give them hope and courage, and he does not attempt to calculate the approach of the end. "I come quickly," is the burden of the revelation of Christ as given to John. The visions of apocalyptic betray their origin; they are the fantasies of men. The visions of John have on them the stamp of genuine visionary experience; they are not products of the study. If apocalyptic may be termed literary meditation on prophetic themes, Revelation is genuine prophecy, a prophecy which uses apocalyptic motifs and forms insofar, and only insofar, as they are legitimate explications of Old Testament prophetic themes and are germane to its own thoroughly Christ-centered proclamation. The Lord in speaking through John speaks in the tongues of men; but He does not think the thoughts of men.

The peculiar advantage or virtue of utterance in this form lies not in the precision and clarity with which the utterance can be made, but in the power with which the thing said can be brought to bear on the whole man — on his mind, his imagination, his feelings, his will. His whole inner life is caught up in the moving terror and splendor of these visions; and the course and bent of his life are determined by them as they could hardly be determined by any other kind of communication. But just this characteristic of the book has given rise to widely divergent interpretations of the book; men have attempted, usually in a one-sided fashion, to be more precise in their interpretation of the book than the book itself by its very nature can be. One group of interpreters has fixed on the fact that the visions have their occasion and basis in real historical events and interprets the book wholly in terms of what had already happened at the time of writing; they see no real prediction anywhere in it, but merely an interpretation of past events in the guise of prediction. This, of course, ignores the prophetic claim of the book itself. Others refer everything but the content of the first three chapters to the very end of time, to the period immediately preceding the advent of Christ, and think of it as still awaiting fulfillment. This ignores the fact that for the author himself all time since the ascension of Christ is the time immediately preceding the advent of Christ and makes the book largely irrelevant for the very people for whom it was first written. Others again see in the visions a more or less detailed predictive portrayal of the successive events of universal history or of the history of the church to the end of time; here again one must ask how such a series of predictions was to be of any aid and comfort to the troubled churches of Asia A. D. 95. Still others renounce all attempts to relate the message of the book *directly* to history and see in the visions rather the enunciation of general principles which will hold good throughout history. But the book itself, with its life-and-death involvement in the crisis of A. D. 95, is anything but the enunciation of abstract principles.

Each of these attempts to interpret the book is, in its one-sidedness, a falsification. A true interpretation will, with the first group, look for the roots of the work in the history contemporary with it, for the book was obviously written for the church's encouragement and strengthening at a certain time and place. It will, with the second group, recognize the fact that the prophecy embraces all time between the now of the church and the return of the Lord of the church. It will, with the third group, take seriously the relevance of the book to all history; but it will, with the last group, be inclined to see in it, not a blueprint of history but a divine light that strikes history and illumines where it strikes, a pointing finger of God to guide men through history and judgment to the end. If the book is so viewed and so taken to heart, its value for the church and the individual will not depend on the completeness of one's comprehension of every detail of its imagery.

Content of the Revelation to John

Revelation is a carefully constructed and elaborately articulated whole, in which the number seven is the dominant unit. An outline such as the following, which views the whole work as a series of seven visions, therefore commends itself as probable. It also seems to be clear that there is a major break between the third and fourth set of visions. This break is constituted not so much by a change of theme as by a change in the vantage point from which the theme is viewed and treated. Important for the understanding of the whole is the observation that each of the units (with the possible exception of the first) spans the whole period between the present and the return of the Lord Jesus, so that we have a set of parallel presentations of the same basic fact and truth, cumulative in effect as each presentation brings in a new aspect of the same basic theme. There is progression in the sense that the end of all things is portrayed with increasing fullness as the visions progress (return of the Lord, last judgment, the new world of God). We have here the same "spiral" thought-pattern that is characteristic of the Gospel and the First Letter of John.

Introduction, 1:1-3

Salutation, 1:4-8

The Seven Visions, 1:9—22:7

I. The First Three Visions: The Church of Christ and the Powers of This World, 1:9—11:19

   A. The First Vision: The exalted Christ in the midst of His church. The seven letters to the churches of Asia: instruction, warning, encouragement, 1:9—3:22.

B. The Second Vision: The vision of the seven seals. God enthroned presides over the history of the universe; the Lamb that was slain opens the seals of the book of the divine decrees, chaps. 4—7. (Chap. 7, an interlude between the sixth and seventh seals, promising security and deliverance to God's people amid God's judgments upon the world.)

C. The Third Vision: The vision of the seven trumpets. In response to the supplications of the saints that God might vindicate His truth, God proclaims the desolations that are to befall the sinful world in which the church bears witness, chaps. 8—11. (10:1—11:14, an interlude which describes the preservation of the witnessing church, despite the apparent triumph of the forces that oppose it.)

II. The Last Four Visions: Christ the Lord of the Church and the Powers of Darkness, 12:1—22:7

A. The Fourth Vision: The church, symbolized by a woman, brings forth the Christ, whom Satan attacks in vain. The assault of Satan upon the rest of the woman's offspring, the church, chap. 12. The two beasts employed by Satan as his agents, chap. 13; the militant church and the advancing stages of Christ's conquest, chap. 14.

B. The Fifth Vision: The vision of the seven bowls of wrath. The sevenfold judgment of God upon a wicked world; the triumph of the saints, chaps. 15, 16.

C. The Sixth Vision: The overthrow of the enemies of God and His Christ. Christ's victory over the city Babylon and over all His enemies. The last judgment, chaps. 17—20. (20:1-10, an interlude between the sixth and seventh scenes of the vision depicting the preservation and security of Christ's martyred people throughout the whole period.)

D. The Seventh Vision: The new heaven and the new earth, the new Jerusalem, 21:1—22:7.·

Conclusion: Dialogue between John and the Angel, 22:8, 9; the last words of Christ, 22:10-16; the prophet's word, 22:17-19; promise, prayer, and benediction, 22:20, 21.

Canonicity: Antilegomenon

Value of the Book

To men sitting in the quiet of their studies and to the church
at peace in the world the Revelation to John presents difficulties
and often brings perplexities. Others in the church have used the
book to feed their fevered dreams. But the book did not originate
as a book to be coolly pondered or as food to feed the dreams
of idle men. It is the cry of victory raised for the cause of Christ
when the cause of the Christ seemed doomed — what was this
pitifully weak assembly of nobodies to oppose the might of Rome?
This book took the word of Jesus, His beatitude upon the persecuted, with absolute seriousness and wrote it into the history
of the church when it was clearly becoming a bloody history:
"Rejoice and be glad, for your reward is great in heaven!" And
so it has happened again and again in the history of the church
that when all secular securities were swept away and all human
guarantees of triumph were lost, men have turned to this book.
They turned to this book, which looks with the same unperturbed
clarity of vision upon the face of Satan and upon the face of God
and His Anointed and sees written in both the triumph of God
and His Christ. Men have turned to this book and have found
the strength not only to endure, but to sing. The doxologies of
the book of Revelation have echoed in the church most mightily
just when men as men could find no cause for songs of praise.

AUTHENTICITY OF THE WORKS ATTRIBUTED TO JOHN

The question of the authenticity of the works attributed to
John, especially the Gospel, has been for more than a century
one of the most warmly debated questions in the field of New
Testament studies. Since the question is in the main the same
for all the works (although the question concerning Revelation
has its own difficulties too), and since the decision concerning
the Gospel will largely determine the decision on the other works,
it can be treated as one question. The debate has been a long
and involved one and has never been conducted along purely
historical lines, but has been deeply influenced by theological considerations (that is, by the nature of the religious content of the
books). Therefore only the main lines of argument can be noted
here. The validity and strength of the ancient tradition which

assigns these works to John the son of Zebedee, the apostle and eyewitness of Jesus, is the first fact to be noted, and the arguments used to discredit that tradition must be the beginning student's first concern. He can judge the strength and weakness of the theologically colored arguments only after he has become thoroughly acquainted with the works themselves.

The Ephesian Ministry of John

The ancient tradition assigns the works of John to the time of his ministry at Ephesus in Asia Minor. If it can be shown, therefore, that John the apostle never reached Ephesus and never worked there, the ancient testimony concerning the authorship of the works attributed to John is, of course, greatly weakened. Many scholars maintain that John the apostle never did reach Ephesus, but died a martyr's death in Judea, either at the same time as his brother James (A. D. 44) or in the 60s at the latest. The following are the chief arguments used to support this contention: (a) The prophecy of Jesus (Mark 10:39) that the sons of Zebedee would drink His cup and share His baptism is held to imply that both James and John must have died a martyr's death. But it should be noted that even if John did die a martyr's death (a question which need not be discussed here) there is nothing in the prophecy to indicate that he died early, in Judea. (b) A ninth-century chronicler, Georgius Hamartolos, following a fifth-century source, the Chronicle of Philip of Side, quotes Papias (second century) to the effect that John was killed "by Jews." This, it is contended, points to an early martyrdom of John and marks the tradition of his Ephesian ministry as legendary. However there is not a syllable, either in the quotation from Papias or in Georgius' own words, to indicate that John was martyred *early, in Judea*. Georgius, in fact, states that John lived on into the reign of the emperor Nerva (A. D. 96—98). (c) Church calendars of the ancient church seem to indicate that John was martyred at the same time as his brother James (A. D. 44). A Syrian martyrology (a listing of martyrs' festivals) remarks on December 27: "John and James, the apostles [died as martyrs], in Jerusalem." Scholars have long ago noted that the ancient martyrologies are not trustworthy guides to history: a Carthaginian martyrology, for instance, contradicts the Syrian one by linking John the *Baptist* with James in the commemoration of December 27. Besides, if the Syrian martyrology be taken at face value, it proves too much; for John, according to the evidence given by Paul (Gal. 2:9), outlived his brother James and was in Jerusalem at the time of Paul's second post-conversion visit to Jerusalem, which falls later than the death of James, the son of Zebedee.

This will perhaps suffice to indicate the nature and the strength of the arguments used to discredit the tradition of the Ephesian ministry of John. The tradition of John's ministry at Ephesus is found first in Irenaeus (c. A. D. 180), who is linked by a direct line of tradition to John himself: Irenaeus drew on the eye-and-ear witness of Polycarp, who had been a disciple of John's in his youth. Irenaeus also knew other "elders," men of the previous generation who had associated with John in Ephesus. This tradition is never questioned or contradicted in the ancient church. Until more valid arguments are brought forward to overthrow it, we may accept it with confidence.

The Gospel

Because the Fourth Gospel differs so strikingly from the Synoptic Gospels in both form and matter and because it gives so high and exalted a picture of the Christ, critical scholarship has for the last century or more questioned or denied the possibility that it is the work of the son of Zebedee; and there has been a strong tendency to discount or discredit the evidence for the apostolic authorship of the Gospel. But both the tradition of the early church and the witness of the Gospel itself are very strong, and both point unambiguously to John the son of Zebedee as the author of the Gospel.

By the end of the second century we find the Gospel of John established as an authority in the church alongside the first three Gospels. It is included in the first Gospel harmony of Christendom, the *Diatessaron* of Tatian (c. A. D. 170), which opens with the first sentence of John and closes with the last. About A. D. 170 Theophilus of Antioch quotes from the Fourth Gospel and names John as its author. About A. D. 180 Irenaeus testifies expressly to the Johannine authorship of the Gospel; as was noted above, his testimony is particularly valuable, for he had in his

youth known Polycarp of Smyrna, who in turn had known John
the apostle in his youth. About the same time the Muratorian
Canon, a listing of the New Testament books accepted as authoritative by the church of Rome, attributes the Fourth Gospel to
John the apostle. A little later Clement of Alexandria records
a tradition of the "elders" (that is, the generation before him)
on the sequence of the four Gospels and adds that John wrote his
Gospel last of all at the urging of his friends.

We have, then, at the close of the second century, evidence
from various quarters of the church (Gaul, Rome, Asia Minor,
Egypt) in favor of the apostolic authorship of the Gospel. And
there is really no *historical* evidence to the contrary. The Gospel
was rejected by members of an obscure sect whom Epiphanius
calls the Alogi and by a certain presbyter Gaius of Rome; but
their reasons for so doing were doctrinal and not historical. There
is no indication that they had any historical evidence which called
into question the Johannine authorship of the Gospel.

Some scholars maintain, on the basis of an ambiguous fragment of Papias, that there were two Johns of note in Ephesus
in the early days, the apostle John and an Elder (or Presbyter)
John, and that Irenaeus mistakenly attributed the Gospel to the
apostle, while it was in reality written by the Elder. If this be so,
not only was Irenaeus mistaken, he succeeded in making the whole
ancient church share in his mistake. But it is not even certain
that the Papias fragment speaks of two Johns at Ephesus; Eusebius
so interprets it and assigns Revelation to the Elder. However,
even if Eusebius is right in distinguishing two Johns, it should
be noted that he does not assign the *Gospel* to the Elder, and
neither does any one else in the ancient church. In fact, on any
interpretation, the Elder remains a very shadowy figure; and the
theory that he is the author of the Fourth Gospel leaves us with
the unanswered question: How could a relatively unknown person,
not an apostle, have added a Gospel (and so different a Gospel)
to the existing three so late and yet win universal acceptance for
it so easily?

The evidence of the Gospel itself, which cannot be recounted
in detail here, is strongly in favor of apostolic authorship. It indicates that the author was a Jew; his style and thought are fun-

damentally Semitic, and he gives evidence of familiarity with the
Hebrew Old Testament (John 13:18; 19:37). The *Jewish Encyclopedia,* which certainly has no pro-apostolic bias, regards this
Gospel as an important authority for rabbinical ideas current in
Palestine before the destruction of the temple A. D. 70. And even
scholars who reject the apostolic authorship insist on the funda-
mentally Jewish character of the work.

The Gospel likewise indicates that the author was a Palestinian.
He is familiar with the culture and geography of Palestine; he
identifies unimportant places with exact detail (e. g., John 3:23).
His notices concerning the pool of Bethesda (John 5:2) have been
confirmed by recent (1932) excavations. And he shows himself
to be familiar with the arrangements of the Jerusalem temple
(John 8:20; 10:23). The recently discovered literature of a Judaic (Essene?) sect at Qumrân has confirmed the findings of those
scholars who saw in the Fourth Gospel, linguistically and historically, a product of Palestine as over against those who disputed
the apostolic authorship on the grounds that its language and
thought betray alien influences.

The Gospel further indicates that its author was an eyewitness
to the events which he records; many graphic details attest this
(e. g., John 9:27 ff.), and in a number of passages this fact of
eyewitnessing is directly claimed by or for the author (John 19:35;
cf. 1:14; 21:24). And the Gospel indirectly declares that this
eyewitness is John the son of Zebedee. In the Fourth Gospel,
and in it alone, there figures prominently a disciple who is left
unnamed, but is referred to as "the disciple whom Jesus loved"
(John 13:23; 19:26; 20:2; 21:7, 20-23). In two passages an unnamed disciple likewise figures, and he is probably to be identified
with the disciple whom Jesus loved (John 1:40; 18:15 f.). Since
this disciple is present at the last supper (John 13:23), he is one
of the Twelve. Since he is on terms of peculiar intimacy with the
Lord and appears together with Peter on a number of occasions
(John 13:23 ff.; 20:2 ff.; 21:20 ff.), we may assume that he is
one of the favored three referred to in the Synoptic Gospels
(Peter, James, and John). Since Peter is excluded by the narrative itself and James is excluded by his early death (Acts 12:2),
there remains only John the son of Zebedee as "the disciple whom

Jesus loved"; thus John 21:24 points to John the son of Zebedee as the author of the Gospel (cf. 21:20): "This is the disciple who is bearing witness to these things, and who has written these things." This identification is supported by the fact that the author of the Gospel never mentions John the son of Zebedee by name and calls John the Baptist simply "John."

In the face of such evidence it seems idle to raise the question whether a Galilean fisherman, an associate of Jesus in the days when He walked the ways of Palestine, could have written so exalted a record and so profound an interpretation of the Christ. The life of Jesus is without parallel in the annals of mankind; the sending of the Spirit is without analogy in the experience of mankind — it is the unprecedented, eschatological act of God. Who is to say what a man who has beheld that life and has been led by that Spirit into all truth could or could not have written? The church from the second to the nineteenth century has accepted the Gospel as the work of the Spirit through John the apostle. If the church of the nineteenth and twentieth centuries is to reverse that judgment, she must have reasons that are cogent indeed.

The First Letter

There can be little doubt that the first letter is by the same author as the Gospel of John. The very first words of the letter seem expressly designed to recall the opening of the Gospel (1 John 1:1-4), and the first letter and the Gospel have so many traits of language and style in common and have so large an agreement in substance that only common authorship serves to explain them, as most modern scholars also have recognized. The answer to the question of the authorship of the First Letter of John is therefore given with the answer to the question of the authorship of the Fourth Gospel. Those features which are peculiar to the first letter, as over against the Gospel, are readily explained by the particular purpose of the letter.

The Second and Third Letters of John

The second and third letters are not so well attested in the ancient church as the first letter; there was, in fact, some doubt as to their authorship. But the evidence of the letters themselves indicates that they are, first, both by the same author. Compare, for example, 2 John 1 and 3 John 1; 2 John 4 and 3 John 3, 4; 2 John 10 and 3 John 8; 2 John 12 and 3 John 13, 14. The evidence further indicates that the two shorter letters are by the same author as the first letter. Compare 1 John 2:7 with 2 John 5; 1 John 2:18 and 4:1-3 with 2 John 7; 1 John 2:23 with 2 John 9; 1 John 3:6-9 with 3 John 11. In the light of such evidence one can understand why Eusebius, surveying the situation in the church as it had developed by the beginning of the fourth century, included the smaller letters of John among those books of the New Testament "that are controverted by some, *yet recognized by most.*"

Since the author of both these short letters designates himself simply as "the elder," some scholars are inclined to ascribe these letters to an "elder" or Presbyter John, distinct from John the apostle. But there are two difficulties in the way of interpreting "elder" as a description of office, that is, as presbyter. For one thing, there were so many presbyters in the churches of Asia that the mere designation "elder" could hardly serve by itself to identify a man. For another, the kind of authority exercised by the "elder" of the letters in congregations obviously not his own far exceeds that which any mere presbyter might exercise or aspire to. It is more natural to see in this word "elder" a self-designation of the apostle in the later days of the church when the men of the older apostolic generation had become few and were distinguished from others by their age. According to tradition, John outlived his co-apostles and could therefore have been known as *"the* elder" (the outstanding man of the first generation) in the churches to which he ministered in his old age.

The Revelation to John

The Gospel and the three letters of John give a unified impression; in thought and language they are patently the creation of one man. The Revelation to John diverges strikingly from the rest of the works of John in both thought and language. Many conceptions which are central for the Gospel and the letters are absent from Revelation (e. g., light, truth, grace, peace, the only Son, the Paraclete or Counselor, as a title of the Holy Spirit;

the antitheses light/darkness, above/below, lie/truth). Instead of
the simple and correct Greek of the other works, Revelation has
the strangest, harshest, and least "correct" Greek in the New
Testament; it is Hebrew thinking transferred directly to Greek,
and the most elementary laws of Greek grammar seem to be
arbitrarily violated.

But if the divergences in thought are striking, a closer examination reveals that the agreements between Revelation and the
other Johannine works are no less so. The Gospel and Revelation
agree in their view of the predicament of man. For the Gospel
man as man is in darkness and the world as world is under the
judgment of God. This is what Revelation too declares with its
visions of judgmental riders, trumpets of doom, and bowls of
wrath. If in the Gospel Jesus calls those who oppose Him
children of the devil and sees the world which hates Him under
the dominion of the prince of this world, the devil, Revelation
makes plain that the powers which persecute the church get their
will and impetus from Satan. In both the Gospel and Revelation
the line between the church and the world, between those who
are Christ's and those who are not, is most rigorously drawn,
with no compromise or mediation: The Gospel speaks in terms
of light, truth, life, and love as contrasted with darkness, lie,
death, and hate; Revelation draws the same line between the
white-robed, adoring saints of Christ united with God in the light,
on the one hand, and the world bewitched by magic, worshiping
the beast, subject to the dark dominion of the devil and under
the wrath of God on the other hand.

And even the language, for all its strangeness and harshness,
does not exclude a common authorship of the Gospel and of
Revelation. This Greek is not bungler's Greek; if it is strongly
Semitic, the Greek of the Gospel and the letters is, despite its
superior smoothness and correctness, strongly Semitic too. If it
diverges from the normal laws of the Greek language, it does so
intentionally and with powerful effect; it consciously recalls the
language of the Greek Old Testament and has a marked poetic
rhythm. Scholars are not so ready as they once were to say that
the Greek of Revelation is impossible for the author of the Gospel.

Given the difference in kind between the two works, the difference between the ecstasy of apocalyptic vision and the quieter, reverent eyewitness report, the difference is not so startling as it at first appears to be. And Revelation has in common with the Gospel a whole series of terms and conceptions which are found only in the Gospel of John: Jesus as the Word of God, Jesus as the Lamb of God, Jesus as the Shepherd, the water of life, the true worship of God independent of any temple (John 4:20 ff.; Rev. 21:22). This does not exhaust the resemblances, but will suffice to indicate the state of the case.

There is one more link between Revelation and the Gospel of John; that is the link of personality. Some have found it impossible to think that the high serenity of the Gospel and the furious intensity of Revelation should be the product of one mind and heart. The two books are not, of course, the product of any human personality; but the problem remains, for when God speaks through men, He does not blank out human personality, but uses it. One should not forget what an amazing range of experiences the life of this passionate Son of Thunder comprehended. He had seen the Word made flesh and had beheld His glory; he had drawn on the fullness of the grace and truth incarnate in Jesus; he had seen the only Son of God go down before the hatred of men who resisted the light and loved darkness. He had seen Him who had proclaimed Himself to be the resurrection and the life risen from the dead, in the unbroken splendor of His eternal life. He had proclaimed this Prince of life to Jerusalem and had seen His own brother killed in the renewed collision between the truth and the lie. He had seen the fury of Nero break upon the church of Rome, and he had seen the judgment of God visited upon Jerusalem and the temple. The high serenity of the Gospel is not the serenity of ignorance or illusion, but the serenity of knowledge, the knowledge of the man who knows Jesus both as the Life of the world and as the Judge of mankind. Only those who shut their eyes to half of John's Gospel, to the dark and fearful shadow of judgment cast by the true light of the world, can think it impossible that John the son of Zebedee should have written both it and Revelation. In both works the judgment and the grace of God go hand in hand and move step for step toward God's wondrous goal. And in both there speaks a man whose vision of the Christ — whether that be the Christ thirsty and weary beside a well in Samaria or the Christ who breaks the seals of God's book and executes His sure and terrible decrees — has given him a unique and enduring authority, the authority of one who can step before the churches with the simple self-disclosure, "I, John."

CHAPTER XII: The Growth of the New Testament Word as a Collection: The Canon of the New Testament

---

The Terms "Canon" and "Canonicity"

By the end of the first century all the New Testament writings were in existence; we have seen how the word of the Lord grew in written form in various places and at various times in the first, decisive half-century of the existence of the apostolic church. But the 27 New Testament writings did not yet exist as a completed collection which as such was the authority for the faith and life of the church. That is, the New Testament writings did not yet exist as the New Testament *canon*. The Greek word *kanon*, from which our term "canon" is derived, developed a wide range of meanings from its original sense of "reed." It came to mean "measuring rod," "rule," "plumbline"; and from this physical sense there arose the transferred sense of "measure," "standard," "norm," or "model." A law, for instance, could be called a *kanon*. From the practice of compiling lists of standard, normative literary works, *kanon* acquired the sense of "list." In the New Testament itself we find the word used in the sense of "standard" (Gal. 6:16). In the Christian literature of the first three centuries it is used in various combinations to express the idea of "revealed truth as normative for the church." About A. D. 350 we find established the practice of referring to Biblical books as "canonical" or as "belonging to, or in, the canon." Two senses of canon seem to have merged here: a book is called canonical both because it is included in a list and because it has the character of a norm or standard. When we today speak of the New Testament canon, therefore, we speak of the New Testament writings as an aggregate, as a list or collection of books which is normative for the church.

Homologoumena and Antilegomena

When we speak of the canonicity of a New Testament book, we refer to its position in this normative list. Those books which were always and everywhere recognized as canonical are termed *homologoumena* ("agreed upon"); those books whose position in the canon was for a time disputed or doubtful are *antilegomena* ("spoken against"). The church fathers Origen (third century) and Eusebius (fourth century) gave the church this terminology; they used the terms to sum up the history of the 27 books up to their time. The terms are therefore a description of the history of the books in the life of the church, not primarily or even necessarily a judgment on their value. The *homologoumena* are: The four Gospels and Acts, the thirteen letters of Paul, the First letter of Peter and the First Letter of John. The *antilegomena* are: the Letter to the Hebrews, the Letter of James, the Second Letter of Peter, the Second and Third Letters of John, the Letter of Jude, and Revelation.

In a very real sense the New Testament church always had a canon, namely in the Old Testament Scriptures, which Jesus and His apostles had interpreted for the church as fulfilled in Jesus Christ and had given to the church as its "holy Scriptures." Christianity did not develop from a religion of Spirit into a religion of the Book, as some have claimed. It was from the beginning a "book religion," and the new book, our New Testament, took its place beside the old, not suddenly and magically, but by a gradual historical process over the years as the church worshiped, did its work, and fought its battles. The story of that process is a complicated one and sometimes difficult to trace; for the process was not uniform throughout the church, and our information is often tantalizingly incomplete. It will be traced here only in broadest outline.

Growth of the Canon: First Stage, A. D. 100—170

In this period there is, for the first, no discussion of the canon as such; that is, no one explicitly asks or answers the question,

"Which books are to be included in the list of those which are
normative for the church?" What we do find in the writings of
the so-called Apostolic Fathers (Clement of Rome, the Epistle
of Barnabas, Ignatius, Polycarp, Hermas, the Teaching of the
Twelve Apostles) is, first, a witness to the fact that the books
destined to become the New Testament canon are *there,* at work
in the church from the first. The books are quoted and alluded to,
more often without mention of author or title than by way of
formal quotation. Secondly, we find a witness to the fact that
the thought and life of the church were being shaped by the
content of the New Testament writings from the first, and moreover by the content of all types of New Testament writings. The
influence of all types of New Testament writings (Synoptic Gospels, Johannine works, Pauline Letters, the Catholic Letters) is
clearly discernible. To judge by the evidence of this period, the
four Gospels and the letters of Paul were everywhere the basic
units in the emerging canon of the New Testament.

And, thirdly, there is some specific witness in these writings
to the fact that the New Testament writings assumed a position
of authority in the church which they share with no other writings.
"The Lord" and "the apostles" appear as authoritative voices
besides the Old Testament Scriptures, at first usually without any
mention of the fact that these voices are preserved in writings.
But these voices of authority are also found directly associated
with the writings that contain them, and once or twice a saying
of Jesus is introduced by the formula regularly used to introduce
Old Testament citations, "It is written." This is high testimony
for authority, for the authority of the Old Testament was unquestioned in the first church.

Further evidence for the authority exercised by the New Testament writings is found in the fact, recorded by Justin Martyr,
that the New Testament writings (or at least the Gospels) were
read in the worship services of the church, interchangeably with
the Old Testament. This is perhaps the most significant bit of
evidence for this period — for one thing, Justin records it as
a well-established regular practice, so that we may fairly assume
that the practice had been long established in the churches. For
another, the fact of public reading in the churches became for

later generations one of the prime criteria of canonicity. This phenomenon is typical of the quiet, unplanned, and unofficial way in which the New Testament writings established themselves in the church. One might almost say that the church had a canon before she began to think about the canon.

Another piece of evidence for the authority exercised by the New Testament writings is the fact that heretics, such as the gnostics Basilides and Valentinus, appealed to them and sought by reinterpretation to base their teachings upon them. They used other sources of their own also, but the fact that they could not simply turn their backs on writings which were, after all, less directly useful to them than their own "tradition" speaks eloquently of the authority which the New Testament writings possessed for the church.

Indeed, it was a heretic who brought the question of the New Testament canon into clear focus and made it a theological concern for the church. Marcion dealt more radically with the New Testament books than did other heretics. He was not content merely to reinterpret and to supplement the existing books. He constructed a canon of his own, a canon consisting of the Gospel of Luke, radically revised by himself, and ten letters of Paul (his canon did not contain the Pastoral Letters). With this revised canon he confronted the church; these books, he claimed, and only these, contained the unadulterated Gospel. The church, which rejected the heresy of Marcion, was thus forced to deal explicitly with the question of the canon. From this time onward the canon is not merely the self-evident but undefined possession of the church; the church now becomes conscious of its embattled possession, and the canon emerges into the clear light of history.

Growth of the Canon: Second Stage, A. D. 170—220

In this period elements already present earlier seem to crystallize and take more definite shape. There is no longer any question as to the existence of the canon as a more or less definite quantity and as a decisive standard; only the extent of the canon is still open to question. Even that question is limited in scope, for about four fifths of the eventual canon of the church is already so firmly established as to be beyond debate.

Two documents from near the beginning of this period are an illustration of the remarkable agreement in various parts of the church concerning the basic limits of the canon. The one is a description of a persecution just past which the churches of Vienne and Lyons in Gaul sent to Asia Minor. The other is the work of a bishop, Theophilus of Antioch in Syria. The Syrian bishop and the Gallic churches have, so far as we can see, a practically identical basic New Testament; neither of them contains all the present 27 books — the absence of some from the lists may be accidental, since neither source is dealing explicitly with the question of the canon. And in neither of them is there any apocryphal material.

Three fathers of this period have in their writings left us a fairly complete picture of the situation in various parts of the church; they are Irenaeus of Lyons in Gaul (who was acquainted with the life of the churches in Asia and Rome also), Clement of Alexandria, and Tertullian of Carthage. Their writings indicate that all but one of the 27 books were somewhere known and accepted in the Christian church; the exception is the Second Letter of Peter. They show also that there was practical unanimity in the churches on all except seven of the New Testament books. The seven are: the Letter to the Hebrews, the Letter of James, the Second Letter of Peter, the Second and Third Letters of John, the Letter of Jude, and Revelation.

The growing self-consciousness of the church regarding its canon is most strikingly reflected in a document called the Muratorian Fragment or the Muratorian Canon. The document gets its name from the librarian of the Ambrosian Library in Milan, Muratori, who discovered the document in 1740. The beginning of the document has been lost, and its curiously corrupt and enigmatic Latin text (probably a rough translation of a Greek original) presents many problems. But the document does give us a clear and fairly complete picture of the canon of the church of Rome about A. D. 170. That canon includes 22 books. The five books omitted are: the Letter to the Hebrews, the First and Second Letters of Peter, the Letter of James, and one of the shorter letters of John.

The most startling omission is that of the First Letter of Peter;

it is startling because this letter is otherwise so widely attested and so generally accepted in the early church. This omission may be due to the mutilated state of the text. The canon includes also a Revelation of Peter, although the document notes that "some of us do not want it read in the church" — another indication of the importance of public reading in the question of canonicity. The Wisdom of Solomon is also included, without comment. The Shepherd of Hermas is rejected because of its recent origin; there is no objection to its content, but it is not to be used in the worship of the church alongside the prophets and apostles. The works of heretics are decisively rejected, as are letters written in support of Marcion's heresy and falsely attributed to Paul: "Gall is not to be mingled with honey." It is clear: The canon is not yet a finished thing. The content is to a large extent fixed; but some books still have not found their place in the canon, and there are some either in the canon or on the fringe of the canon which will not maintain their place.

Growth of the Canon: Third Stage, A. D. 220—400

The first part of this period, the third century, marks no decisive stage in the growth of the canon. The three chief witnesses for the state of the canon in this century are Origen, Dionysius of Alexandria, and Cyprian of Carthage. Origen is of special importance because of the immense range of his learning and because of his wide acquaintanceship with various branches of the church; he knew what writings were normative for the church, not only in his home Alexandria, but also in Rome, Antioch, Athens, and Caesarea. Origen knew and used all 27 books of our New Testament canon. He is the first ancient authority to take notice of the Second Letter of Peter; there is none of the *antilegomena* which he rejects, although he knows that they have not all won equal acceptance in the churches. His tendency is to be inclusive rather than exclusive; consequently it is difficult to determine the outer limits of his canon.

Dionysius of Alexandria, the pupil and successor of Origen, likewise was in communication with many branches of the church. His canon includes, besides the *homologoumena,* the Letter of James, the Letter to the Hebrews (which he, unlike Origen, considers Pauline) and the Second and Third Letters of John. He argues, on the basis of vocabulary, style, and content, that Revelation is not by John the Apostle, but he is not inclined to question its authority; the author is in his view another John, "a holy and inspired man," who "beheld the revelation and had knowledge and the gift of prophecy." Dionysius does not notice the Second Letter of Peter or the Letter of Jude.

Cyprian of Carthage is our witness for the West in this century. In his writings he cites all books of the New Testament except Paul's Letter to Philemon, the Letter of James, the Second Letter of Peter, the Second and Third Letters of John, the Letter of Jude, and the Letter to the Hebrews. This does not necessarily mean that these books were all unknown at Carthage or unacknowledged. There is evidence that the Second Letter of John, for instance, was accepted at Carthage during Cyprian's time. Of the *antilegomena* Cyprian frequently used and held in high esteem the Revelation to John.

Two things are noteworthy in the third century. One is the fact that the *antilegomena* are slowly gaining ground in the churches. The other is the absence of any official action on the canon: No commission of theologians, no church council defines the canon or imposes a canon on the church. The canon is not being *made;* it is growing and being recognized. This remains the case in the fourth century also, when the canon assumed the form that it was destined to retain ever after in the Western church. When the historian Eusebius of Caesarea early in the fourth century (A. D. 325) came to consider the canon of the church, he had nothing "official" to which he could appeal, no conciliar decrees, no definitive pronouncements that had behind them the authority of the whole church. His discussion of the canon is in essence a historical survey of what had happened to the various books in the church. What had happened was this: 27 books had assumed a place of authority in the life of the church. But the evidence indicated that the process had not been uniform, and Eusebius seeks to deal fairly with the evidence by dividing the books into three classes, the *homologoumena,* the *antilegomena,* and the "spurious." (This third classification is really a subdivision under *antilegomena* and includes the Acts of Paul, the Shepherd of Hermas, the Revelation of Peter, and the Epistle of Barnabas.) He lists 21 books as *homologeumena:* the four Gospels, fourteen Letters of Paul (Eusebius includes the Letter to the Hebrews among the Pauline Letters), the First Letter of Peter, and the First Letter of John; he includes the Revelation to John also, but with the reservation, "if it seems good," and indicates that he will give his own opinion on this point later. He lists five books as *"antilegomena,* but known to (or acknowledged by) the majority," namely, the Letter of James, the Second Letter of Peter, the Second and Third Letters of John, the Letter of Jude. He lists Revelation twice, once among the *homologoumena* and again under the "spurious" books, noting that some reject the work, while others list it among the *homologoumena.* This hesitation is curious; Eusebius seems to be trying to be scrupulously fair in assessing the evidence both for and against the book without being unduly swayed by his own opinion of the book, which was not favorable to it.

Some 25 years later (A. D. 350) Cyril of Jerusalem in his catechetical lectures recommends to his catechumens a 26-book canon of the New Testament. His canon differs formally from that of Eusebius in the omission of Revelation. More remarkable is the fact that the distinction between *homologoumena* and *antilegomena* plays no role whatever in the canon of Cyril. The 26 books *are* the *homologoumena,* "the books agreed upon by all," in contrast to apocryphal works against which he warns his hearers: "Do not read for yourself what is not read in the churches." Again it is noteworthy that Cyril appeals to no official action of the church but only to the general consensus of the churches.

In A. D. 367 Athanasius, bishop of Alexandria, in his Thirty-ninth Paschal Letter (so called because it announced the official date of Easter to the churches) warns the churches against heretical writings and lists the 27 books of Eusebius' canon as the "wellsprings of salvation, from which he who thirsts may take his fill of sacred words." Like Cyril, he draws a sharp line between canonical and heretical works with their fictitious claim to antiquity and authenticity. Like Cyril, he makes no distinction between *homologoumena* and *antilegomena.* Like Eusebius, he finds the authority for the canon in the history of the canon, not in any decree of the church. It is noteworthy too that Athanasius expressly states that he is not introducing any novelty in thus defining the canon: "Permit me," he says, "to remind you of what you know." With the Paschal Letter of Athanasius the canon of the church is practically determined. The 27-book canon remained the canon of the Greek church. Before the end of the fourth century the Western church, strongly influenced herein by Jerome and Augustine, likewise had a definitive 27-book canon. Local divergences persisted here and there for a time, as the content of some of our New Testament manuscripts indicates, but only the Syrian church persisted in using an essentially different canon, one in which the Catholic Letters and Revelation had no firm position.

Even so sketchy and incomplete an account as the one here given indicates that the New Testament as a collection has a curiously informal and almost casual sort of history. The book that was destined to remain the sacred book for millions of Christians for century upon century came into the church without fanfare, in a quiet, shuffling sort of way. Its history is not all what *we* should expect the history of a sacred book to be. The story of the Book of Mormon is a good example of how man thinks a sacred book should come to man — miraculously, guaranteed by its miraculousness. The canon is a miracle indeed, but a miracle of another sort, a miracle like the incarnation of our Lord, a miracle in servant's form. Only a God who is really Lord of all history could risk bringing His written word into history in the way in which the New Testament was actually brought in. Only the God who by His Spirit rules sovereignly over His people could lead His weak, embattled, and persecuted churches to ask the right questions concerning the books that made their claim upon God's people and to find the right answers: to fix with Spirit-guided instinct on that which was genuinely apostolic (whether written directly by an apostle or not) and therefore genuinely authoritative. Only God Himself could make men see that public reading in the churches was a sure clue to canonicity; only the Spirit of God could make men see that a word which commands the obedience of God's people thereby established itself as God's word and must inevitably remove all other claimants from the scene.

This the 27-book canon did. It established itself in the early centuries of the church and maintained itself in the continued life of the church. It survived the questionings of both humanists and reformers in the sixteenth century; it is a remarkable fact that a Scripture lesson read in Lutheran churches on the Feast of the Reformation is taken from one of the books which Martin Luther himself seriously questioned, the Book of Revelation. And it will maintain itself henceforth. The question of the limits of the canon may be theoretically open; but the history of the church indicates that it is for practical purposes closed. The 27 books are *there* in the church, at work in the church. They are what Athanasius called them, "the wellsprings of salvation" for all Christendom. And in the last analysis, the church of God can become convinced and remain assured that they are indeed the wellsprings of salvation only by drinking of them.

BIBLIOGRAPHICAL NOTE

The beginning student is often tempted, in his first enthusiasm, to buy more books than he needs. It is ominously easy to slip into the habit of reading books about the New Testament rather than the New Testament itself. A bibliographical guide is therefore a good investment. If the student has access to a good library, it is well also to sample a book before buying it. In many areas of study, such as Introduction, the area of overlapping and repetition between books is often very large, and the law of diminishing returns begins to operate early. A relatively small library of solid books, read and re-read, underscored and annotated is, in my experience, better than a large array of books that are merely nibbled at — or read to the exclusion of the New Testament itself. The following list confines itself to books which are likely to be useful to the student of the New Testament in English. The bibliographical guides treat also the works designed for the student of the New Testament in the original Greek.

Bibliographical Guides

Danker, F. W. *Multipurpose Tools for Bible Study*. St. Louis, 1960.

Kelly, B. H., and D. G. Miller, eds. *Tools for Bible Study*. Richmond, 1956.

New Testament Introduction

Wikenhauser, A. *New Testament Introduction*. New York, 1958.

This is a major scholarly work in the field, one which provides a good introduction to its many problems and is rich in references to the pertinent literature in English, German, and French. For those who read German the following two works, similar in scope and make-up to Wikenhauser's, can be recommended:

Feine, P., and J. Behm. *Einleitung in das Neue Testament*. Heidelberg, 1950.

This has long been my favorite. It is not "easy reading" even for those who know German, for the style is compressed and abbreviations are staggeringly abundant. But page for page there is hardly a book which will reward the reader so richly as this one.

Michaelis, T. W. *Einleitung in das Neue Testament.* Bern, 1954.
Devotes more space to the discussion of various theories than the two
previous works.

Somewhat more popular and easily readable is

Rutenborn, Guenter. *The Word Was God,* trans. Elmer E. Foelber. New
York, 1959.

Tenney, M. C. *The New Testament: An Historical and Analytical Survey.*
Grand Rapids, 1953.

The following is not, technically, a book on Introduction but nevertheless
provides a highly original and extremely valuable contribution to the historical understanding of the New Testament:

Schlatter, A. *The Church in the New Testament Period,* trans. P. Levertoff.
London, 1955.

Concordances

Of the Authorized Version:

Strong, J. *The Exhaustive Concordance of the Bible.* New York, 1894.
The claim made in "exhaustive" is hardly an exaggeration.

Walker, J. B. R. *The Comprehensive Concordance to the Holy Scriptures.*
Boston, 1894.

Young, R. *Analytical Concordance to the Bible.* New York, 1902.

A concordance is an invaluable tool to Bible study. Besides a word concordance the student might well invest in a thought concordance such as

Joy, C. R., ed. *Harper's Topical Concordance.* New York, 1940.

Miller, D. M., ed. *The Topical Bible Concordance.*

Of the Revised Standard Version:

*Nelson's Complete Concordance of the Revised Standard Version of the
Bible.* New York, 1957.

Bible Dictionaries and Encyclopedias

Gehman, H. S., ed. *The Westminster Dictionary of the Bible.* Philadelphia,
1954.
A reliable one-volume, moderately priced work, good to have at one's
elbow. A valuable feature is the set of indexed maps at the end of the
volume.

Orr, J., ed. *The International Standard Bible Encyclopedia.* 5 vols. Chi-
cago, 1930.
Scholarly and full, but not too technical for the average reader.

Archaeology and Geography

Finegan, J. *Light from the Ancient Past: The Archeological Background of
Judaism and Christianity.* Second, revised edition. Princeton, 1959.

Wright, G., and F. Filson, eds. *The Westminster Historical Atlas to the Bible.* Philadelphia, 1956.

Two good basic works.

Commentaries

The student will do well to begin with a one-volume commentary such as Davidson, F., A. M. Stibbs, and E. F. Kevan, eds. *The New Bible Commentary.* Grand Rapids, 1954.

Among modern series of commentaries on the New Testament the following will be found useful:

Stonehouse, N., ed. *The New International Commentary.* Grand Rapids, various dates.

Tasker, R., ed. *The Tyndale New Testament Commentaries.* Grand Rapids, various dates.

All three of the above works will be found to be Calvinist in their treatment of passages dealing with the sacraments.

A series recently begun which gives promise of solid usefulness is Kelley, Balmer H., ed. *The Layman's Bible Commentary.* Richmond, 1959.

An older work which continues to render good services to many Bible students, especially when supplemented by one of the newer commentaries, is Jamieson, Fausset, and Brown. *Critical and Explanatory Commentary on the Whole Bible.* Grand Rapids, 1934.

For further help in selecting commentaries, see F. W. Danker's *Multipurpose Tools for Bible Study.* (*Tools for Bible Study,* by Kelly-Miller, does not offer much help for the beginner in this area.)

TOPICAL INDEX

INDEX OF SCRIPTURE PASSAGES